Narratives of Trauma and Moral Agency among Christian Post-9/11 Veterans

Thomas Howard Suitt, III

Narratives of Trauma and Moral Agency among Christian Post-9/11 Veterans

palgrave
macmillan

Thomas Howard Suitt, III
Franklin, TN, USA

ISBN 978-3-031-31081-2 ISBN 978-3-031-31082-9 (eBook)
https://doi.org/10.1007/978-3-031-31082-9

This Palgrave Macmillan imprint is published by the registered company Springer Nature Switzerland AG.
The registered company address is: Gewerbestrasse 11, 6330 Cham, Switzerland

To those who served the United States in our post-9/11 conflicts.

Contents

About the Author

Thomas H. (Ben) Suitt III is a graduate from Boston University and the author of "Finding Resonance Amid Trauma." A contributor for the Costs of War Project (2022 US Peace Prize recipient), his white paper "High Suicide Rates Among United States Service Members and Veterans of the Post-9/11 Wars" received international attention. He has been featured on NPR, NBC, *New York Times*, and other major news outlets. Suitt resides with his family in Franklin, TN, where he teaches English at Franklin Road Academy.

List of Figures

CHAPTER 1

Introduction

The military is an institution that cannot escape moral concern. Moral dimensions infuse every decision in war because military action has wide-ranging consequences. Whether for good or ill, military actions burden the decision-maker, their peers, subordinates, civilians, and enemies (Thompson & Jetly, 2018). These concerns are not new. Indeed, they have been the subject of moral debate since Aristotle (Orend, 2006: 10). As Navy LCDR Ian Davison[1] told me in an interview, "moral stain" and "guilt" are inevitable while participating in a system of violence. In his estimation, "the consequences of your daily work could also lead to life or death for somebody else, even if it's somebody on the other side; that's a lot of free-floating emotion that could inappropriately … cause you to treat people unjust, suspicious or cruel." Making decisions in war affects many lives that have moral, mental, and physical consequences.

Among the ethical meaning-making systems from which military service members[2] draw to make decisions amid these dilemmas are religious

[1] For the confidentiality of the participants, culturally appropriate pseudonyms have been assigned to each of them. Their reflections remain unchanged.

[2] I will rely on the terms "service member" or "warrior" to denote members of the US Armed Forces. "Soldier" is often used in scholarship, but I am leaning on these alternate words at the behest of participants who preferred being designated as a marine, sailor, or airman rather than a soldier.

T. H. Suitt, III, *Narratives of Trauma and Moral Agency among Christian Post-9/11 Veterans*,
https://doi.org/10.1007/978-3-031-31082-9_1

ones, most notably a Christian one. The percentage of service members who identify with some form of Christianity is not small. The Defense Equal Opportunity Management Institute (DEOMI) reports that about 66% of the current US military claim some form of Christian affiliation, and many veterans find faith after service even as others lose their faith upon serving (Hunter & Smith, 2010: 3).[3] A pacifist religion in origin (Wogaman, 1993), Christianity has supplied prescriptions for just cause for war and just actions in war since the time of Augustine of Hippo in the fifth century. Christian thought has informed the long influential just war tradition that forms the basis of modern international humanitarian law, the law of armed conflict (LOAC), rules of engagement (ROE), and operational law. However, service members bring a range of Christian faith commitments, beliefs, and narratives to the military, many of which are at odds with participation in violence. When faith cannot make sense of the moral dimensions inherent to the military experience, a cognitive disconnect can produce dissonance, or the feeling of a psychologically distressing mismatch between two cognitions (Harmon-Jones & Mills, 2019: 3). In these cases, faith itself can be the source of distress.

This project began with questions about the role of religion in veterans' lives, particularly those who served in the "Global War on Terror."[4] For those who once or currently identified as Christian, how has religious belief shaped their military experience? How did it impact veterans' transition from civilian life to the military and back? Despite having access to vast religious resources in the military that make meaning of experience and "successful" measures intended to supply moral frames that preempt potential moral trauma in war, what accounts for the epidemic of moral injury, a dimensional problem associated with moral challenges during the military experience, and other lasting traumas affecting post-9/11 Christian service members and veterans?

There is a wealth of scholarship exploring theological and normative ethical claims concerning the religio-ethical conflict characteristic of war.

[3] The DEOMI study found that 42.05% identified with some form of Protestantism, 20.51% with Catholicism or Orthodox, and 3.28% identified as other Christian. The second largest group in the study was for those with no religious preference at 25.5%. Other major religions found much less representation, with 1.09% identifying as Jewish, 0.45% as Muslim, and 0.87% as part of an Eastern religion.

[4] With the drawdown of US troops in Afghanistan in August 2021, the initial phase of the war is over; however, the continued presence of the US military in Syria and Pakistan provokes my presentation of the Global War on Terror as ongoing.

What is missing in the scholarship, and one of my guiding motivations for undertaking this project, are the stories of veterans who must enact (or ignore) these principles. What do those narratives suggest about military training, culture, and norms that might, then, guide our understanding of just war theory as it confronts the Global War on Terror?

To explore these questions, I interviewed forty-eight veterans and six military chaplains of the post-9/11 era who once or currently identified as Christian, and I relied on a narrative approach to ground this project in their stories. This narrative approach is a way of seeing "whole persons" and allows us to understand "multiple aspects of an individual's life and experiences over the life course in historical time" (Maynes et al., 2008: 10). Telling stories about religion reveals how the individual uses religion in different spaces over time in different contexts. Their narratives reveal the multitude of identities (warrior, citizen, and Christian) they must navigate before, during, and after military service.

As we will see, a large part of the story they tell is that not everything about religion is beneficent. It can intensify or even be the source of trauma itself. While there is variation, foremost is how the military uses its religious culture. From the use of chaplains as religious guides and counselors to explicit moral training and ethics education rooted in Christian justificatory frames to the religious practices, beliefs, values, narratives, symbols, and objects it supplies, the military exercises its religious culture to support the pervasive and all-encompassing warrior identity.

Military training and culture work in complex ways to alter a life. From basic training through service members' careers, they participate in an institution designed to keep them "ready to engage in technically complex and physically demanding labor, exercise organized violence, and be exposed to harm" (MacLeish, 2019: 193). The military institution's culture persistently promotes "strict adherence to its values" that makes it difficult "to anticipate the moral quandaries of killing" among other moral concerns (Wood, 2016: 71, 186). Indeed, the military organization is efficient at supporting the warrior identity, which may limit individual agency. It decentralizes the salience of other identities a service member maintains, and it uses everything from narratives and values to remote weaponry to *religion* to do it.

As the veteran narratives will show, chaplains, moral training, and other religious resources aim to make service members courageous, supplying them with explicit beliefs and narratives to keep them in the fight, often even after a traumatic experience. They present service members' work and participation as "good." In so doing, they often skirt the ethical dimension inherent in exposing service members to persistent trauma. Military service limits moral agency, and military religious culture and resources contribute to this limitation despite earnest efforts by chaplains to help service members through trauma.

This book shows how personal moral and religious identities were shaped and reshaped in the context of military training, combat experience, and trauma. As you will see, the interaction among previous religious narratives, military religious culture, and traumatic events can either help to avoid or anticipate trauma in some while it exacerbates it in others. Military experience can confirm pre-enlistment religious and moral expressions, but it can also deny or contradict them, leading to moral dissonance and trauma. When religious identities are central and salient, they may be integrated with other identities and demand reconciliation when conflict arises. Alternatively, service members can learn (or are trained) to compartmentalize, to keep their Christian, civilian, and veteran identities (among others) separate from one another to avoid dissonance. Still others find that the disruption of the military experience drives them to seek faith and faith communities for the first time. Moreover, some veterans do not find the military experience to be a disruptive one. This book will unpack each of these descriptive narratives at the crossroads of the religious identity and military and civilian identities.

By identifying patterns of experience and post-hoc justifications for actions, we can explore the complex ways religious resources play a role in veterans' lives, particularly amid trauma. The retelling of veteran stories will reveal the ambivalence of service members and chaplains toward service and religion as these frameworks simultaneously support and undermine their struggles amid the moral complexities of participation in war. Together, this discussion will illuminate the lived religio-ethical landscape of the US military. What will emerge is a communitarian approach that invites service members to find meaning-making and moral frames rooted in the memory of their stories and aimed at restoration.

Identity, Agency, and a Narrative Approach

Understanding the interplay of moral agency and identity requires understanding the nature of the "warrior identity" the military inculcates. Identity, however, is itself a contested term. Psychologist Hubert Hermans (2001: 44) contends that we can usually break identity into two main modes of inquiry: the public features of an individual (like their age, race, denomination, and others) or "a psychological construction which represents a continuity through time as opposed to a discontinuity." In the first case, knowing these public features of an individual's identity allows a social scientist to determine a person's social position, allowing us to talk about power dynamics or understand social movements. However, there is a shortcoming of this sort of labeling approach to identity. Sociologist Margaret Somers (1994: 605) posits that there is an "inadvertent tendency to conflate identities with what can often slide into fixed 'essentialist' singular categories," but people "do not always obey the social expectations which are associated with these roles." That is, as sociologist Nancy Ammerman (2003: 212) explains, "we are always many things at once," and focusing on static identity labels does not capture the full reality of one's ongoing life narrative, which is always in flux and adapts to new surprises.

That complexity is captured by sociologist John Hewitt's (1989: 152–3) construction of identity as including four elements—"continuity, integration, identification, and differentiation"—that are the "essence" of humankind. Continuity is the sense that a person maintains a sense of self over time. Integration is the feeling of "wholeness" a person has, incorporating all of the various memories, feelings, and experiences. Identification is a feeling of "being like others"—as in the sense of belonging to a community. Finally, differentiation is a feeling that, despite a feeling of belonging to a group, a person is still an individual. Whether a person has most or all of a singular identity's attributes, there is always more to the story. Amid different roles, labels, and communities, there is a "tension" between identifying with a particular solidarity but then "doing something that emphasizes our uniqueness, our differentiation" (Ammerman, 2003: 210–11). That tension plays out throughout a life in numerous ways, especially as competing solidarities come into conflict or new challenges reshape existing continuities. What is "essential is to move beyond the notion that any single category of experience … defines identity or action"; instead, we must focus on self-narrative continuity that individuals possess as they navigate different solidarities.

One question to be addressed in examining military identities involves examining individual agency. How much control does a person have within a context? For instance, military culture demands a specific type of behavior of a service member and provides resources at every turn that form and reinforce those behaviors. Simultaneously, a service member is free to practice whatever religion she wants and think her thoughts, perhaps invoking evaluations brought to the military experience from the civilian sector. Upon leaving the military, there is more freedom to construct a day-to-day civilian identity, but fewer compatriots and resources to help integrate the military experience into that new civilian-veteran identity. How, then, do we locate agency?

Ammerman (2003: 212) locates agency "not in freedom from patterned constraint but in our ability to invoke those patterns in nonprescribed ways, enabled … by the very multiplicity of solidarities in which we participate." The different communities with which the service member has identified provide frameworks—the ways of behaving, the ethical norms, the things she values—and these frameworks shape how the service member acts. Indeed, these cultural values, beliefs, and habits provide "strategies of action" from a broader cultural "toolkit" that organizes action even when desired ends change or are out of sync (Swidler, 1986: 277). Different situations call for different strategies for action, and individuals pull from different cultural toolkits for appropriate action within different contexts. Agency is the ability to choose how to act drawing from these different cognitive frameworks.

However, individuals also carry with them bodily, cognitive, and social behaviors and dispositions that constitute what Pierre Bourdieu (1990: 53) calls their *habitus*, which can itself be hybrid and draws unconsciously on different cultural packages when the need arises (Ignatow, 2009). Building on Mills' (1940) and others' pragmatist tradition, this theoretical approach emphasizes patterned habits of behavior (Dewey, 1922). Individuals likely do not consciously choose how to act in every moment; they rely on deeply held unconscious habits of behavior. Motivation for action, then, includes both a history of personal experience that produces one's behaviors and beliefs as well as a discursive consciousness when situations interrupt habit (Dewey, 1922: 215; Winchester & Green, 2019; Guhin, 2016). Novel situations can force a reflexive period in which persons must draw on different cultural packages to determine a new strategy for action, replacing an interrupted habit.

An individual subconsciously navigates socially ingrained ways of behaving as different settings dictate, revealing ebbs and flows in agency within an ongoing narrative. Sociologists Mustafa Emirbayer and Ann Mische (1998: 1012) contend, "Actors are always living simultaneously in the past, future, and present, and adjusting the various temporalities of their empirical existence to one another … in more or less imaginative or reflective ways." It is their ability to choose how to act during discordant, unsettled times that marks their agency. This emphasis on choice and the transitions between different solidarities is critical in understanding the veterans' moral and religious narratives that are the focus of this project. They are choosing "how and whether to be religious, including choosing how central religion will be in their lives" (Ammerman, 2003: 207). However, moral action in war can be a different matter when the warrior identity takes centrality. The tension between *habitus*, which can be multiple or "split" (Vest, 2013: 605), and reflexive deliberation and agency will shape these stories.

The question of agency, by needs, raises questions about moral norms and expectations. Different communities in which the service member finds herself provide moral frameworks—ways of behaving, ethical norms, and values. These frameworks help her differentiate between oughts and nots, what she should approve and what she should reprove. By defining herself as a warrior or a citizen or a Christian, she is not merely revealing her background or viewpoint; she is providing "the frame within which [she] can determine where [she] stand[s] on questions of what is good, or worthwhile, or admirable, or of value" (C. Taylor, 1989: 27). Additionally, these frames show her commitment to particular value judgments, orient her to a specific moral space, and suggest what is good or bad, what is essential and what is not.

However, because different cultural packages can have different moral commitments—different frameworks for what is important—there can be conflict. Distinct morals and expectations compose different social spheres in one's life, and when values and beliefs between them compete and collide, navigating the moral order can be difficult (Wuthnow, 1987). Morals can overlap and comingle between different producers of morality, but they can also be at odds, leading to inner levels of contestation and competition among expected moral narratives, identities, and institutions (Hitlin & Vaisey, 2013). For instance, a veteran who enters the military with a certain sense of who he is may experience tension, even trauma, if deemed a persona non grata in the military for holding onto beliefs from home and acting contrary to the warrior identity.

In the spirit of Somers, Ammerman, and Taylor, my narrative approach will allow us to explore and understand this potential tension. We will listen to how a person emplots life events and other characters into a story or stories. Sociologist Daniel Winchester (2017: 86) describes emplotment as "the selective integration of social actors' experiences and actions into a more or less coherent life story." To do this, we must include the dimensions Somers (1994: 607–614) contends unsettle identity—"time, space, and relationality"—and attend to "overlapping networks of relations that shift over time and space." In other words, this narrative approach includes attention to continuity over time, the impact of spaces (public and private), and the relationships between different networks that affect a life. It includes attention to the social world where people assemble identities "by locating themselves or being located within a repertoire of emplotted stories." In their stories of being a mother, of being a warrior, of being a Baptist, of being a man, individuals emplot themselves in a more or less coherent narrative, and it is that "autobiographic narrative" that will be the focus of how we approach understanding identity and the tensions between commitments to multiple solidarities (Ammerman, 2003: 214).

By understanding identity in this narrative mode, this study will show how veterans describe their autobiographical narrative amid their participation in military culture and various religious communities along the way. In looking at veterans' narratives from before their service through their careers and eventual reintegration into the civilian sector, this project will capture a more nuanced understanding of veterans' multiplicity of identities, allowing us to understand the complex ways religious resources and military experience shape, reshape, or otherwise alter their life trajectories in significant ways.

Religious Military Narratives and the Independent Variables of the Study

An essential feature of this research was an interview process that invited a co-construction of narratives about veterans' lives before, during, and after military service. These reveal an interplay between many different solidarities, roles, and social positions (that I will call "identities"), each of which came with cultural, religious, and moral frameworks. This book will analyze religion's role in Global War on Terror service members' navigation of these identities. Emphasizing the multiple identity narratives will account for variation in congruence and dissonance between different identities, particularly religious, civilian, and warrior ones. From the stories these veterans shared with me, I have constructed narratives structured around a "typical" military life cycle: before joining, training, career, return to civilian sector. My analysis of these narratives allows me to identify significant tension points considered incongruous or traumatic. When no dissonance or trauma occurred, I will attend to the same places in their timelines to determine what accounts for the differences between the different narrative groups. Because the narratives are explicitly about religion amid the military experience, I will refer to them mostly as "religious military narratives," although they will also include times before and well after military service ended.

Looking for explanations for differences in these religious military narratives sent me in surprising directions. Scholarship on religion and trauma led me to predict that differences would revolve around participants' religiosity and combat exposure. I imagined a clear two by two grid of high and low religiosity compared with high and low levels of combat exposure. Surely, combat experience would naturally be the source of trauma—whether combat trauma, physical trauma, or morally traumatic experiences—and I imagined that the individual's religiosity level would be a factor in the dissonance created. Of course, the reality was far more complicated than a simple grid structure, and the apparent factors at play were not combat exposure and religiosity. Instead, they were trauma (more broadly conceived) and variation in religious resources. Exploring those concepts will be the task of this project, and some initial definition is important here.

The trauma we will explore is far from rare. In any given year since 9/11, the VA reports that between 11% and 20% of US veterans of Iraq and Afghanistan have PTSD ("How Common Is PTSD in Veterans?": 2018). While one may assume that combat exposure would be the most likely source of trauma and PTSD in the military experience, this is not necessarily true. Combat experience, while indeed a source of trauma, is far from the *only* source. Military training is itself traumatic, even deliberately so, and is designed to "break down the minds of the recruits" (Gutmann & Lutz, 2010: 48). Many service members in support roles experience the horrors of war. For example, fellow service members can threaten their lives or assault them. Service members can see the injured and the dead brought in from the battlefield. Indeed, knowingly participating in violence—even in a secondary sense—can be traumatic. The Diagnostic and Statistical Manual (DSM-5) diagnostics for PTSD were expanded in 2013 to "include vicarious traumatization" (Howley, 2019). Previous editions of the DSM suggested that one could only develop PTSD after being traumatized oneself and needed to include life-threatening risks. The revised DSM acknowledges that one does not have to be the person threatened. Simply witnessing a traumatic event can leave persons traumatized.

Moreover, trauma includes *morally* traumatic events. Moral injury—the term which has come to describe the trauma one feels when one's sense of right has been betrayed in some way—leads to a different form of trauma from, though often accompanied by, PTSD. While moral injury is not yet officially diagnosable under the DSM-5 at VA hospitals, it is a phenomenon that has dominated new scholarship in trauma and accounts for the moral wounds with which many veterans return home.

Many veterans I spoke with experienced military sexual trauma (MST) or had their lives threatened or were subject to sexual harassment. MST affects over 23% of women veterans, although somewhere between 80% and 90% of those sexual assaults go unreported ("How Common Is PTSD in Veterans?: 2018"; Conard et al., 2014). In addition to sexual assault, sexual harassment is common among women (55%) and men (38%). MST can lead to PTSD or moral injury. However, some psychiatrists and mental health researchers are careful to designate MST as a unique traumatic phenomenon distinct from morally injurious events, combat trauma, or other traumatic experiences, even if the other forms of trauma can accompany it. That is to say, the ways of approaching MST can often be different from other forms of trauma common to the military experience.

Physical trauma and complications—like a traumatic brain injury (TBI)—affect tens of thousands of veterans. Since 9/11, over 53,000 have officially been listed as wounded while in the service (US Department of Defense, 2021), and this does not include roughly 7000 service members killed during combat operations or those additional service members wounded in training or who have hidden wounds, like the growing number of veterans who have developed lung disease after exposure to burn pits. There are numerous ways military service members experience trauma, many of which overlap and interact, further making the military experience disruptive for those who serve.

In addition to the disruption of navigating between the civilian and military sectors, these traumatic events can also force transitions of identity, complicating how veterans navigate the rest of the military experience or transition back to civilian life. Indeed, homecoming and reintegration "is the time of greatest risk" for service members (Hautzinger & Scandlyn,

2014: 136). PTSD, moral injury, long-term effects of TBIs, depression, substance abuse, and vicious behaviors can all present significant issues in the life of a veteran. In the civilian sector, veterans' warrior identities have little purchase, and the loss of identity, status, and purpose can be a trauma unto itself. In all these cases, it was clear that combat exposure is only one piece of a much larger tragic puzzle of trauma.

Just as combat and trauma proved more complicated than initially expected, so did religiosity. It became clear that access to and kinds of religious resources was much more important than mere religiosity. Religiosity accounted for a portion of the differences, to be sure. However, it also mattered when and whether religious support was available and whether those resources were congruent or dissonant with military values and culture or existing religious identities. It also depended on whether those resources could satisfy existential questions or act as a salve for trauma.

We can understand religion as a complete meaning-making system that is a cultural sphere unto itself.[5] Religion provides a sense that we live in a "meaningful cosmos" and relies upon different cultural tools and communities to do so (Weber, 1946: 281). By "religious resources," then, I describe those cultural objects religion provides, including institutional structures, interpretive strategies, and social dimensions that produce, enforce, and reinforce beliefs, values, and practices. Notably, religious resources can have different sources. Religious cultural toolkits are not monolithic, and service members and veterans interact with multiple religious toolkits during their religious military narratives. Moreover, the cultural package that "religious resources" represents is just one toolkit of many that service members and veterans employ for strategies of action (Swidler, 1986; C. Smith, 2003). While the military has its own religious culture within it, the stories of service members, veterans, and even military chaplains show competition between these packages. Religious military identities were shaped by a wide range of trauma experiences and a complex range of religious resources.

[5] The definition of religion has remained a topic of persistent debate among religious studies scholars (e.g., Geertz, 1973; Durkheim, 1995; Weber, 1946, 1958; Asad, 1993). However, this book will focus on religion as a meaning-making system and producer of culture.

Sitting with Trauma and the Need to Remember, Retell, and Reimagine

Part of the work of this project will be to make something of these religious military narratives, to listen to the stories veterans and service members tell and suggest a possible pathway forward. This book begins with military religious culture's part in that process but then turns to the impact of that system on service members' lives. As we will see, a large part of that impact is trauma, and it is what we do with the memory of their trauma that can inform new theological and ethical possibilities for service members.

However, sitting with service member and veteran trauma is difficult. Military religious culture supplies its troops with narratives and "interpretations that continually cover over the wounds," thus emphasizing salvation over suffering, protection over solidarity, good work over tragic necessity (Rambo, 2017: Location No. 273). These frames produce facile justifications that are "successful" in keeping warriors in the fight but challenge the plausibility structure of their moral beliefs about themselves, the military, and God. These narratives and frames demand a creative reimagining.

To do this work, I draw from ethicist Walter Fluker's (2016: 29) analytical schema of "remembering, retelling, and reliving … stories" corresponding to a "spiraling … counterclockwise turning of memory, vision, and mission." In a sense, this process is a way for us to collectively draw up the discursive consciousness and attend to the open wound of trauma unsettling the military community. It calls us to remember the history, narratives, and frames that have produced the modern military religious culture: chaplains, ethics education, and military religious life. It invites us to retell narratives in the words of service members themselves who have lived amid those persistent cultural frameworks alongside trauma: moral, physical, mental, spiritual, and sexual. Finally, it demands that we live out a new reimagined mission, calling on memory, experience, and revised metaphors to develop "new enfleshed approaches and practices that speak to our contemporary situations" (Fluker, 2016: 29).

Moreover, this schema can normalize remembering, retelling, and acknowledging traumatic experiences by transforming this process into a communal experience. Engaging with trauma, with wounds, has great theological and ethical potential for service members, and "it emphasizes the importance of a collective and the formation of a community of witnesses" (Rambo, 2017: Location No. 3045). By meeting them in their stories and conjuring new ethical and theological frames that account for the suffering inherent in war, this book can suggest a possible starting place for service members to acknowledge the tragedies of war.

Methodology and Sample

For this project, I used an inductive qualitative approach using interviews to garner an experiential understanding of faith's role in veterans' lives. I sought out those who served during the Global War on Terror and at one time or currently identified as Christian. The interviews were semi-structured, relying on interview guides while allowing the discussions to expand with follow-up questions and anecdotes to invite deeper meaning. Additionally, as a complete outsider to the military community, it was vital to allow the interview guide to develop with each encounter, providing space to gain trust and open avenues for dialogue. The interviews lasted about one hour each, ranging from forty-five minutes to over two hours. The result was about 3250 minutes of recorded conversations.[6]

I chose post-9/11 veterans for their historical context and related moral implications. First, these are people who ostensibly chose to enlist and were not conscripted (by contrast to Vietnam,[7] Korean, or World War II veterans). Indeed, many people who served in earlier wars volunteered, and much has been said about the ways the military coerces people to enlist today (Fransen, 2019); however, the post-conscription era was nonetheless a factor in determining the focus of this study. Second, the post-9/11 conflicts have a built-in religious dimension that makes questions about religious experience more palpable within this context. Between an enemy characterized mainly in religious terms and a war that former President Bush (2001) described as a "crusade" against terrorism five days after 9/11, religion remains a defining feature of the US involvement in the Muslim world.

That the research was not comparative across religious traditions was a conscious choice. By centering my work on one specific, though diverse

[6] This entire project was IRB-approved through the Institutional Review Board offices at Boston University and abides by the high standards of protocol and safety demanded of such a project.

[7] While this study will not emphasize the Vietnam era, parallels to the work of Mahedy (1986) are clear. As this study will show, the spiritual readiness of warriors for military experience remains inadequate.

and complex, religious tradition, I can address the interplay of Christianity's ideas and structures with service members' experiences. Nevertheless, the different denominations and possible experiences with Christianity that veterans described provided ample intra-religious comparison opportunities. This proved to be very useful, as I found many different forms of Christianity (from Catholicism to Mainline Protestantism to evangelicalism and the Church of Jesus Christ of Latter-day Saints) and believe this provides a significant critical perspective.

The screening protocol for the veterans, then, was very straightforward. I would ask them if they at one point identified as Christian and if they served in the Global War on Terror. The beginning of my interviews always included a statement to make sure they understood I would be recording them and that questions could bring up past trauma. I then asked questions about their frequency of combat experience and questions regarding their religiosity. I gauged religiosity by having the veterans answer the Duke University Religion Index (DUREL) questions, a five-item scale used to assess religious/spiritual beliefs.[8] I would then ask if they were comfortable with me turning on the recorder. Completed interviews were then transcribed and coded around inductive themes, allowing for the co-construction of their religious military narratives.

There were fifty-four total participants in this study. The self-selecting sample represented many different branches of service, lengths of careers, ranks, and Christian denominations, and while not a demographically representative sample, the participants provided a channel through which to identify the social processes at work. Forty-seven were post-9/11 era veterans, six were military chaplains, and one participant was a former West Point professor and veteran.

Of the forty-seven veterans, the Army was overrepresented with twenty-two soldiers. Seven were sailors in the Navy, six were Marines, six were airmen in the Air Force, and six were National Guardsmen. Of the twenty-two participants who served in the Army, six were Army Special Forces.[9] Thirty-six of the participants enlisted, while eleven commissioned as

[8] This scale measures the three major dimensions of religiosity—organizational religious activity (ORA), non-organizational religious activity (NORA), and intrinsic religiosity (IR). ORA and NORA are assessed on a six-point scale while IR is measured on a five-point scale over three questions. See Koenig and Büssing (2010).

[9] While the service branch of the National Guard is technically separate from that of the Army, all the National Guardsmen were Army National Guard and deployed under the Army's purview.

officers. Of the forty-seven veterans, thirty-five identified as men, eleven identified as women, and one identified as gender fluid (they/their/them). Women were slightly overrepresented in the study at 23% compared to the military (17% in Department of Defense, 2015). Twenty-two of the participants were between thirty-one and forty years of age. Three were between twenty-six and thirty. Twelve were between forty-one and fifty. Seven were between fifty-one and sixty, and three were over the age of sixty. The shortest career length was two years, while the longest was forty years. Twenty-four of the participants served for over ten years, meaning over half were career military men and women. Significantly missing are the voices of the military's (40%) non-white population. All but one participant presented as white, and that participant was Hispanic. Overall, the study sample and their narratives are primarily those of Euro-American Christians and represent only a starting point for understanding the social processes at work here.

In a Department of Defense demographic study (2015) of the US Armed Forces, approximately 40% of active-duty personnel were made up of racial and ethnic minority groups (17.3% Black, 11.8% Hispanic, 6.6% Other, and 4.2% Asian).[10] That nearly every participant in my sample was white presents significant limitations worth addressing immediately. I did not sufficiently anticipate the need to reach out to non-white communities and believed my recruitment approach would produce a more diverse sample than it did. In so doing, I failed to capture important voices that represent a significant portion of service members and veterans. It is unclear what about the recruitment process led to the dearth of non-white participants. There may have been distrust of a white researcher or hidden factors related to social media algorithms for ad placement, the demographics of veterans who participate in veteran groups, and my geographical location. It may simply be a shortfall of self-selection. In any case, it is my failure to foresee the need for more targeted outreach that is to blame.

Unfortunately, this is a perennial issue in the field. For example, Robert Bellah et al.'s (1985) *Habits of the Heart* drew criticism for their targeted focus on an all-white, middle class population while simultaneously claiming their work answered fundamental questions concerning "what it

[10] These numbers include enlisted and officers combined. The numbers are different for officers where racial and ethnic minorities make up approximately 30% of commissioned active-duty personnel (8.1% Black, 7.6% Hispanic, 8.2% Other, 5.2% Asian). See Kamarck (2019).

means to be an 'American'" (Harding, 1987: 2). Such a narrow focus misses "a major portion of the painful reality, the ambiguous richness and the anguished integrity of this nation's past and present—as well as a full sense of the magnificent possibilities of the future." Such a criticism is true of this project as well. Those experiences will simply be missing in the accounts that follow and remain an area in need of future study.

The limitations of my sample should be kept in mind in your reading of this research. However, I invite the reader to consider that the stories included here are worth telling. They point to significant trends among white Christians in the US military representing a range of socio-economic backgrounds, ranks, ages, genders, and denominational affiliations. This project does not capture the whole story of religion in the military amid competing identities, moral toolkits, and trauma, but it is an important *part* of the story. It is a beginning and will necessitate and invite further investigation of these questions in the lives of minority service members and veterans in the future.[11]

Of course, there were many denominations represented in the population, which I tracked over the full narrative of the veterans' lives. Many changed denominations during or following military service. However, at the time of speaking with me, nine identified with Mainline Protestant denominations (American Baptist (1), Presbyterian (3), Methodist (4), and Episcopalian (1)). Seven identified with Catholicism. Fourteen identified with various evangelical groups, including Southern Baptist. Four identified as either having no denominational affiliation or as other Christian.[12] One identified with Church of Jesus Christ of Latter-Day Saints (LDS). Finally, twelve claimed no preference or stated they were taking a "break" from organized religion altogether.

[11] To my knowledge, there is little research on moral injury or investigations of moral frameworks specific to BIPOC perspectives in the context of post-9/11 wars and conflicts among Christian veterans and service members interacting with modern military religious culture. However, psychology and trauma scholarship has focused on war-related PTSD among Black and Hispanic Vietnam veterans (Dohrenwend et al., 2008) as well as racial trauma and sexual harassment (Settles 2012) and the impact of racism and bias (Burk & Espinoza, 2012) among Black military personnel in the Global War on Terror era.

[12] Having no denominational affiliation was not necessarily indicative of a lower religiosity. Some relied exclusively on non-church-specific Christian veterans' groups and refused to identify with a denomination. Others claimed no affiliation because they were no longer attending services at church but were still firmly Christian. They were different from the No Preference group because they did actively claim Christianity as their faith.

To create a snapshot of the military's religious life, which will be the focus of the next few chapters, I also interviewed six chaplains. One served only in the Canadian Armed Forces[13] but had unique experiences that proved relevant. The remaining five all served the US Army. Each of the five were commissioned officers, as all chaplains in the Chaplain Corps enter as officers. Their ranks ranged from Major (2) to Lieutenant Colonel (1) to Colonel (2), meaning they were all high-ranking chaplains during their careers. Four of the chaplains were white, while one was Latino. All of them were men. They were also all above the age of forty, with two between fifty and sixty and one above sixty. Four were from Mainline Protestant denominations (two Episcopalian, one Lutheran, and one Presbyterian), while one chaplain was evangelical. Finally, their experience spanned the historical period under study, with the shortest length of service being thirteen years and the longest being thirty-six years.

Book Structure

This book has eight chapters. Following this introduction, it will investigate three major locations where service members interact with military religious culture: military chaplains, ethics education and moral training, and the broader military religious life. Chapter 2 will investigate the history and role of military chaplains. Commonly treated as a synecdoche for religion in the military, chaplains have been a central and essential part of the US military since 1775. Their role has changed and transformed over our nation's history, and they have taken on more formalized and even non-religious roles. The chapter will explore how military chaplains manage competing moral commitments to the military organization and their call to serve individual troops.

Chapter 3 will focus on ethics education and moral training. As service members enter the military, training plays a vital role in instilling military cultural frameworks in cadets and academy students in an intense process of establishing the warrior identity. Alongside intensive training on rules, norms, combat, and the like, ethics education and moral training find varied relevance. With deep roots in Christian theology, religion is not

[13] I have included him in the study because he was a US veteran of Vietnam and has spent his life working with veterans after becoming a minister after that war. Our conversation guided much of my conclusions. I will not use his interview while talking about the religious life of the post-9/11 US military.

absent from such training, even if it remains implicit. This chapter will look at the influence of Christianity in military ethics education and the differences between training provided to enlisted versus that of officers. It will reveal the mismatch between the military's taught "virtue ethics" and its utilitarian commitments.

Chapter 4 will then look at what formal and informal religious resources veterans have available to them. From chapel services to prayer groups to persistent institutional myths and stories related to material objects to private prayer, the military contains a vast and varied range of religious resources that remain on offer. Of course, service members bring a range of religious beliefs, practices, and expectations with them to the military as well. This chapter will examine how formal and informal beliefs, practices, and symbols play out and interact amid the military experience. The result will be a picture of the rich and deeply embedded religious military culture of the US Armed Forces and the ways it supplies service members with narratives, values, beliefs, and objects that keep them ready to fight.

Chapters 5 and 6 will turn the conversation toward trauma as we hear veterans retell their religious military stories. The military experience presents novel moral dilemmas and traumatic experiences in the lives of service members. Chapter 5 will look at how service members use religious beliefs and practices in the context of potential moral trauma. Exploring the concept of moral injury, I will investigate what accounts for religion's role in mitigating moral trauma in some while exacerbating it in others. This investigation and the stories therein reveal a social process of belief maintenance amid moral trauma that contributes to our understanding of culture in action and moral injury in war. Chapter 6 will then discuss other forms of trauma and the development of PTSD. In stories of physical injury, MST, or traumatic exposure, religion tended to play a more "positive" role in service members' lives.

Chapter 7 will explore the difficulty of new veterans transitioning back to the civilian sector, where their warrior identity has less purchase in daily life. Looking at the big picture and identifying the extensive process of identity maintenance amid trauma and varied religious resources, seven religious military narratives emerge. These narrative trajectories, stemming from veteran stories, suggest complementary and competing ways veterans navigated the military experience. These narratives I will identify as *Religion Maintained Amid Trauma*, *Religion Adapted Amid Trauma*,

Religion Maintained Absent Trauma, *Religion Found Post-Trauma*, *Religion Found in Community*, *Religion Lost in Trauma*, and *Religion Lost to Irrelevance*. Each shows the process of identity maintenance over a "typical" life cycle of a veteran, following their transition from civilian to warrior to veteran and the role of a religious identity alongside that process.

Finally, in the concluding chapter, I will make an ethical claim about the military institution, its culture, and the role of religion in the military revealed by this study. Having analyzed the lived religio-ethical system that emerged from veterans' narratives, I will argue that the all-encompassing nature of the warrior identity and the effects of an institution that uses its resources—including religious ones—to aim and re-aim service members at strategic goals severely limits the moral agency of individual service members. As a result, we must consider changing military organizational frameworks toward help-seeking attitudes and collective or organizational moral responsibility.

Bibliography

Ammerman, N. T. (2003). Religious Identities and Religious Institutions. In M. Dillon (Ed.), *Handbook of the Sociology of Religion* (pp. 207–224). Cambridge University Press.

Asad, T. (1993). *Genealogies of Religion: Discipline and Reasons of Power in Christianity and Islam*. Johns Hopkins University Press.

Bourdieu, P. (1990). *The Logic of Practice* (R. Nice, Trans.). Stanford University Press.

Burk, J., & Espinoza, E. (2012). Race Relations within the US Military. *Annual Review of Sociology, 38*(1), 401–422.

Bush, G. W. (2001). Remarks by the President upon Arrival. *The South Lawn*. Retrieved http://georgewbush-whitehouse.archives.gov/news/releases/2001/09/20010916-2.html.

Conard, P. L., Young, C., Hogan, L., & Armstrong, M. L. (2014). Encountering Women Veterans with Military Sexual Trauma. *Perspectives in Psychiatric Care, 50*(4), 280–286.

Department of Defense, Office of the Deputy Assistant Secretary of Defense for Military Community and Family Policy. (2015). *2015 Demographics: Profile of the Military Community*.

Dewey, J. (1922). *Human Nature and Conduct: An Introduction to Social Psychology*. Henry Holt & Company.

Dohrenwend, B. P., Turner, J. B., Turse, N. A., Lewis-Fernandez, R., & Yager, T. J. (2008). War-related Posttraumatic Stress Disorder in Black, Hispanic, and Majority White Vietnam Veterans: The Roles of Exposure and Vulnerability. *Journal of Traumatic Stress, 21*(2), 133–141.

Durkheim, E. (1995). *The Elementary Forms of Religious Life* (K. E. Fields, Trans.). Free Press.

Emirbayer, M., & Mische, A. (1998). What Is Agency? *American Journal of Sociology, 103*(4), 962–1023.

Fluker, W. E. (2016). *The Ground Has Shifted: The Future of the Black Church in Post-Racial America*. New York University Press.

Fransen, M. (2019). Selling Military Service during Wartime: U.S. Army Recruitment Advertising and Enlistment Motivation during the War against Terror. *Scandinavian Journal of Military Studies, 2*(1), 178–192.

Geertz, C. (1973). *The Interpretation of Cultures*. Basic Books.

Guhin, J. (2016). Why Worry about Evolution? Boundaries, Practices, and Moral Salience in Sunni and Evangelical High Schools. *Sociological Theory, 34*(2), 151–174.

Gutmann, M. C., & Lutz, C. (2010). *Breaking Ranks: Iraq Veterans Speak Out Against the War*. University of California Press.

Harding, V. (1987). To the Authors of "Habits of the Heart," A Letter of Concern, an Invitation to Re-Creation: Toward a Darkly Radiant Vision of America's Truth. *CrossCurrents, 37*(1), 1–16.

Harmon-Jones, E., & Mills, J. (2019). An Introduction to Cognitive Dissonance Theory and an Overview of Current Perspectives on the Theory. In E. Harmon-Jones (Ed.), *Cognitive Dissonance: Reexamining a Pivotal Theory in Psychology* (pp. 3–24). American Psychological Association.

Hautzinger, S., & Scandlyn, J. (2014). *Beyond Post-Traumatic Stress: Homefront Struggles with the Wars on Terror*. Routledge.

Hermans, H. J. M. (2001). Conceptions of Self and Identity Toward a Dialogical View. *International Journal of Education and Religion, 2*(1), 43–62.

Hewitt, J. P. (1989). *Dilemmas of the American Self*. Temple University Press.

Hitlin, S., & Vaisey, S. (2013). The New Sociology of Morality. *Annual Review of Sociology, 39*(1), 51–68.

How Common Is PTSD in Veterans? (2018). Retrieved from https://www.ptsd.va.gov/understand/common/common_veterans.asp

Howley, E. K. (2019). Statistics on PTSD in Veterans. *U.S. News & World Report, U.S. News & World Report*.

Hunter, C., & Smith, L. (2010). Military Leadership and Education & Religion's Role in the U.S. Military Mission. *Defense Equal Opportunity Management Institute Research Directorate*, 2–18.

Ignatow, G. (2009). Why the Sociology of Morality Needs Bourdieu's Habitus. *Sociological Inquiry, 79*(1), 98–114.

Kamarck, K. N. (2019). *Diversity, Inclusion, and Equal Opportunity in the Armed Services: Background and Issues for Congress*, fas.org/sgp/crs/natsec/R44321.pdf.

Koenig, H. G., & Büssing, A. (2010). The Duke University Religion Index (DUREL): A Five-Item Measure for Use in Epidemiological Studies. *Religions, 1*(1), 78–85.

MacLeish, K. (2019). Imagining Military Suicide. In C. Lutz & A. Mazzarino (Eds.), *War and Health: The Medical Consequences of the Wars in Iraq and Afghanistan* (pp. 190–208). New York University Press.

Mahedy, W. P. (1986). *Out of the Night: The Spiritual Journey of Vietnam Vets.* Ballantine Books.

Maynes, M. J., Pierce, J. L., & Laslett, B. (2008). *Telling Stories: The Use of Personal Narratives in the Social Sciences and History.* Cornell University Press.

Mills, C. W. (1940). Situated Actions and Vocabularies of Motive. *American Sociological Review, 5*(6), 904–913.

Orend, B. (2006). *The Morality of War.* Broadview Press.

Rambo, S. (2017). *Resurrecting Wounds: Living in the Afterlife of Trauma.* Baylor University Press.

Smith, C. (2003). *Moral, Believing Animals.* Oxford University Press.

Somers, M. R. (1994). The Narrative Constitution of Identity: A Relational and Network Approach. *Theory and Society, 23*(5), 605–649.

Swidler, A. (1986, April). Culture in Action: Symbols and Strategies. *American Sociological Review, 51*(2), 273–286.

Taylor, C. (1989). *Sources of the Self: The Making of the Modern Identity.* Harvard University Press.

Thompson, M. M., & Jetly, R. (2018). Battlefield Ethics Training: Integrating Ethical Scenarios in High-Intensity Field Exercises. In *Moral Decisions and Military Mental Health* (Vol. STO-TR-HFM-179, pp. 8-1–8-15). NATO Science and Technology Organization.

US Department of Defense. (2021, March 8). *Immediate Release: Casualty Status as of 10 a.m. EST Mar 8, 2021* (Rep.). Retrieved https://www.defense.gov/casualty.pdf

Vest, B. M. (2013). Citizen, Soldier, or Citizen-Soldier? Negotiating Identity in the US National Guard. *Armed Forces and Society, 39*(4), 602–627.

Weber, M. (1946). *From Max Weber: Essays in Sociology* (H. Gerth & C. W. Mills, Trans.). Oxford University Press.

Weber, M. (1958). *The Protestant Ethic and the Spirit of Capitalism.* Scribner.

Winchester, D. (2017). 'A Part of Who I Am': Material Objects as 'Plot Devices' in the Formation of Religious Selves. *Journal for the Scientific Study of Religion, 56*(1), 83–103.

Winchester, D., & Green, K. D. (2019). Talking Your Self into It: How and When Accounts Shape Motivation for Action. *Sociological Theory, 37*(3), 257–281.

Wogaman, J. P. (1993). *Christian Ethics: A Historical Introduction.* Westminster John Knox Press.

Wood, D. B. (2016). *What Have We Done: The Moral Injury of Our Longest Wars.* Little, Brown and Company.

Wuthnow, R. (1987). *Meaning and Moral Order: Explorations in Cultural Analysis.* University of California Press.

CHAPTER 2

Military Chaplains and the Two-Collar Problem

A religious component within the American military has existed longer than the US itself. From the beginning of the republic, service members have had access to military chaplains and were free to practice their faith, albeit only a Christian one in the early days. However, the military chaplaincy has changed considerably, and the modern Chaplain Corps looks much different. The military has formalized the role of chaplains in the last 200 years. Pluralism has ensured a greater breadth of endorsed religious, spiritual, and humanitarian chaplains to provide accommodation for a diverse service member population. Concurrently, the military has experienced an overwhelming and disproportionate influx of evangelical chaplains and a conservative ideology. Amid a culture conflict in the Chaplain Corps, military chaplains now operate at a moral crossroads between serving as strategic assets for military goals and attending to the needs of individual service members. Ultimately, the dilemma rests on how the military institution has come to define the role of chaplains.

Despite the constitutionally mandated separation of church and state, the military has provided religious accommodation to its ranks over its long history while claiming such accommodations do not establish a

T. H. Suitt, III, *Narratives of Trauma and Moral Agency among Christian Post-9/11 Veterans*,
https://doi.org/10.1007/978-3-031-31082-9_2

religion.[1] The major branches of the military have likewise expressed the value of religion in the lives of service members and reinforced the importance of religious accommodation (Department of the Air Force, 2006; Secretary of the Navy, 2008; Department of the Army, 2009). Although undoubtedly slow to expand accommodations beyond Protestant Christianity, the Department of Defense (DoD) now recognizes 221 faiths and belief systems (Hebert, 2017), including humanism and pantheistic groups, accommodating the free exercise of each albeit with varied breadth of available resources. With most service members still claiming a religious affiliation of some kind (Hunter & Smith, 2010), religion remains an important part of the military experience in various ways, providing religious resources to service members that can shape and inform their moral expectations and beliefs as well as their military experience overall.

However, except for the growing research on religion and trauma, scholarship on religion in the US military is relatively scarce. Opening the field up to the militaries of other nations expands the universe of available scholarship, but not much. A clear consequence of this dearth is that current scholarship does not yet understand "the roots, characteristics, or consequences of religious practices in the Armed Forces" (Hassner, 2014: 2). In what is otherwise a vast topic, the only piece of the military religious resource puzzle with persistent attention is the role of military chaplains.

Indeed, military chaplains are—in both scholarship and among my participants—often treated as a synecdoche for religious resources overall. Chaplains are mental healthcare providers. They are moral educators. They are spiritual guides. They wear many hats and often draw considerable respect for their reverence, dedication, and bravery, providing much needed counsel for enlisted infantrymen and high-ranking commanding officers alike. Whether or not I raised the subject of chaplains myself in interviews, conversations inevitably led to reflections on them. Navy officer Catherine Bakker, for example, reflected on religion in the military by saying, "I guess religion and military life can be really tricky in the sense that … chaplains have a really difficult job in ministering to communities

[1] See, for instance, US DoD (2009), which states, "The US Constitution proscribes Congress from enacting any law prohibiting the free exercise of religion. The Department of Defense places a high value on the rights of members of the Military Services to observe the tenets of their respective religions. It is DoD policy that requests for accommodation of religious practices should be approved by commanders when accommodation will not have an adverse impact on mission accomplishment, military readiness, unit cohesion, standards, or discipline."

of all faiths. … I think individuals definitely will have different experiences with their religion in the military based on the religious life, based on how accessible faith leaders are." The chaplain is the marked symbol of religion in the military, facilitating it while simultaneously representing religion overall.

Recent scholarship, too, focuses most of its attention on the positive role of military chaplains in the post-9/11 era. Military chaplains, of course, help service members navigate traumatic experiences (Kopacz, 2014). But they also act as religious intermediaries (Adams, 2006), playing a crucial role in foreign military operations, including acting as indigenous religious liaisons (Lee et al., 2005). A. Thompson (2011), Patterson (2014), Moore (2014), and Gutkowski and Wilkes (2011), for example, each show that military chaplains can be crucial guides in understanding the importance of religion to Afghan culture, mediating relationships between service members and civilians, and legitimizing the democratic Afghan government. In this scholarship, chaplains exist at the moral crossroads of faith communities in the military and combat operations, providing military personnel with resources for multiple facets of the mission.

While scant scholarship addresses the complexities of chaplains navigating that crossroads, some literature explores how chaplains' moral commitments interact with their military ones, a reality with varying consequences. For example, Peter French, a moral philosopher, taught week-long ethics intensives to US military chaplains. Among the dilemmas often brought up in his classes was that chaplains felt beholden to the military organization rather than the needs of individual service members. As one chaplain in his course said, "The right collar outranks the left" (French, 2011: 36). Specifically, this refers to a former chaplain uniform of the Navy where the right collar has the chaplain's rank, a symbol of one's role within the military organization, and the left has her religious affiliation, a symbol of commitment to one's faith. The oft-referred to "two-collar problem" symbolizes the tension between loyalty to one's faith and loyalty to the military organization. In my estimation, this is at the root of the Chaplain Corps from the beginning, as chaplains have, throughout the entire history of the US, been precariously positioned between the state and the religion service members practice. As religious leaders, they are a symbol for the dilemma of religion's use in the US military overall, representing both military objectives and those of their respective faiths.

Episcopalian Ch. (Maj.) John Williams knew the two-collar problem well, although he admitted the term has become a cliché and has outlived the Navy uniform that produced the saying. Still, he reflected, "people who mentioned that, seemed to me to always be like the ones who were really good at the military part of it but not real good at the cross side of it. … The assumption was we're totally part of the military system. Anyone who would say that we're not, like it's just ridiculous. We're so embedded in the system. The cross thing comes in the sense of like faithfulness to one's church, which for most people, is fairly compatible with the military service." When it's not, however, he said, "they did not stay long." In his view, to be able to support the troops, chaplains had to support troop actions, and sometimes that came at the cost of religious and even moral considerations.

Despite its dated reference, the two-collar problem is a metaphor for the military chaplaincy that sums up their role in the lives of post-9/11 service members well. It is a dilemma that looms large over their job and daily interactions, influencing their relationship with service members and their approaches to spiritual guidance and even moral advice. As *the* symbol of faith in the military, chaplains operate in a unique position, one tiptoeing the line of meeting service members' needs and representing the military organization as well as the line between free exercise and no establishment. With their unique place in the history of the US military and their position as a pulse-read on the spiritual lives and overall well-being of many service members, a significant portion of the story of religion in the military is theirs. As such, this chapter will explore the history of the US military chaplaincy, the realities of their job today, and their role in the lives of post-9/11 service members. Chaplains are but one part of the religious resources that the US military provides its service members, yet they are simultaneously the best starting point for an investigation of military religious resources overall.

Military Religious Resources and the History of Military Chaplains

Represented in every branch of the US military today, the Chaplain Corps of the Army, Navy/Marines/Coast Guard, and Air Force all have their roots in the naval chaplaincy established by the Continental Congress in November, 1775. As early as September, 1775, George Washington had the subject of religious freedom on his mind. In a letter to Col. Benedict Arnold, Washington wrote:

> As the Contempt of the Religion of a Country by ridiculing any of its Ceremonies or affront its Ministers or Votaries has ever been deeply resented, you are to be particularly careful to restrain every Officer and Soldier from such Imprudence and Folly and to punish every Instance of it. On the other hand, as far lays in your power, you are to protect and support the free Exercise of the Religion of the Country and the undisturbed Enjoyment of the rights of Conscience in religious Matters, with your utmost Influence and Authority. (Boller, 2012: 55)

General Washington was adamant that the military simultaneously show respect for differing religious views while also affording service members the ability to practice their faith. By November, he helped institute the Navy Chaplaincy. By May 1776, he ordered a day of rest followed by chapel attendance with "their respective chaplain" (Drazin & Currey, 1995: 11). Finally, by May 27, 1777, Washington and the Continental Congress proposed that there "should be one chaplain to each brigade of the army, nominated by the brigadier general, and appointed by Congress, with the same pay as colonel" (L. Johnson, 1856: 9). The support for and maintenance of chaplains and free exercise in the US military continued in the early decades of the US. By 1838, there was to be at least one chaplain per brigade in the Army with a limit of thirty in the Army and twenty-four in the Navy.

The number of chaplains has ballooned to include today over 5000 chaplains between active-duty and the Reserves in all branches of the US military combined, increasing by 75% since 2009 (Torpy, 2021)—the largest Chaplaincy Corps being that of the Army at about 2900. With certain limitations stemming from staffing or remote locations, every unit has an assigned unit ministry team (UMT) made up of one chaplain and one chaplain's assistant. When units without UMTs require religious support, a chaplain section will supply religious ministry support (US Marine Corps, 2015: 1–4). That is to say that chaplains remain and have been a staple of the US military since its conception, and to talk of the history of chaplains in the military is to talk about the history of religion in the US military overall. They appear to be the clear through-line and have, from the beginning, been at the heart of constitutionally protected free exercise of religion in the military overall.

In addition to their role in protecting religious tolerance and free exercise in the early years of the nation, chaplains were also thought important for the comfort they would bring service members and for their ability to instill good values. It was thought they had important moral effects which could also benefit strategic ends (Maurer, 2005). Theologian Ed Waggoner (2014: 705) proposes that early chaplains were a part of the military because it was generally thought that "all US military personnel would be Christians who need the solace of their faith in martial contexts," and "military-wide affirmation of Christian religions would nurture winning traits in individual fighters." By extension, a stronger Christian faith supplied by military chaplains would inspire military personnel to be better Christians and, therefore, better warriors. Thus, chaplains provided some strategic benefit to the military while also aligning with constitutional aims of free exercise. If being a good Christian made someone a better combatant, then this helped ensure the strategic goals of the nation.

The modern religion of the US military and the religious resources it provides have morphed and matured over time to become integral to the military strategic mission. The biggest changes over time that have shaped modern military religious culture and resources are: (1) the formalization of who can become a chaplain, (2) the move toward religious pluralism, (3) the concurrent rise and influence of evangelicals, (4) the significant expansion of chaplains' roles to serve as symbols of a civil religion, and (5) their consequent function as strategic assets for military goals. In combination, these changes have embedded chaplains in essential strategic positions within the military, often in ways that remove them from fulfilling the nominal purpose of bringing comfort and morality to service members as religious guides. Instead, many chaplains, mostly those at higher positions of authority, have limited interaction with service members, though they have a large role in shaping the ways service members, even high-ranking officers, understand moral decision-making and questions of conscience. What follows, then, expands on these themes to account for the place of religion in the military today, particularly the push and pull chaplains face between the organization and the military personnel they serve.

The Formalization of Chaplains and the Rise of Pluralism

Washington's vision of chaplains serving as religious guides for service members conjures up kindly images of ordained ministers leading Sunday services for engaged soldiers; however, the reality is that there were not many rules or regulations governing who could become a military chaplain or what they should do. Before 1861, chaplains did not have to be ordained, nor did they receive formal training for life among service members. In the early to mid-nineteenth century, chaplains were "poorly trained, some were political appointees, and almost all spent a good deal of their time serving as secretaries to the ships' captains" (Weil, 1950: 8). Many were learned teachers and not clergy at all. While chaplain activity increased during early American conflicts, vacancies in both the Army and Navy were common. Viewed as a "political plum," many clergymen sought out the role, but apart from wartime, chaplains had little role beyond schoolteacher for service members and secretaries for high-ranking officers (Weil, 1950: 6). Consequently, congressmen did not feel the need to fill chaplain positions. The ad hoc "decisions about selection, training, duties, and status" of chaplains characterized the period, with many clergymen volunteering without commissions (Waggoner, 2014: 705). There was also political pressure to abolish clergy from the military on the grounds that it was unconstitutional and because chaplains appeared to be lazy or even hedonistic, but the charges lobbed against military chaplains soon took a backseat as the need for them ramped up during the Civil War.

To combat criticisms against military chaplains and fill chaplain positions as the Civil War escalated, legislation began to tighten rules on who could become a military chaplain. In August of 1861, Congress passed an act that included the provision "that none but regularly ordained ministers of some Christian denomination shall be eligible to selection or appointment" (US Congress, 1861: 288). A year later, they added language to specify further that "no person shall be appointed a chaplain in the US Army who is not a regularly ordained minister of some religious denomination *and* who does not present testimonials of his good standing as such minister" (Weil, 1950: 6 [emphasis my own]). In concert with these changes, commanding officers were pressured to remove the chaff among the ranks of the military chaplaincy, clearing them of bad eggs taking advantage of the position. This left some chaplain positions unfilled. Running concurrently with a renewed desire for religious guidance amid moral concerns in war time, officers began to see the benefit of having a chaplain among their men, making them more discerning about whom they appointed into chaplain positions ("Traveling Preachers", 2015: 615).

In addition to the more stringent rules for appointing chaplains, officers also had more willing chaplains to choose from in wartime as literally thousands of itinerant preachers followed troops during the war, offering services and gaining favor with service members. Mostly evangelical

Methodists, traveling preachers filled the void left by the unfilled military chaplain positions. With renewed importance, chaplains took on more official roles, making "regular reports to the colonel of the regiment on the 'moral and religious condition of the regiment, and such suggestions as may conduce to the social happiness and moral improvement of the troops'" (Weil, 1950: 6). This marked the true beginning of chaplains taking on advisory roles to higher ranking officials.

Along with the rise of committed, ordained clergy in the ranks, the military also began to include other religions apart from Protestantism. Despite the establishment and free exercise clauses, recall that the 1861 act required military chaplains to be ordained in "some Christian denomination." Even with freedom of religion, early years favored supporting Christian service members alone. This changed during the Civil War when Jewish soldiers and sailors enlisted in the Union army. When the 5th Pennsylvania Cavalry attempted to commission a Jewish rabbi, Reverend Arnold Fischel, as their military chaplain, the Secretary of War rejected his application. A Jewish rabbi could not be a military chaplain under the law. This alarmed the American Jewish press, who relocated Rev. Fischel to Washington, DC to minister to wounded Jewish service members in military hospitals. As his reputation grew, Fischel and the Jewish press lobbied to President Lincoln to change the act, and Lincoln obliged. In July 1862, Congress accepted a change to the chaplaincy law proposed by Lincoln that included "the appointment of brigade chaplains of the Catholic, Protestant and Jewish religions" (Feldberg, 2009). While this change notably leaves out many religions, it does represent a significant shift in the history of chaplains as it marks the military becoming more explicitly pluralistic.

Near the turn of the century, the role of military chaplains became still more formalized with acts of Congress in 1898, 1899, and 1901 that made changes to pay, rank, age limit, physical requirements, and, most importantly, a requirement that appointed chaplains meet specific ecclesiastical qualifications by taking a test upon commission. Extending from the changes made in 1861 and 1862 (that chaplains be ordained by a civilian religion), this marked the origins of ecclesiastical endorsing agencies that are still used today for aspiring military chaplains (Hedrick, 1990: 41–2). The Protestant Episcopal Church, Methodist Episcopal Church, Presbyterian Church (USA), and the Catholic Church all formed endorsing agencies, and they, along with the Federal Council of Churches (now the National Council of Churches), helped the military commission new chaplains. As the military became significantly larger during World War I, these agencies placed hundreds of chaplains into new positions, growing the ranks from the original seventy-five chaplains in the Army to 2300 by 1918, reflecting more modern numbers. As the needs of service members changed, and with more religions represented in a larger military, a 1917 act of Congress authorized the appointment of chaplains of religious minorities, paving the way for the Jewish Welfare Board also to endorse new chaplains (Weil, 1950: 7).

For the rest of the twentieth century and early twenty-first century, the military chaplaincy continued to become even more formalized. The National Defense Act of 1920 created the position of Chief of Chaplains to oversee the entire Army Chaplaincy Corps and act as a chief advisor to high-ranking officials in the military, like the Chief of Staff, a four-star general. Additionally, the chaplaincy became formally established as a corps in 1920 with members receiving rank and commensurate pay. A Reserve training program and component also soon followed. By 1949, the US military established the Air Force Chaplain Corps, bringing the military chaplaincy to its modern form with corps in each branch. With expanded roles as counselors in the 1960s, the military chaplaincy became what it remains today with chaplains acting as ministers, teachers, moral guides, counselors, and strategic advisors.

Despite large and expedient expansions to the military chaplaincy, representation of minority religions did not keep pace with growing diversity among service members. Jewish rabbis were endorsed and included in the ranks since the early twentieth century, but the first Muslim military chaplain, Chaplain Abdul-Rasheed Muhammad, was not commissioned until 1994. The first Buddhist chaplain, Thomas Dyer, was not appointed until 2008. The first Hindu chaplain, Pratima Dharm, was not appointed until 2011. These represented major religions in the world and a fair proportion of service members. For even smaller minorities, like Wiccans, there remain no appointed military chaplains at all. While the number of service members affiliated with minority religions in the US military has remained small, the slowness in appointing diverse chaplains belies the chaplaincy's roots specifically in fostering religious free exercise. It further illustrates the dilemma of military chaplains, caught between commitment to the frames of the military organization (and its history therein) and the needs of service members.

This history of slowly adding in chaplains from minority religions reveals two major trends. The endorsement of minority chaplains shows the growth of pluralism in the military; however, the slowness of this process points to firmly rooted strains of Christianity, particularly the overrepresentation of conservative evangelical groups. Military chaplains are overwhelmingly evangelical, making up 69.01% of the Chaplain Corps as of 2017 (See Fig. 2.1). Other Protestants fill 21.82% of posts and Catholics 7%. Non-Christian minority religions make up only 2.16% of military chaplains (Torpy, 2019). They are also overwhelmingly white (79.1%) and male (93%) (Malana, 2016).[2]

The number of active evangelical service members is harder to track because, until 2017, DoD questionnaires included religious categories for "Protestant, no preference" and "Protestant, other churches," so many non-denominational—but evangelical—service members may not have been properly captured in DEOMI statistics (Shellnutt, 2017). According to the Military Association of Atheists and Freethinkers (MAAF), only about 13% of all service members identify as evangelical—down from about 20% in 2009 (Torpy, 2019). Others claim that about 40% of service members are evangelical (Brady, 2005; Shellnutt, 2017). While the disparity between 13% and 40% is quite large, it raises an important question about why military religion overrepresents evangelicals among its chaplains in either case. The dominance of evangelicals is an important part of the larger picture of what US military religious resources look like today.

The Rise and Influence of Evangelicals in the Chaplain Corps

By evangelical, I am referring to an ideal type. Sociologist Meredith McGuire (2008, 70) explains that the most important features of defining evangelicalism are "the conversion or 'born again' experience" and the "expectation of certain specific kinds of ongoing experiences of the divine in one's life." Evangelicalism is found in various denominations, including strains of Baptist, Holiness-Pentecostal, Reformed-Confessional, and Anabaptist traditions. For McGuire, the historical denominational divisions are less important than "how individuals select, interpret, and use

[2] Malana (2016) draws on 2015 Navy Manpower Programming Budget System and Officer Personnel Information Systems data to show some Chaplain Corps population trends. Among non-white military chaplains, 7.9% were Black/African American, 5% were Asian, 3.7% declined to respond, 3.2% were "multiple," 0.7% were indigenous, and 0.4% were Hawaiian/Pacific Islander. The data did not include Hispanic/LatinX.

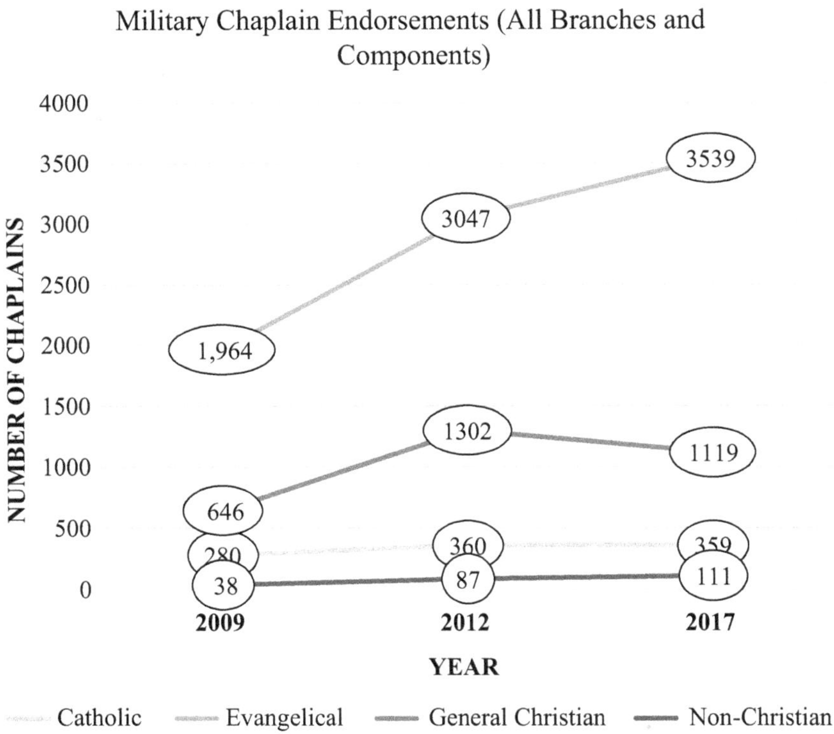

Fig. 2.1 Military chaplain endorsements. (DoD data obtained from Torpy (2021) via the Military Association of Atheists and Freethinkers. "General Christian" here includes all non-Catholic, non-Evangelical Christian traditions, including Mainline, Orthodox, and others. Non-Christian includes all other religious traditions with military endorsing agencies, including Judaism, Islam, Hinduism, Buddhism, etc.)

evangelical traditions … in their religion-as-lived" (McGuire, 2008: 71). This is important, particularly for my sample, where "non-denominational" became shorthand for evangelical for some of the participants but not others. Treating evangelicalism as a strain of practice and thought rather than denominational affiliation makes sense in understanding the religious experiences of these veterans.

Evangelicals were outsiders to the military and military culture in the late nineteenth and early twentieth centuries. The large number of wandering ministers during the American Civil War who were largely evangelical Methodists or came from post-Third Great Awakening era denominations largely refused appointments when asked. Indeed, there was not a clear push for evangelicalism in the US military or even a front-running evangelical endorsement agency until 1942 with the formation of the National Association of Evangelicals (NAE) and their endorsing agency, the Commission on Chaplains (NAECC). That is not to say evangelicals and evangelical chaplains were disinterested parties in the military to that point. Southern Baptists and the Southern Baptist Convention had endorsed chaplains since the Civil War—for the Confederate Army—but they did not establish their endorsing procedures for the US military until 1941. This meant that most chaplains entering the military during World War II and leading into the Cold War were Mainline Protestant. Accordingly, most military leaders and chaplains in the 1950s and 1960s belonged to Mainline Protestant groups. According to Hansen (2012: 122), "evangelicals were few, were considered outsiders, and were wary of the military establishment." It took some time for evangelicals, and the NAE specifically, to change the landscape of the military.

Evangelical concern had been kindled by a perception that post-World War II (WWII) service members were coming home "physical, mental, moral and social wrecks, having been infected with venereal diseases" and "coddled by a complacent service attitude which encourages promiscuity" (Weinstein & Seay, 2006: 41). A report back from a group of evangelicals visiting US occupation forces in Europe in 1947 only enhanced this feeling when they witnessed "the extent of venereal disease, drunkenness, vulgarity, and black marketing among American troops" (Loveland, 1996: 1). The NAE became concerned for what happens to young men "removed from home and church influences" in a world divided (Weinstein & Seay, 2006: 42). The Armed Forces were the frontline against the perceived godlessness of Communism, and the NAE and other evangelical endorsing agencies believed they needed to prepare service members to defend Christian democracy.

As the purported moral leader of the world during the Cold War, the US projected a message that "God is an American" (Stahl, 2017: Location No. 3360). President Dwight Eisenhower's election win marked a turning point in the rise of evangelicalism. Cast as "one of their own" by Billy Graham and other conservative evangelical leaders, Eisenhower was outspoken against the threat of communism and the clear solution for it: "spiritual convictions" (Loveland, 1996: 36). By 1955, he "ratcheted up his rhetoric, arguing that the founding fathers had recognized that all rights came from God and it was merely the state's duty to defend those rights" (Kruse, 2015: 75). He explicitly placed the very existence of the American way of life in God's hands.

Along with other overtly religious political moves like adding "nation under God" to the Pledge of Allegiance, Eisenhower also explicitly supported evangelical enterprises during his presidency, including the 1953 March of Freedom—a "year-long campaign to proclaim the Gospel to the American people"—the American Legion's "Back to God" movement, and the initiation of the National Prayer Breakfast (Loveland, 1996: 38; Kruse, 2015). In the military, evangelical elites began to shape troop education and training. For example, John Broger, a director at the Pentagon and head of Troop Information, saw communism as a "'dynamic ideology' that could be defeated only by 'a stronger dynamic ideology,'" evangelical Christianity. By 1961 and the slow ramping up of combat operations in Vietnam, evangelical leaders began to have more political influence, including over and in the military.

To expand their influence, evangelicals relied on several major strategies. They used the NAECC to overfill military chaplains' roles along with publication and outreach programs to promote awareness among possible recruits. Where the NAE placed only about 100 chaplains "from various evangelical and fundamentalist denominations" by the late 1940s, they, along with other evangelical endorsing groups like the Christian and Military Alliance, Assemblies of God, the Southern Baptist Convention, and others, endorsed over 500 military chaplains by the late-1960s (Loveland, 1996: 16, 26–7). Evangelicals outpaced Mainline Protestant chaplains by double. The US military nominally worked on a quota system and attempted to fill chaplain positions commensurate with the proportion of the general population's denominational affiliations.

However, in the 1960s, Mainline Protestant support for the Vietnam War dwindled even as Mainline numbers declined overall in the US. Mainline leaders and chaplains often opposed the war while evangelicals "clung fiercely to the belief that America was a Christian nation [and] that the military was a force for good" (Kobes Du Mez, 2020: 10). As a result, Mainline Protestant endorsing agencies failed to meet their quotas of new chaplains, leaving some positions unfilled and ready for conservative evangelicals to take instead. The NAECC lobbied to fill the positions left open, and "the military, seeking to meet the demand for chaplains caused by increased draft calls and recruiting drives during the Vietnam

War, encouraged them to do so" (Loveland, 1996: 23). In a bid to fill even more positions, certain evangelical denominations purposefully stopped using the NAECC as their endorsing agency, creating new ones instead. For example, the Assemblies of God and the Church of God formed their own endorsing agencies, which increased their individual number of military chaplain slots. This, on paper, made it appear that the NAECC was not dominating the open positions; however, this greatly expanded the number of evangelical chaplains in the military. The NAECC perhaps only had a little over 100 newly endorsed chaplains at the time, but others had 10s to 100s more as well.

Inside the military itself, evangelicals more actively established a place for themselves. They employed letters, publications, and fellowships to create positive attitudes toward evangelicals. Organizations like the Officer's Christian Fellowship (OCF) and the Christian Military Fellowship (CMF) helped to entrench their influence in the religious life of the military. These fellowships existed on top of the military's own religious infrastructure. By taking advantage of vacancies, overfilling chaplains' positions, and establishing outreach programs and fellowships, evangelicalism found its foothold.

With decades-long efforts to grow evangelical influence and power across secular institutions, evangelicals used various organizations to cultivate elites in the military (Lindsay, 2007a: 208). Fellowships like OCF at officer candidate schools and the influence of evangelical chaplains in authoritative positions in the three Chaplain Corps, evangelicals gained access to elite leadership positions as high-ranking military officials. Sociologist D. Michael Lindsay (2007b: 165, 173) contends that the influence of elite evangelicals in the military accounts for the "increasingly evangelical ethos of the armed services." As high-ranking officers attended chapels and participated in fellowships, meetings "provided informal forms of fellowship and support for evangelicals in the higher circles." Evangelical elites in the military could continue to gather and promote their interests in formal religious settings alongside other military meetings. These sorts of organizational developments allowed evangelicalism to flourish. Where once evangelical chaplains could have been called "outsiders" to the military, from the 1970s to today, evangelicals in the military (chaplains and service members alike) have dominated military culture. While the military and its religious culture are not unilaterally evangelical, their influence does not appear to be declining, even if the number of service members who claim an evangelical affiliation remains stagnant.

The continued disproportionate number of evangelical chaplains allows evangelicalism in the US military to continue to hold influence. That said, it would mischaracterize the situation to claim that religion in the military is entirely evangelical in nature. In fact, both the number and the activities of evangelical chaplains have created tensions with those who are not evangelical. Indeed, certain commitments to endorsing agencies motivate an additional difficulty in the two-collar problem. Progressive Mainline Protestant military chaplains actively push for pluralism and pastoral care, while conservative evangelical chaplains promote sectarianism and evangelism, creating a culture war within the Chaplain Corps, even as Mainline Protestant and especially Catholic military chaplain numbers dwindle (Shinkman, 2013). Alongside that struggle are consistent public outcries over the perception of an establishment of religion in the military. Press articles and even court cases (Cooperman, 2006; Weinstein & Aslan, 2007) have challenged these practices.

That is not to say that the cultural differences between progressive and conservative lines means evangelicals are unilaterally against pluralism. Again, I am describing an evangelical ideal type. There are indeed evangelical chaplains who proselytize among the ranks for example, but there are also those who only proselytize those who have no religious preference and evangelical chaplains who actively provide ways for people of other faiths to worship. For instance, one chaplain interviewed by Goodstein (2005) avowed, "I am an Assemblies of God, pound-the-pulpit preacher, but I'll go to the ropes for the Wiccan." Some evangelical chaplains do actively attempt to convert people of different religions and even denominations, but modern concern among evangelical chaplains tends to be over the higher and higher percentage of individuals joining the military with no religious affiliation or who are undecided. Evangelical religious resources, then, are varied. They supply and promote beliefs, values, and narratives that support military operations and ensure the influence of religion on military culture.

Toward a Civil Religion: The Expanded Role of Chaplains in the Military

Despite the significant influence of evangelicalism over the past seventy years, military policy and its guiding frames do aim to promote pluralism and protect the establishment clause. That said, what results from this is the promotion of a civil religion in its place, and the reality of this can be found no more clearly than in the expanded role of chaplains from simply faith leaders and moral teachers to walking symbols and propagators of the US civil religion.

By civil religion, I mean to rely on Robert Bellah's (2005) formulation of it. While the term originates from Jean-Jacques Rousseau's *The Social Contract*, Bellah reformulates Rousseau's "dogmas of the civil religion: the existence of God, the life to come, the reward of virtue and the punishment of vice, and the exclusion of religious intolerance" to serve the civil religion of America better (2005: 43). This view of civil religion is one accounting for the "religious dimension for the whole fabric of American life … expressed in a set of beliefs, symbols, and rituals" (2005: 42). Reverence for the American flag, the induction of a President with oath on a Bible, the National Day of Prayer (for which the President is legally required to sign an annual proclamation announcing citizens may "turn to God in prayer and meditation" according to 36 U.S. Code § 119), the National Anthem, the constitution qua holy text, and the hero worship of military personnel all constitute the American civil religion. It may, at times, look like Christianity. But Bellah is quick to point out that the civil religion of America is not the same as Christianity. For example, the "God of the civil religion is not only rather 'unitarian'; he is also on the austere side, much more related to order, law, and right than to salvation and love" (2005: 45). While it has many clear Judeo-Christian archetypes underlying it—and this certainly factors into its ability to work often seamlessly atop the beliefs and aims of the Christian Right—it is also "genuinely American" with its "own prophets and its own martyrs, its own sacred events and sacred places, its own solemn rituals and symbols" (2005: 54). In the absence of an established religion but with an abundance of religious military personnel, chaplains find themselves at the crossroads between their religion and a conservative American civil religion, an extension of the two-collar problem for some and a merging of the two allegiances for others.

While chaplains bring either progressive or conservative concerns from their respective denominational affiliations, they may or may not take issue with the conservative strain of civil religion the military promotes. But it would make their jobs exceedingly difficult if they did not support a conservative view of the American civil religion. As Hansen (2012: 31) asserts, "their constant identification of the United States with freedom and democracy, the flags on their uniforms, and most of all their dedication to the American Constitution that is acted out in their oath of office" demonstrates their promotion of an American civil religion; to do otherwise would undermine the strategic aims of the military as it calls for self-sacrifice in defense of an idealized nation.

To that end, military chaplains have found their roles expanded beyond the confines of Sunday services. Chaplains began their time in the military as moral support, religious leaders, and educators. The Army website, for instance, lists "providing advice in matters pertaining to religion, morals and morale"; "overseeing a full program of religious ministries, including workshops, counseling sessions, religious [and ethics] education and special events." But these initial roles have expanded greatly, as special events now include "officiat[ing] official ceremonies such as military functions, funerals, and memorials." Their most basic duty of "provid[ing] religious ministry to a variety of armed service personnel" is on the bottom of the list and also includes "civilians from the US, foreign nations and agencies" (GoArmy.com, 2018).

Much of the expansion of their role can be mapped atop the rise of evangelicals' expanded influence over military elites and policymakers along with the formalization of chaplains as officers in the military. However, it is critical to see, too, the ways expanded influence has been consistently constrained by policies promoting pluralism and maintaining the establishment clause, effectively relegating chaplains to functionaries of the American civil religion. This is, in fact, baked into rules and regulations of the military. Army Regulation 165-1 (US Department of Army, 1998), for instance, explains, "the Army chaplaincy, in providing religious services and ministries to the command, is an instrument of the US government to ensure that soldier's religious 'free exercise' rights are protected. At the same time, chaplains are trained to avoid even the appearance of an establishment of religion." Again, this places chaplains at the junction between free exercise and establishment. They must be able to minister to everyone but not establish their own religion.

At face value, this regulation guarantees constitutionality and pluralism. Tacitly, however, it frees the military up to use chaplains toward the end of promoting American civil religion. The regulation continues, "Military and patriotic ceremonies may require a chaplain to provide an invocation, reading, prayer, or benediction. Such occasions are *not considered to be religious.*" As such mandatory military gatherings take place, the military uses chaplains to facilitate religious practices that ought not be considered religious. And while there has been a class action lawsuit over the inability of chaplains to use "in Jesus' name" at the end of a prayer at such events (Hansen, 2012: 104; Goodstein, 2005)—illustrating the upholding of the Establishment Clause—this regulation points to the chaplains' use of the "neutral deistic language" of Bellah's (1975: 45) conception of American civil religion. Religion is still happening at military ceremonies and gatherings, just not necessarily a Christian or otherwise specific one.

Chaplains as Strategic Assets for a Civil Religion

Modern military chaplains are no longer merely moral and spiritual guides; they are now implicated in the US military's goal of "global, 'full-spectrum dominance' by promoting among military personnel the practices, values, moral sensitivities, and self-appraisals that the military thinks conducive to the projection of national power" (Waggoner, 2014: 712). Chaplains, originating in the civilian sector and accredited by a civilian endorsement agency, enter the military ready to serve the religious needs of service members, yet they are reoriented toward strategic aims of the military, reshaped to support and disseminate the institutional frames of the military organization. Theologian Ed Waggoner (2014: 703) sees the reframing as a form of "bricolage." In his estimation, "just as an artist imbues existing elements with new, context-specific meanings" in the form of a novel mixed media creation, the military "reconfigures civilian practices and ways of speaking to generate functions and meanings for religion that support [its] institutional aim." By taking existing civic materials, ordained and endorsed chaplains, the military can re-socialize their public roles along with the symbols of religion to channel the Chaplain Corps toward its strategic ends. The result is military chaplains who are ministers of the American civil religion to service members, influencing their participation in the military in both tacit and explicit ways. An essential part of that narrative chaplains promote, as we will see, is an "ideology of the necessity of war-as-sacrifice" where violence is necessary; other diplomatic options are "unreliable, ineffective and effeminate" (Denton-Borhaug, 2011: 93).

Underlying this reframing, I argue, is the promotion and establishment of the American civil religion "stressing what the United States has to offer the world" (i.e., freedom and democracy as virtue) rather than how the US can participate in a global community (Hansen, 2012: 31). It is clear from how the Armed Forces use military chaplains that they are aware of the motivating quality chaplains have. Their message is one of spreading freedom around the world, rather than spreading specific religious convictions. According to sociologist Robert Wuthnow (1989), there is no greater guiding principle for understanding the American way of life than the US's nominal moral exceptionalism in its spread of freedom and democracy, as it requires no actual religious values or justifications to explain it. That the military has chaplains who spread American civil religion is seen as a strategic benefit and force multiplier. While the oft-mentioned two-collar problem represents a complex dynamic of tensions—competing cultural values, questions of responsibility and authority, institutional needs versus congregational ones—it is perhaps no more clearly manifest than in the evolution of chaplains into force multipliers rather than simply spiritual caretakers. It is the promise of peace reframed as the promise of national power.

This tension is not an easy one for chaplains to navigate. It means that they become eyes and ears for officers hoping to understand if their men are combat ready or not. As moral guides for service members and officers alike, they are uniquely situated to speak to whether service members are on board with the immediate goals of a mission, but they are sidelined from moral assessments of the mission itself or the actions service members will be called to undertake. In my estimation, this, too, is a way of being ministers of the American civil religion. It relegates the moral compass of chaplains to that of promoting the US ideals of freedom and democracy. The nominal virtues explicit in the cultural stories of American exceptionalism give way to a terrible calculus of results. It is the incoherence philosopher Alasdair MacIntyre describes in *After Virtue* (2007: 8) concerning twentieth-century moral discourse: "premises which invoke justice and innocence are at odds with premises which invoke success and survival." The narratives of civil religion and the ostensible role of chaplains as moral guides are at odds with the military's teleological focus. The success of a mission trumps adherence to virtue. As we will see, this is a significant factor underlying many stories of trauma in later chapters of this book.

The Military Chaplain Career

Looking now at the careers and stories of those chaplains that I interviewed, it is clear that there is not one monolithic military chaplain experience. However, there are some commonalities. Would-be military chaplains have requirements they must possess before being considered for the position, assuming they have never served in the military. These requirements are set by the Chaplain Corps for the Army (along with the National Guard), the Navy (along with the Marine Corps and Coast Guard), and the Air Force. Like those branches, there are also active and reserve components to the three Chaplain Corps. All three have roughly the same stipulations (see US Army, 2018; US Navy, 2019; US Air Force, 2018). Chaplains must have a baccalaureate degree from an accredited institution and must have completed (or nearly completed) a Master of Divinity or similar degree. They must also have at least two years of pastoral leadership experience and must be endorsed by one of the DoD's recognized endorsing agencies. While they are nominally open to a pastor representing any religion, the endorsing agency factor manifestly limits the number of faith representations allowed to commission as a chaplain. Wicca, for example, does not yet have an Ecclesiastical Endorsing Agency in the military, although they are recognized by the VA. In addition, prospective chaplains must be US citizens, younger than forty-two (in the Army and Navy) or forty-six (Air Force), able to meet physical and medical standards, have a clear disciplinary and legal record with no convictions or history of domestic, child, or drug abuse. Assuming they meet the above requirements and pass a security clearance and credit check, they must then attend an officer training program and commission as officers, marking the beginning of a chaplain's military career.

As chaplains enter the military as officers corresponding with their level of education, they begin their careers with high ranks. With ranks as high as a two-star general (Navy Rear Admirals or Army/Air Force Major Generals), new ranks bring greater authority over subordinate chaplains, overseeing chaplain operations, and giving spiritual and even strategic guidance to other non-chaplain high-ranking officers. While these high ranks afford them more power, prestige, and pay, chaplains continue to have the designation of "chaplain" alone. Even the two chaplains at the rank of colonel I interviewed maintained the designation of "Chaplain Sandberg" or "Chaplain Granger." The reason for this is that military chaplains do *not* have command authority, even if they are the only remaining officer on the battlefield. A way to ensure a separation of church and state, this important distinction is a part of Title X of the US Code, section 7231 (1956) "Command: chaplains," which states clearly, "A chaplain has rank without command." Additionally, chaplains who enter the military without previous military experience only learn to fire a weapon if it is a requisite for completing a military training school (like Army Rangers) but otherwise do not learn to fire a weapon and do not carry weapons, as they are designated as non-combatants in official military policy (see, e.g., Dept of the Army, Army Regulation 165-1, 3-1f, 2015) and in Geneva Convention I, Article 24 (1949). They do not attend service academies unless by happenstance—as in the case of an officer becoming chaplain later in her career—and they rely on civilian divinity schools for their theological training. This non-combatant status and lack of command authority places chaplains in a unique position as both authoritative and revered yet set apart.

The duties and locations of chaplains run the gamut. On one end, there are battalion chaplains going into the theater of war under threat of fire, chaplains teaching courses at officer candidate programs, and hospital chaplains praying with service members at their bedside. On the other end of the array of jobs are higher ranking chaplains that advise the topmost officers, delegate responsibilities to subordinate chaplains, and generally do not interact with nearly as many service members day to day. Chaplains are retirement eligible after their twenty-first year of active-duty, assuming they did not leave the military before that time.

To illustrate what a military chaplain career looks like, consider Chaplain (Col.) Thomas Sandberg, who, at thirty-three years, had the longest career of the chaplains interviewed for this project. He became an Army military chaplain in the late 1980s after two years as a Lutheran pastor in a small midwestern church. In reflection of his long career, he recalled doing the jobs "most chaplains do. I've been a battalion chaplain. I was usually in the combat arms units. I've been airborne, air assault. I've also served, of course, brigades, division, division minus elements. ... I've had a large variety of experiences." As he moved through his career and climbed in rank, so did the number of military personnel he needed to ensure had access to religious resources, from the smallest being a battalion (hundreds of service members) to the largest at a division (more than 25,000 service members).

Beyond overseeing the needs of service members' religious lives, delegating to subordinate chaplains, meeting with his chaplain assistant, and providing guidance to individual service members, he also had several "outside the box" assignments. He was an ethics instructor, a command chaplain for the US Army Medical Research and Development Command (USAMRDC), and a command chaplain for the First Army, the training command of reserve components. With many different divisions and commands across the US Armed Forces, Ch. Sandberg's different ranks and roles were illustrative of all the chaplains I interviewed, even those with a career half the length of time.

Sandberg's career snapshot is also helpful in understanding how and where ministry happens in the military. Early in his career as a battalion chaplain, he reflected on having the most interaction with soldiers on a day-to-day basis through in-person ministry both in the chapel and in other settings. "The battalion chaplain, that was my ministry. That's what always appealed to me about being in the military ministry was this ministry of presence." He felt that over the course of his career that religious "nones," or those who mark "no preference" as their religious preference in the military, were a growing demographic. He felt his "ministry of presence" allowed him to interact with them with empathy regardless of their religious convictions. This was a real highlight of his career. He recalled, "What you find with the no preference is they really don't care if you're Presbyterian or Roman Catholic, but they'll accept you as a chaplain. They'll accept a spiritual dialogue with you. They will approach you. They'll talk with you. They'll counsel with you. But they don't identify with you as their parish pastor. And I've always found that really comforting and challenging, truthfully. That's why I really loved battalion ministry."

In addition to chapel services and spiritual counseling, Sandberg felt he often functioned as a social worker for his battalion. While making the rounds with service members, some would often ask him for his time, and it was "off to the races … about anything under the sun." Non-religious questions would come up about marriage care or interpersonal or financial issues or concerns over feelings of fear. "Oftentimes the counseling for most chaplains will bring spiritual content into those conversations. And the soldiers will be very receptive to those things. But they won't identify it as 'religious' even though it has a definite religious foundation and intent behind it." There are social workers in the military; however, this pastoral care was a large part of his ministry and interaction with soldiers, who he began to believe were less religious as time went on. Often this work (spiritual or social) would be preemptive and spurred on by superior officers, if need be, to address trauma or loss at crucial moments in the lives of service members.

Shifting roles to become a brigade pastor was difficult for him because he had less interaction with Army soldiers. A brigade usually has about six battalions within it, so just by the numbers, he could not interact with the same proportion of service members. He explained:

> Understand that through a career of a chaplain battalion is your most heavy interactive role with soldiers. As you move from the battalion up to the brigade, your role or hands-on with soldiers gets less and less. And the role you do have with soldiers, tends to be more and more senior and higher-ranking soldiers as you move up to brigade, to division, to above division level stuff.

As a brigade pastor, he had six battalion chaplains and six religious affairs specialists under him that he had to lead and mentor, so his time was spent helping them to do the hands-on ministry and smaller religious services, while his ministry was focused more on higher ranking officers and speaking and praying at larger gatherings like memorial services.

By the time he reached the division level, he oversaw ministry for about 36,000 soldiers. His ministry became something much different. "When you start thinking ministry, you have less and less hands-on ministry because you're not walking around where these people are working. But you're trying to help large programs for broad numbers of people," Sandberg said. He does not lead chapel services at all anymore, and the command headquarters at the division level did not have chapels. "My involvement in chapel on Sunday mornings has actually been going to local congregations as just another congregant." What direct ministry remained for him was relegated only to very senior officers (colonels and future generals) and senior noncommissioned officers (sergeant majors). At such a high level, his time was mostly spent developing curriculum programs with a spiritual dimension and teaching in classrooms or coordinating the deployment of military chaplains according to need. A high-ranking chaplain's amount of interaction with service members becomes extremely limited, yet higher ranking chaplains have much more influence over the spiritual content and religious resources available to military personnel.

The Relationship Between Service Members and Chaplains

With chaplains representing the face of religion in the military, it became clear that speaking with veterans about religion would bring up some strong opinions, both of praise and of criticism, on the quality, value, and role military chaplains provide. While most of the research on religion in the military portrays chaplains as uniformly beneficial, not all chaplains are equally effective, empathetic, or committed to the needs of individual service members. My interviewees voiced both positive and negative assessments of the chaplains they encountered. Service members described different levels of access to chaplains, sought them out more and less often, and had differing opinions of the value of that interaction. By presenting both sides, this section gives a fuller, critical view of the role of chaplains in the lives of service members.

Among my participants, there was significant variation in terms of both access to chaplains and cause for interacting with them. Over half of the participants (twenty-six) sought out a chaplain at least once over the course of their careers, with only two of those stating it was solely on behalf of subordinates. Of those twenty-six, about 75% felt the interaction was helpful. They felt that chaplains were "well-respected" and beneficial to the needs of religious or struggling service members overall as well as to commanding officers—for example, Army Sgt. Joseph Daniel reflected, "We all had a good view of the chaplains," and that view came down to perceptions of their insight, presence, care, and an adaptability to different service roles.

Among the most important roles of the chaplain was as a counselor, aiding both commanders and their subordinates. The ability of commanding officers to use chaplain insight appeared to be what set successful leaders apart. Special Forces SFC Martinez emphasized their importance for command. "The good commanders listen to the chaplains," he said. "It's the bad commanders that don't." Chaplains, in his and others' view, had a real pulse on the needs of lower ranking service members and were "a great resource for them to be able to talk to someone who they could trust, and be a counselor, a mentor or advisor," as Captain Russo put it. He felt it was the fact that chaplains were in the military that they were so useful. He said:

> They're also soldiers, they're also in the service, they understand to some extent what someone goes through. In their job, in their role, they have to understand what it's like to be in the Army, be a soldier, have to deploy, have to go to war, have to see this stuff. But, they also take in that faith perspective, and they're able to kind of talk about the higher calling, maybe a higher order, ability of someone to transcend good and bad or evil.

As part of the military organization, they share an identity with service members that they can rely upon to relate with personnel.

This shared identity also sets them apart from civilian cultural resources, especially in dealing with potential military moral dilemmas. In Captain Marcus Russo's estimation, "If you were to go talk to a normal priest or something, the priest may not have an understanding or appreciation of what you go through as a soldier. ... A [military] chaplain understands that there are terrible things that happen in this world that we may ask our soldiers and our people to be a part of. That doesn't necessarily make them a bad person." That reliance on shared military identity, even military *habitus*, permeates military culture and all sorts of interactions between chaplains and service members. Marine Col. Owen Gray's described his favorite military chaplain: "I just thought it was funny. He would drink and smoke and do all the crazy things everybody else did and I just used to think it was so funny because my preacher at home would never drink and smoke or anything else." That feeling of shared identity allowed Gray to have a strong relationship with his chaplain. He called the chaplain's friendship a "real source of comfort," a point which benefited his entire unit when the chaplain would go on convoys with Gray and his men, often near significant danger.

That comfort and relatability shows how this shared identity comes up in so many ordinary ways. Accordingly, a consequence of that shared identity is that the role distance between service members and chaplains disappears, which also initiates the loss of critical distance. Chaplains then become a megaphone for beliefs, frameworks, and other strategies for action supplied by military culture. Service members trust chaplains to be the confidante supplying them with the right frameworks and prescribing just behaviors. They find "success" because they have beliefs and advice ready at hand that connect with service members who have questions of faith, social problems, experiences of trauma, and the like.

In addition, many service members reflected on the resilience of chaplains. Special Forces Sgt Dean Chamois, for instance, asserted, "They bear the burden of everybody. It's a mentally tough job." He added, "The chaplain role is crazy. You're out there without a gun, that's fricking crazy. That's some faith right there." In stories of trauma and in regular daily life, most of the high opinions of chaplains came down to this mental fortitude and their presence, both a spiritual and actual presence often near or even in dangerous locations. Sgt. McDaniel recalled, "They were even on the battlefield with us. [They] didn't necessarily go on mission with us all the time, but on a few occasions they did. They were in Iraq with us; they'd pray with the guys before we left. While we were there, they had services."

In these stories, chaplains often huddled up with men before missions or even accompanied them in a vehicle through the warzone. Their willingness to be in danger so long as they could serve troops appeared to have a lasting impact on veterans; they noticed the amount of faith and resilience it would take to be a non-combatant in dangerous areas.

Off the battlefield, chaplains were often described as empathetic and non-judgmental, providing a caring confidante when needed. In those stories, the effective chaplains were those who could provide solidarity, pathways to forgiveness, and a sense that God ought not be blamed for the suffering. Army mechanic Taylor Vaught, for example, said of chaplains, "They're the only people that don't judge you. No matter what it is. They're better than a medic. They're better than a counselor. They're your everything when you're in crappy situations." After her traumatic experiences with a superior officer, she felt a chaplain was the only one on her side despite the fact that she was not a person of faith at the time.

Beyond providing understanding in difficult situations and general counsel to command, officers were quick to relate their appreciation for chaplains' ability to provide tangible support amid everyday concerns. Marine Corps officer Arthur Hazel, for example, explained that as a Company Commander, having a military chaplain who could be a religious figure, a counselor, and a social worker was a boon. The chaplain "focused on being an advisor, counsel, someone that people with problems can go talk to." That chaplain helped Hazel navigate his subordinates' diverse issues, including two men who were suicidal and one whose wife outside the service was abusing their children. While the chaplain connected the first two men with mental health professionals, he worked with Child Protective Services to help the other Marine move his children to safety while he was many miles away. "He gave me a lot of guidance on where to turn, who do we need to talk to, how do we need to give his family the right resources, all of those kinds of issues," Hazel said. The positive stories about military chaplains often placed them in the role of counselor or social worker, emphasizing their care and ability to navigate many roles, not just their religious one.

The positive role of chaplains, particularly as counselors, has been well-documented (Hufford et al., 2010; Besterman-Dahan et al., 2012; Carey et al., 2016). As frontline workers for the mental health and social needs of service members, military chaplains have the essential role of connecting troops with mental healthcare professionals and staff social workers. Besterman-Dahan et al. (2012: 1032) point out the importance of the "collaborative model" that allows the much-needed relationships of trust to take place, thereby connecting service members with resources of care—mental, social, and spiritual. By extension, chaplains can play their role in establishing spiritual fitness (Hufford et al., 2010), a key aspect of resilience training, to ensure service members can continue to participate in the military. On the whole, it does appear that military chaplains play a vital and largely positive role in the lives of service members. It is no wonder then that their availability, relatability, and success in sorting out mental health and social problems were all major points of praise from my participants.

However, not all chaplains were as "successful" as others in serving as counselors, social workers, and spiritual guides. Seven of the participants who sought out a chaplain reported negative experiences. In addition, two felt that they did not have access to a chaplain upon having a need for one. While consensus in the literature does show chaplains as having a positive role in the lives of service members, it is worthwhile to explore cases where they fell short to determine what was destructive in the management of troops' needs. The seven who reported finding experiences with chaplains "unhelpful," along with others who had mixed positive and negative interactions, highlighted inexperience, forced religious engagement, different needs, and lack of availability as the common problems.

Many of the participants felt that chaplains did not have enough life experience when offering spiritual guidance or counseling to service members. Most lower ranking enlisted service members and officers interact with lower ranking chaplains after all, and inexperienced chaplains came across as "inauthentic" by contrast to experienced chaplains who more clearly shared the military identity. For example, Army counterpropaganda specialist Sgt. Edward Roberts felt good chaplains were those who could "speak to someone's condition or position." In his view, that ability only came from experience. "I have consistently found throughout my entire military career that most chaplains really don't have enough life experience to speak to someone's condition." A significant reason for this is that the chaplains most interacting with service members day to day, particularly lower ranking service members, were themselves lower ranking chaplains. Air Force LTC Maddie James proposed this very point. "The chaplains were usually younger chaplains," she said, "they may have been older in age, but they were younger in the field, and they were captains, and so therefore, they were sort of new in their ministry. And so, a lot of them were just bringing God to them and doing a lot of evangelizing." This, according to her and to the others with similar complaints, made it difficult for chaplains to relate to service members.

Extending from that failure to relate was a persistent complaint that military chaplains would promote Christianity to those who were not Christian adherents. Despite moves toward pluralism in recent decades, some service members felt alienated by the pervasiveness of Christianity at official military services. Christian rhetoric and symbols at required services created tension for service members who had lost their Christian faith or maintained different belief frameworks. For example, Air Force MP Joe Guthrie, who lost his faith while serving, reflected on awards ceremonies. “Everybody’s required to attend, which is cool,” he said, but “the chaplain shows up and leads everybody in prayer. Well, if it’s a mandatory formation, and the chaplain shows up and leads everybody in prayer, I don’t think that’s legal. It’s, in fact, not legal, and the military does it routinely. You know? So, that stuff always bothers me.” Explaining that he had never noticed it until he became an atheist, he felt it established religion in the government. As noted above, Guthrie is not wrong for noticing the parallels between civil religion and Christianity; they use many of the same symbols and language. While much of the Chaplain Corps takes pluralism and free exercise seriously, it is simultaneously part of their job to be functionaries at such events, and that role creates distance between them and service members who do not share their religious commitment—civil or otherwise.

Beyond the confines of official military ceremonies, however, service members also found some direct interactions with chaplains troubling as well—for instance, Sgt. Paul Callaghan, who led a SKT and saw frequent combat, recalled how chaplains were always mandatory after a killed-in-action (KIA). He said, “It was kind of just falling on deaf ears. Out of respect for who the chaplain is and what he represents, we would sit and listen but never take it to heart. It’s like water off a duck’s back. Let us go through the motions, and then when he’s out of here, we’ll talk about how f’d up God is and why He doesn’t exist.” Characterizing the prayers and reflections as well-meaning but ultimately damaging, Callaghan was critical of chaplains who used trite religious rhetoric to make meaning of the death of a brother-in-arms, particularly because the meetings with chaplains were mandatory in such a situation. Like Callaghan, others felt some military chaplains pushed their faith on them—often in times of distress—when such a tack was not welcome. While some instances could be characterized as the problem of proselytizing in the military (Hansen,

2012), it also illustrates how bureaucratic policies that purposefully send post-combat service members to see military chaplains can create an establishment problem when counseling is otherwise needed. Military chaplains can be a boon for service members of faith in need of care, but that religious connection can simultaneously be the reason some service members do not seek help. This likely underlies the military's push since April 12, 2014, for commissioning secular Humanist chaplains who speak to the needs of the non-religious (Banks, 2014).

Of course, even with the efforts to which chaplains will go to be present for troops, even in extremely remote areas, their presence down range, much like that of social workers and mental health counselors, can be limited. Many service members genuinely had good relationships with chaplains while at larger bases or stateside, but they, too, had complaints about a lack of available chaplains. Army mechanic Taylor Vaught, who had positive experiences with chaplains, called their general lack of availability "the dirty little secret in the military." Calling them "ghosts," she claimed, "you don't ever see them." Worse, she felt that despite training on "soldier readiness, and what to do, and how to get medical attention, how to call in for a nine-line medevac, and all these different things," she never heard mention of access to counselors or chaplains. She reflected, "I believe that if we had more chaplains, and they were more readily available, … we'd come back not so broken mentally and spiritually." Despite having about 5000 active and reserve military chaplains among the different Chaplain Corps, they cannot make close relationships with or be available for the more than 1.3 million service members in the US Armed Forces.

It was not just experience and availability, then, but also the match between the religious world of the service member and the religious position of the chaplain. The successful chaplains connected with service members with responses that spoke to their particular beliefs and experiences, offering empathy and paths to forgiveness that affirmed their participation in the military and otherwise reinforced or provided worldviews that captured the realities of war. They were available to provide a space for deliberation, and they reported to commanding officers to help those officers support their subordinates. They had success because more experienced chaplains developed a compatible military identity with those of other religious service members; they could articulate religious beliefs and ideas that reflected the military life they, too, experienced. In addition, their ability to connect service members with other resources was key to their success. Complaints of chaplains establishing a religion, in contrast, speak to a dissonance between competing cultural packages—a distinctly Christian or Christian-like toolkit supplied by the military and a service member's different religion or non-religion.

Conclusions

Much like the rest of the military, the Chaplain Corps' hierarchical structure means that higher ranks deal more infrequently with lower ones, and those they associate with and minister to hold higher ranks as well. This also equates to less experienced chaplains interacting with lower ranking service members on a day-to-day basis and less experienced chaplains deploying to the theater of war with combatants. With many lower ranking service members potentially interacting with unseasoned chaplains, those with the greatest need for counseling and spiritual guidance find those with the least experience coming to their aid.

While religion in the military certainly extends well past interactions with chaplains, they provide an important window into the active role of military religious resources in the lives of service members. Military chaplains have a complex relationship with service members and a unique role within the military overall. It is one that can have clear positive benefits for service members in need of positive religious coping and spiritual fitness (Hufford et al., 2010; Besterman-Dahan et al., 2012; Carey et al., 2016). It is also one that challenges these beneficent assumptions. Chaplains, as I have noted, are also strategic assets (Waggoner, 2014). They are an important institutional tool for service member retention and readiness while simultaneously counsel for troops facing the challenges of military life.

That they can be a tool of the institution to help the military promote its own civil religion while motivating service members to be willing to participate in combat operations is a shocking claim. It suggests that chaplains make a conscious decision to serve the military institution and support civil religion. My interviews, however, suggest that this is not a conscious decision so much as an unconscious accommodation to military roles and culture. Military chaplains vehemently believe what they preach and believe their pastoral counseling is all in the best interest of service members, and there is no reason, from my investigation, to doubt their faith commitments. Chaplains are simultaneously committed to mission goals and subject to the traumas of service. They are neither nefariously tricking service members into fighting the enemy nor are they helpless dupes reading off sanctioned scripts. They are people who have gone through the pathways available to them to help service members navigate the spiritual perils and social problems that arise from military participation. It is from this difficult position that they attempt to serve as moral and spiritual guides, not to mention as ethics teachers in OCS and other training programs.

However, they are not off the hook. The two-collar problem is worth further exploration. While presented as a dilemma between a commitment to one's pastoral ministry and a commitment to the military, we must investigate the influence of military culture on this issue. Chaplains absorb military *habitus* and culture much in the way that other service members do, and their moral and religious commitments—their moral responsibility in the context of war—has been defined by military frameworks. The two collars do not carry the same weight; the first collar (denomination and ministry) bows to the second. This uneven weighting inherently sets up a moral issue.

Two chaplains interviewed believed chaplains were called to serve the military and had to do their jobs right by their leadership. Ch. (Col.) Granger explained that his job was to make service members courageous. He claimed:

> Courage is the ability to gather your fears and tuck them in and go about doing what [is] the duty that you're called to do. And sometimes that's what we did. We were there to garner their spiritual backbone to help them be able to do what they needed to do, which marks the chaplain as culpable. You know, we're non-combatants, but the reality is that I've become just as culpable as anybody who pulls the trigger. And, so, you know, you'd better have a good reason to go to war.

By contrast two said they were obviously committed to the individual service members over the organization. Col. Sandberg, for instance, said his commitment was to "the individual soldier, without a doubt," yet both mentioned it was more complicated than that. Finally, one claimed he was equally committed to both, although he was at such a high rank that helping very high-ranking officers, in effect, was helping the organization. What commitment to the organization effectively looks like, how its emphasis on military readiness motivates service members' moral decision-making, and its ethical implications will be a major part of the following chapters.

The point Ch. Granger raises himself is worth further investigation. If the chaplain role is to "garner [service-members'] spiritual backbone" to motivate them to do what the military requires of them, are military chaplains not as culpable as military leaders making decisions in war or "anybody who pulls the trigger"? He mentions the macro-ethical question of just cause to go to war, but his account of the moral work chaplains do ought also to extend to the actions in war, which chaplains convince service members to perform again and again. They have moral culpability that extends beyond the imperative to comfort and advocate for service members. They are morally responsible for the justifications, beliefs, and moral narratives they supply. War is steeped in moral concern, and military chaplains provide service members with the religious tools to navigate them. When those tools demand tremendous contortions to keep service members in the fight, it is the chaplains who require a "spiritual backbone" to attend to the moral needs of service members in a manner that reflects the realities of war.

Chaplains have always been a part of the US military, but their roles were once much more limited. As spiritual guides and moral educators, they serviced the spiritual needs of service members during American wars and conflicts. Over the years, however, their roles have grown and become more formalized. They have taken on new roles and facilitated new functions. More than that, they have been integrated into the military ethos. As we begin to look at other locations where religion happens into the military, it will be important to continue to remember the place chaplains have in religious military life.

Bibliography

Adams, G. (2006). Chaplains as Liaisons with Religious Leaders: Lessons from Iraq and Afghanistan. *Peace Works, 56*(1), 1–56.

Banks, A. M. (2014, April 22). *Army Approves 'Humanist' as Religious Preference.* Retrieved from https://religionnews.com/2014/04/22/army-approves-humanist-religious-preference

Bellah, R. N. (1975). *The Broken Covenant: American Civil Religion in a Time of Trial.* Seabury Press.

Bellah, R. N. (2005). Civil Religion in America. *Daedalus, 134*, 40–55.

Besterman-Dahan, K., Gibbons, S. W., Barnett, S. D., & Hickling, E. J. (2012). The Role of Military Chaplains in Mental Health Care of the Deployed Service Member. *Military Medicine, 177*(9), 1028–1033.

Boller, P. F. (2012). *Essays on the Presidents: Principles and Politics.* TCU Press.

Brady, J. (2005, July 27). *Evangelical Chaplains Test Bounds of Faith in Military.* Retrieved from https://www.npr.org/templates/story/story.php?storyId=4772331%3FstoryId

Carey, L. B., Hodgson, T. J., Krikheli, L., Soh, R. Y., Armour, A., Singh, T. K., & Impiombato, C. G. (2016). Moral Injury, Spiritual Care and the Role of Chaplains: An Exploratory Scoping Review of Literature and Resources. *Journal of Religion and Health, 55*(4), 1218–1245.

Cooperman, A. (2006, December 11). Inquiry Sought over Evangelical Video. *Washington Post.* Retrieved from https://www.washingtonpost.com/wp-dyn/content/article/2006/12/10/AR2006121000883.html

Denton-Borhaug, K. (2011). *U.S. War-Culture, Sacrifice and Salvation.* Routledge.

Department of the Air Force, Air Force Policy Directive 52–1: Chaplain Service intro. (2006).

Department of the Army, Army Regulation 600–20: Army Command Policy para. 3–3. b. (4). (2009).

Department of the Army, Army Regulation 165–1: Army Chaplain Corps Activities. (2015, July 23).

Drazin, I., & Currey, C. B. (1995). *For God and Country: The History of a Constitutional Challenge to the Army Chaplaincy.* KTAV Publ. House.

Feldberg, M. (2009). *Jewish Chaplains in the Civil War.* Retrieved from https://www.myjewishlearning.com/article/jewish-chaplains-in-the-civil-war/

French, P. A. (2011). *War and Moral Dissonance.* Cambridge University Press.

Geneva Convention I, Diplomatic Conference for the Establishment of International Conventions for the Protection of Victims of War. *Geneva Convention for the Amelioration of the Condition of the Wounded and Sick in Armed Forces in the Field.* 6 U.S.T. 3114. (1949, August 12).

GoArmy.com. (2018, May 24). *Careers & Jobs: Chaplain (56A). U.S. Army.* Retrieved www.goarmy.com/careers-and-jobs/browse-career-and-job-categories/administrative-support/chaplain.html.

Goodstein, L. (2005, July 12). Evangelicals Are a Growing Force in the Military Chaplain Corps. *New York Times.* Retrieved from https://www.nytimes.com/2005/07/12/us/evangelicals-are-a-growing-force-in-the-military-chaplain-corps.html

Gutkowski, S., & Wilkes, G. (2011). Changing Chaplaincy: A Contribution to Debate over the Roles of US and British Military Chaplains in Afghanistan. *Religion, State and Society, 39*(1), 111–124.

Hansen, K. P. (2012). *Military Chaplains and Religious Diversity.* Palgrave Macmillan.

Hassner, R. E. (2014). *Religion in the Military Worldwide.* Cambridge University Press.

Hebert, L. J. (2017, April 20). Faith and Belief Codes for Reporting Personnel Data of Service Members [Letter written March 27, 2017 to Memorandum for Deputy Assistant Secretary of the Army for Manpower and Reserve Affairs, Deputy Assistant Secretary of the Navy for Manpower and Reserve Affairs, Deputy Assistant Secretary of the Air Force for Manpower and Reserve Affairs, Director, Reserve and Military Personnel, US Coast Guard, and Director, Defense Manpower Data Center]. In *Office of the Assistant Secretary of Defense*. Retrieved from http://americanhumanist.org/wp-content/uploads/2017/04/Faith-and-Belief-Codes-for-Reporting-Personnel-Data-of-Service-Members.pdf

Hedrick, C. W. (1990, Winter). The Chaplaincy as a Professional Army Branch. *Military Chaplains' Review*, 19–52.

Hufford, D. J., Fritts, M. J., & Rhodes, J. E. (2010). Spiritual Fitness. *Military Medicine, 175*(8S), 73–87.

Hunter, C., & Smith, L. (2010). Military Leadership and Education & Religion's Role in the U.S. Military Mission. *Defense Equal Opportunity Management Institute Research Directorate*, 2–18.

Johnson, L. D. (1856). *Chaplains of the General Government: With Objections to Their Employment Considered*. Sheldon, Blakeman, &.

Kobes Du Mez, K. (2020). *Jesus and John Wayne: How White Evangelicals Corrupted a Faith and Fractured a Nation*. Liveright Publishing.

Kopacz, M. S. (2014). Moral Injury – A War Trauma Affecting Current and Former Military Personnel. *International Journal of Social Psychiatry, 60*(7), 722–723.

Kruse, K. M. (2015). *One Nation Under God: How Corporate America Invented Christian America*. Basic Books.

Lee, W. S., Burke, C. J., & Crayne, Z. M. (2005). *Military Chaplains as Peace Builders: Embracing Indigenous Religions in Stability Operations*. Air University.

Lindsay, D. M. (2007a). *Faith in the Halls of Power: How Evangelicals Joined the American Elite*. Oxford University Press.

Lindsay, D. M. (2007b). Evangelical Elites in the U.S. Military. *Journal of Political and Military Sociology, 35*(2), 161–176.

Loveland, A. C. (1996). *American Evangelicals and the US Military, 1942–1993*. Louisiana State University Press.

MacIntyre, A. (2007). *After Virtue* (3rd ed.). University of Notre Dame Press.

Malana, J. (2016). *Navy Chaplain Corps*. Lecture presented at 2016 Military Chaplain Endorser Conference. Retrieved from https://www.spirit-filled.org/documents/NavyPersonnelBrief-2016January.pdf

Maurer, C. F. W. (2005). *Dragoon Diary: The History of the Third Continental Light Dragoons*. AuthorHouse.

McGuire, M. B. (2008). *Lived Religion: Faith and Practice in Everyday Life*. Oxford University Press.

Moore, S. K. (2014). *Military Chaplains as Agents of Peace: Religious Leader Engagement in Conflict and Post-Conflict Environments*. Lexington Books.

Patterson, E. (Ed.). (2014). *Military Chaplains in Afghanistan, Iraq, and Beyond: Advisement and Leader Engagement in Highly Religious Environments*. Rowman & Littlefield.

Secretary of the Navy. (2008). Secretary of the Navy Instruction 1730.8B: Accommodation of Religious Practices para. 1.

Shellnutt, K. (2017, May 30). *Why the US Military Wants Fewer Generic Christians*. Retrieved from https://www.christianitytoday.com/news/2017/may/why-us-military-fewer-generic-christians-216-religions.html

Shinkman, P. D. (2013, October 30). The Catholic Crunch: Inside the Shortage of Catholic Military Priests. *U.S. News & World Report*.

Stahl, R. Y. (2017). *Enlisting Faith: How the Military Chaplaincy Shaped Religion and State in Modern America*. Harvard University Press.

Thompson, A. (2011). Religious Leader Engagement in Southern Afghanistan. *Joint Forces Quarterly, 63*(1), 95–101.

Torpy, J. (2019, November 14). *Report by MAAF of Religious Demographics and Chaplain Endorsement Distributions*. Retrieved from http://militaryatheists.org/news/wp-content/uploads/MAAF-Demographics-20191114.pdf

Torpy, J. (2021, March 5). Military Association of Atheists and Freethinkers Data on DoD Military Chaplain and Service Member Demographics.

Traveling Preachers. (2015). In L. T. Frank (Ed.), *The World of the Civil War: A Daily Life Encyclopedia* (pp. 615–618).

US Air Force. (2018). *Chaplain Officer: Providing Spiritual Care*. Retrieved from https://www.airforce.com/careers/specialty-careers/chaplain?gclsrc=aw.ds&gclid=EAIaIQobChMIvYuuwpDQ6gIVU8DICh18Wwy2EAAYASAAEgLcE_D_BwE

US Army. (2018). *Overview of Army Chaplain*. Retrieved from https://recruiting.army.mil/MRB_ReligiousServices/

US Congress. (1861). Senate. *An Act providing for the Better Organisation of the Military Establishment*. 37th Cong. 1st sess. S. 7. Washington.

US Department of Defense. (2009). Department of Defense Instruction 1300.17: Accommodation of Religious Practices within the Military Services para. 4.

US Department of the Army. (1998, March 27). *Reg. 165–1*. Chaplain Activities in the United States Army.

US Marine Corps. (2015). *Religious Ministry in the United States Marine Corps*. Dept. of the Navy, Headquarters U.S. Marine Corps.

US Navy. (2019). *Navy Chaplain Careers*. Retrieved from https://www.navy.com/careers/navy-chaplain

Waggoner, E. (2014, September). Taking Religion Seriously in the U.S. Military: The Chaplaincy as a National Strategic Asset. *Journal of the American Academy of Religion, 82*(3), 702–735.

Weil, F. L. (1950). The Military Chaplaincy: A Report to the President, October 1, 1950. The President's Committee on Religion and Welfare in the Armed Forces.
Weinstein, M. L., & Aslan, R. (2007, August 22). Not So Fast, Christian Soldiers. *Los Angeles Times*. Retrieved from https://www.latimes.com/opinion/la-oe-aslan22aug22-story.html
Weinstein, M. L., & Seay, D. (2006). *With God on Our Side: One Man's War against an Evangelical Coup in America's Military* (1st ed). Thomas Dunne Books.
Wuthnow, R. (1989). *The Restructuring of American Religion: Society and Faith since World War II*. Princeton University Press.

CHAPTER 3

Christian Influence and Variation in Military Ethics Education

Army National Guard Major Chris Herder was a member of an Embedded Training Team (ETT) and was tasked with training the Afghan National Army and 15 other service members as part of Task Force Phoenix in the mid-2000s. A captain at the time, he was an infantry officer and former medic working with a small group of Army National Guard troops to train about 100 Afghan soldiers and lead them in combat against Taliban opposition forces. After a two-decade career, he had been trained extensively and had facilitated hundreds of others' training. Training does not *only* happen in boot camp, and he had training throughout his years of service as an officer. He, of course, learned how to shoot. He had medical training early in his career. He received leadership training at various points. However, when I asked him about moral training and ethics education, he stopped me to say the question reminded him of a joke.

"There's a running joke," he said. "I've heard it many times, and that kind of relates to that. There's a weapon called the M2 .50 caliber, and it's a big rifle. It's a rifle that you can't carry. It's too big. And it has to be mounted because it's so violent when it shoots. It's a beast. You can shoot tanks with it. ... And because of that, because of its power, I guess the simplest way to describe it is it's not meant to be used on personnel. You don't shoot people with that rifle. You shoot vehicles and equipment. You don't shoot individuals because it's ... overkill. It's like dropping a nuclear

T. H. Suitt, III, *Narratives of Trauma and Moral Agency among Christian Post-9/11 Veterans*,
https://doi.org/10.1007/978-3-031-31082-9_3

bomb on a group of Taliban." He called it a problem of "proportionality," meaning the use of such a weapon would far exceed the required sufficient use of force to subdue a combatant. He continued, "So, what they always say in training is you can always use this to shoot at equipment and vehicles, so shoot at the equipment they're wearing on their back. Shoot the equipment on the belt they have on. It's like a joke. It's a joke."

While Herder was familiar with the Hague and Geneva Conventions—formal declarations of the international laws and rules of war—and claimed he took that training very seriously, he did not feel the average enlisted service member received much ethics education. Calling it "lip service" meant to "check the box," any training on ethics of war was accompanied with a "wink, wink, nod, nod." Ethics education, in his estimation, for the average enlisted infantryman consisted of required PowerPoint decks and pamphlets that fell on deaf ears of those who joined "to kill bad guys. They're not there to follow the freaking Geneva Convention." That is, the "joke" he shared with me was indicative of a larger issue in the US Armed Forces where the machismo of military culture and its attendant warrior identity clashes with serious ethical considerations in the context of war as well as the moral beliefs, narratives, and expectations service members bring to and find during their service.

The US military presents itself as "moral light to a nation lost in a morass of moral relativism and decay" (Cook, 2008: 57), yet they function amid a moral pendulum swinging between the promotion of Christian virtues, core warrior values, and a notion that a "good soldier, even a good officer, *could be a bad man*" so long as he was loyal and effective (Wilson, 2008: 32). This contradiction is between a belief in American exceptionalism and a military culture that aggressively aims service members at strategic ends (Waggoner, 2014). Service members, officers in particular, are considered moral by default in their willingness to serve and lead. In fact, until World War II and the Korean War, moral and ethics training was carried out exclusively by chaplains to benefit enlisted men, not officers (Brinsfield, 1997: 41). Officers were gentlemen, after all. The military presupposed military leaders had good moral character, and moral decision-making and ethical thought remained in the realm of that leadership. Their good character would trickle down to the enlisted by their actions, and chaplains would shore up good character among them besides. Enlisted infantrymen could confidently embody the tip of the spear in combat, knowing officers aimed it in a moral direction. Officers receive most of the moral training and ethics education today, yet the contradiction remains. The "joke" still draws a laugh despite the military's "moral light."

Irrespective of this contradiction, moral concerns pervade military experience; war is inseparable from moral harm. Morality and moral decision-making are of such consequence in the military because every decision in war burdens decision-makers, commanders, cohorts, subordinates, civilians, and enemies (Thompson & Jetly, 2018). Despite this reality, formalized moral training and ethics education beyond the purview of military chaplains alone and ROE that govern right action in war for service members are a relatively new phenomenon. Spurred by the Vietnam War's moral travesties but solidified in various scandals in the late 1980s and 1990s, ethics education has only been a requisite part of military training—particularly in the academy—for roughly 30 years (Wertheimer, 2010; Wilson, 2008). These include philosophical ethics courses and values-based education at various points through an officer's career with the hopes of instilling moral decision-making and behavior in military leaders. While officers receive the most ethics education by far, enlisted service members do receive a rules-based approach to ethics education focused on LOAC and, of course, ROE, along with military Core Values, Resilience training, and the Code of Conduct. Depending on the location of the education and its recipient, Judge Advocate lawyers (JAGs), high-ranking officers, civilian professors, and (very often) military chaplains teach these courses.

In trying to understand the role of religion in the lives of post-9/11 veterans and the religious military narratives they develop, the contents of their ethics education may well play a part. While rarely explicitly religious, ethics education in the military has clear religious roots and is often imparted and promoted by religious guides and taught in a way that creates religious justifications for action. Furthermore, this education is a major part of the wider military cultural toolkit with which service members operate. The religious resources, if any, they bring with them to the military along with any moral narratives, beliefs, and expectations will interact with this training—likely when the military forges their warrior identity. It is a central piece in understanding how military service can alter the moral trajectory of a life.

This chapter will explore the brief history of ethics education in the military, its contents, the reports of its utility among my interlocutors, and its potential significance as an organizational framework in moral decision-making. The result will be an investigation into the explicit ethical norms and moral frames that the military inculcates in its troops and an exploration of the apparent contradictions between the military's projected virtues, warrior values, and the call to violence. As we will see, the contents and utility of ethics education and moral training have significant variance across branches and ranks, particularly between enlisted service members and officers.

Moral Questions in War and the Roots of Modern Military Ethics

Ethical problematics are part and parcel of war and the military profession; violence of any kind perpetrated for good or ill has a moral dimension. It should be no surprise, then, that moral questions about and in war—whether wars can be "just" or not—extend at least to the writings of Aristotle and Cicero (Orend, 2006: 10). Prescribed ethical limitations on war comprise likely the most comprehensive convention of war, just war theory, which has its roots in St. Augustine of Hippo and his teacher, Ambrose Ambrosius, writing in the early days of Christianity and addressing statecraft in the Roman Empire in the late fourth and early fifth centuries CE. Developed and institutionalized over hundreds of years and embedded within modern military ethics, LOAC, and international law, these prescriptions and laws are taken as a fact of American (and Western) military operations.

Truly, the just war tradition and its role as a convention of warfare "in the service of the powers" is the bedrock of all modern laws of war and military ethics education (Walzer, 2010: 15). Understanding its development and how it became secularized and institutionalized will help clarify the organizational frameworks that the military supplies its service members. It is an approach to limiting warfare with deep roots in the early Christian church as Christianity grew into its place as the Roman Empire's official religion. Throughout the history of the US military, Christianity has had a persistent place in its organizational frameworks and the lives of service members, with Christian chaplains often teaching its precepts to service members. Philosophers, political scientists, and political and military leaders have secularized the just war tradition over time, but its Christian influence remains.

According to many historians, Christianity was entirely pacifist during its first 200 years. Although there are limitations to having a complete picture of this time in the Christian tradition, there is evidence to support this claim. The first time a Christian even served in the Roman imperial army was 170 CE (Wogaman, 1993: 34). Augustine of Hippo, however, was the reason just war theory came to prominence in the Roman Empire and shifted Christianity from a religion largely of pacifism to one supporting "just" wars. In the early fifth century, he felt a Ciceronian model for society could be useful and was inspired by Cicero's writings and many other Neo-Platonic thinkers. For him, the Roman striving for glory was a potential model for the Christian, but only in the case of the City of God, not the earthly city. Striving for the glory of the earthly city would be a form of patriotism that would be unjustifiable to the Christian. However, this linking of Christian values with Roman society showed that a Christian could use violence if it were "clearly recognized that it was a deeply unfortunate duty brought about by a clear case of injustice in the world, and that the violence was intended to protect 'those things in accordance with the law by which peace and human society are preserved" (Tuck, 2001: 55). Augustine made it clear that a Christian could not participate in violence if it were for self-glory or even self-preservation. War was a means of defending the state or revenge for aggression, and Biblical justifications (e.g., Romans 13: 4) lent such formulation credence.

The early days of the tradition largely focused on *jus ad bellum*—or justice of the war—considerations rather than much *jus in bello*—or justice in the war—prescriptions and limitations. In other words, Augustine emphasized just cause for going to war rather than just means for fighting a war. He claimed a state should only fight in wars that are defensive or retributive against an aggressor, and wars should only be for the end of achieving a just peace. Participating in wars should be a bothersome prospect, but a Christian can participate because it is the more loving act to strike back at an aggressor than to do nothing to bring about peace, a prescription rooted in Christ's love commandment (Augustine, 1984). To the extent that he did write on *jus in bello*, Augustine claimed soldiers and police should act with mercy and restraint when doling out punishment or participating in a violent conflict. Importantly, it is here where the once pacifist Christianity changed. Augustine showed how Christian moralism and Roman society could overlap, leading to a justification for participation in war.

Alexander of Hales, a Franciscan, and Thomas Aquinas, a Dominican, extended the tradition and systematized it in the thirteenth century. Alexander's treatise argued that one declaring war must have both "right *affectus*"—or the right state of mind—and the authority to do so (Finnis, 1996: 18). He added that those fighting the war must not be religious officials and must have "right *intentio*"—or right intention. Finally, he claimed that the opponents in war must be deserving of it ("*meritum*") and that the war itself has a just cause ("*causa*"). Where Augustine was not systematic in his rendering of what a just war would look like, Alexander of Hales began to add these specifics, outlining how a just war would be undertaken in practice.

Soon after, Thomas Aquinas undertook a similar project and formulated an even more systematic approach to just war doctrine. Aquinas was aware of Alexander's work, but his formulation of just war theory went much deeper and was more straightforward than the Franciscan's. Instead of six preconditions, Aquinas narrowed it down to three. In summary, his preconditions were "authority, *causa iusta*, and *intentio recta*" (Finnis, 1996: 18). Aquinas wrote that it is solely the right of the sovereign to declare war, "for it is not the business of a private individual to declare war" (Forell & Childs, 2013: 95). In addition, it would be wrong for an individual to gather up armies; that, too, is the responsibility of the sovereign. The just cause (*causa iusta*) refers to the need for the enemy to have done something blameworthy. Finally, *intentio recta* refers to the need that the "belligerents should have a rightful intention, so that they intend the advancement of the good, or the avoidance of evil" (Forell & Childs, 2013: 95). Like Augustine, Aquinas claimed that the only just war would be one that aimed at establishing a just peace. The persistent goal of establishing the City of God through peacemaking continued to underlie these prescriptions and maintained the ideal that the more Christ-like loving act was to limit war as much as possible. If the intent of the war was unjust, even if the other two pieces of his formulation were met, then the war was entirely unjust.

In addition to the systemization of the just war tradition, Aquinas developed two concepts that are now inextricably linked to just war theory: proportionality and double effect. Although Aquinas does not name proportionality, he laid the foundation of the principle. He argued, for instance, that a people ought only to depose a tyrant if the cost of remaining under that tyrant's rule was greater than the cost of revolution (Wogaman, 1993). In other words, the means must not exceed the costs. The rule of proportionality is a key feature of modern just war theory and is a major determining factor for many military operations. As it has developed over time, the idea is that an act of aggression or destruction should be proportionate to the benefit the actor hopes to achieve. Consequently, it is also at the heart of the "joke" that looms over this chapter.

Proportionality is tied very closely with another concept called the rule of double effect, which Aquinas also developed in a circuitous manner. While discussing the merit of killing in self-defense, Aquinas wrote, "Nothing hinders one act from having two effects, only one of which is intended, while the other is beside the intention" (quoted in Wogaman, 1993: 96). In such a case as self-defense, the good intention of protection from harm was morally significant. The unintended consequence of the assailant's death was not. Aquinas described this in terms of self-defense, but it has come to be a major part of operational law in modern warfare. Its modern application describes a situation wherein the intention of a military action is good (like the completion of a mission); therefore, the action is morally justified despite unintended losses—so long as the harm is proportional to the benefit of acting.

Eventually, by the sixteenth and seventeenth centuries, Francisco de Vitoria, Francisco de Suárez, Bartolomé de las Casas, Sepulveda, Hugo Grotius, and others had bridged the gap between secular and religious interpretations of the theory, allowing the tradition to influence both morality and civil lawmaking (Orend, 2006: 16–18). Grotius, a popular Dutch diplomat and jurist—and one who philosopher Jeff McMahan calls the "greatest writer in the tradition of just war theory"—brought the just war tradition squarely into civil society in particular (McMahan, 2009: 16). One of the veritable fathers of international law—the other being Vitoria—Grotius sought to secularize the just war tradition and apply it to the international landscape. "Focusing it on the preservation of state sovereignty," Grotius' secularization of the historically Christian tradition in his *On the Law of War and Peace* and other works transformed just war theory into one with philosophical and legal bases needed to inform the law of the time (Hartle, 2004: 95). Although not codified for some time yet, Grotius' contributions allowed the just war convention to extend beyond the confines of Christian peacemaking into the realm of post-Christendom statecraft and international politics. Importantly, he also flipped just war theory on its head in an important way. Rather than focusing on the rights of sovereigns to declare war, he emphasized the right of individuals to defend themselves, which then extended to sovereigns. Further, should a sovereign fail to defend its people, the citizens would have just cause to go to war. This emphasis on individual rights effectively moved the just war tradition's earlier emphasis on *jus ad bellum* to *jus in bello*. It also marked the beginning of placing blameworthiness for actions *in* war on individuals on the ground.

Grotius' novel applications of just war theory in the international landscape paved the way for its eventual codification in the nineteenth century as the tradition remained a part of the international law discourse. However, Grotius' natural law influences fell out of fashion with the rise of positivism (Forde, 1998). In the following two centuries, just war theory was, on the one hand, a dated natural law approach criticized by realists like military theorist and Prussian General Carl von Clausewitz. War was a political tool; it "was not a question of legality or legitimacy" (Simon, 2018: 118). On the other hand, it received sharp criticism from moral philosophers like Immanuel Kant, who could not reconcile justice and war (H. Williams, 1995)—at least not in the same manner as the historical just war tradition. By the time the just war tradition was finally codified in the later part of the nineteenth century, its natural law roots had given way to positive law interpretation. Where Christianity produced and modified the tradition on moral grounds determined by nature or by God, the eventual codification of just war theory was one "where law is made by humans through legislatures, courts, or treaties" (Crawford, 2013: 162). This puts a distance between morality and law that still lingers. To this day in the US Armed Forces, moral justifications and prescriptions promoted and reinforced by spiritual guides stand opposed to organizational frameworks that define military operations in terms of legal and illegal rather than right or wrong.

The shift in moral philosophy that led to the just war theory's secularization also initiated other lasting changes that still affect modern military ethics. During the Enlightenment, the philosophical project of providing "an independent rational justification of morality" became an essential concern of Western culture (MacIntyre, 2007: 39, 50). Indeed, the Kantian and Clausewitzian responses to the just war tradition as well as its secularization as a rational convention of warfare extend from this Enlightenment project where "religion could no longer provide … a shared background and foundation for moral discourse and action." As the Enlightenment project failed, religion did not reprise its same role as a rational foundation. Instead, other prominent ethical theories like utilitarianism and emotivism emerged. As will become clear, although the military professes core values, moral virtues, and just war precepts—often using religious rhetoric—they adhere to utilitarianism in practice. MacIntyre (2007: 65) explains, "utilitarianism … left its mark upon a variety of social roles and institutions. And these remained as an inheritance long after utilitarianism had lost … philosophical importance." The US military is one such institution, and determining net positive gain against potential losses has come to define the military's strategy even if they continue to use just war rhetoric. That is, the secularization and codification of the just war tradition coupled with the lasting influence of utilitarianism explain, in part, the mismatch between the military's expressed virtues and their practiced commitment to results.

The actual codification of just war theory into law in the US came in the form of Army General Orders No. 20 in 1847 during the Mexican-American War, which stipulated just conduct in war according to an unwritten code, "the rules and articles of war" (Scott, 1847). General Orders No. 100 followed in 1863, or what has more commonly been called the Lieber Code—named for Dr. Francis Lieber, who developed its laws. The code was reflective of the customs of warfare of the time (Hartle, 2004), and they were largely based on underlying moral principles long prescribed by the just war tradition and brought to the international political landscape by Grotius in the early seventeenth century. The code provided what is the first example of a field manual for combatants for just conduct in war, and it set the laws for conduct among Union soldiers during the American Civil War. It was "for half a century the official Army pronouncement on the subject" and formed the basis for the 1899 and 1907 Hague Conventions (T. Taylor, 1973: 6). Of course, the Lieber Code did not exist in a vacuum, and a similar process of codification came just a year later in 1864 with the first Geneva Convention, convened at the behest of International Committee of the Red Cross founder J. Henry Dunant (Hartle, 2004). These two initial codification processes, steeped in the just war tradition's moral precepts, formed the basis and greatly influenced modern international law concerning warfare, including the later Geneva and Hague Conventions and Protocols I, II, and III. Furthermore, the Lieber Code was an influence on all future US military laws—LOAC and operational law—and codes of conduct and ROE. By the Vietnam War, these laws were a fundamental part of military operations, yet that war also marks a significant turning point where positivist attitudes and moral concerns came to a head.

Ultimately, the just war tradition's codification does not necessarily equate to just wars or just actions in war. As political scientist Neta Crawford (2003: 12, 20) posited about the early years of the Global War on Terror, "normative beliefs and just war talk permeate official U.S.

discourse in the counterterror war, influence how the conflict is understood, [and] affected U.S. conduct." However, the US's inability to appropriately distinguish combatants and non-combatants in a counterterror war—among other moral shortcomings—reveals the "U.S. strategy for the War on Terror is, on balance, not just in the moral sense, despite the administration's pronouncements."[1] Even if just war considerations are deemed important in discourse and undergird LOAC, that does not mean they will not be stretched, bent, and abused beyond their palliative purpose. Just war prescriptions are a part of the military cultural toolkit, to be sure, and organizational frameworks ensconce the just war rhetoric. Nevertheless, those frames exist alongside many others in the modern military toolkit and are not necessarily the ones commanding officers draw from in military decision-making to pursue institutional goals.

The same tradition that supplied the US military with moral foundations and concepts like double effect and proportionality can also, over time, bend these principles for self-serving ends, and their failure does not upend the organization and change those frameworks. On the contrary, the military organization can continue to reinforce those organizational frames again and again because they are perceived to have a moral basis and are deeply engrained in military organizational culture. It is another instance of what Waggoner (2014: 703) refers to as "bricolage," wherein the US military takes civilian practices and meaning-making systems and aims them anew at institutional goals. Just war theory is explicitly part of officer ethics education and still often taught by military chaplains, but, as I will show, that has little bearing on the military organizational frames that guide action.

A Brief History of Modern US Armed Forces Ethics Education

Although ethics education and moral training may have mixed results in terms of outcomes, it is worthwhile to investigate what they look like in content and practice. They house the military's moral frames that ostensibly influence decision-making, even if those decisions bend the rules

[1] Crawford (2003) critiques the Bush administration, but just war rhetoric has remained a constant in the last twenty years. Even President Biden's administration has cited a "proportionate military response" in its early days concerning strikes on Syria (Cooper & Schmitt, 2021).

toward strategic goals. Moreover, as the Global War on Terror continues, we ought to be concerned with and critical of the training and education future service members will receive. The matter of their moral consciences—not to mention our own—is at stake, and this training is their first contact with the explicit military moral beliefs and expectations.

The great turning point toward the development of ethics education in military academies and other training sites came in the later part of the twentieth century. Before then, in the time from the Revolutionary War through the Vietnam War, ethics education existed only in a smattering of moral education programs and training was largely headed up by chaplains and targeted at enlisted men. Critical moral discourse on ethical decision-making in war was relegated to top military brass, chaplains, theologians, and philosophers. Military ethics scholarship surged following the invention of the atomic bomb, but such moral discussions did not influence military ethics education and training. Moral leaders, it was thought, would produce moral subordinates.

The historical pattern of training enlisted men in morality continued with chaplains taking on education duties—a role they had maintained since the days of the Continental Army under General Washington (Brinsfield, 1997: 41). Officers received little ethical education of any kind, as it was presumed that they were educated gentlemen. In fact, even when professional schools like the Naval Academy attempted to introduce "moral science" courses into their curriculum for officers in the nineteenth century, it was met with derision, and the courses were eventually dropped soon after in favor of more practical coursework (Clark, 2004: 6). It would be more than a century before ethics education for all service members, including officers, became the norm.

For the better part of the US Armed Forces' history, military chaplains and religious activities were home to the military's moral formation efforts. Chapel attendance was mandatory for all faiths until 1972. There, military chaplains could extoll moral values and behaviors to the enlisted service members who were deemed to need it (Brinsfield, 1997: 133). As moral training became more formalized between World War II and the end of the Vietnam War, chaplains continued to teach "Character Guidance" classes to thousands of enlisted troops (Brinsfield, 1997: 41). In the wake of the Vietnam War, however, officers were finally included in moral training, and the military began to take moral development and ethics education—beyond the chapel—more seriously. When atrocities of the Vietnam

War became public knowledge, the military took more explicit steps to rethink how it understood ethics education and moral training.

Perhaps best encapsulated by the success of philosopher Michael Walzer's 1977 book *Just and Unjust Wars*, certain moral failings of the Vietnam War brought just war questions into the public eye. The persistent view of the military as a "moral light" (Cook, 2008: 57) faced challenges in the post-Vietnam landscape of America. In the escalation of conscription that characterized the Vietnam War between 1965 and 1970, there was a "corresponding decrease in attention paid to ethics education and training" leading, as Jeffrey Wilson argues, to widespread vicious behaviors, racial violence, and moral relativism (Wilson, 2008: 33). Emblematic of those problems was the My Lai Massacre of 1968. On March 16, soldiers of Charlie Company, First Battalion, murdered at minimum 347 non-combatants in the Son My village in South Vietnam as they were "encouraged to kill without making careful discriminations—encouraged to do so by their own officers" (Walzer, 2006: 309). Charlie Company fired on non-combatants, including women, children, and even infants, yet only one officer, Lieutenant William Calley, served any jail time at all. When news of the massacre reached the public in 1969, the US military had to correct its course.

News of the My Lai Massacre shocked the American public, including news of its coverup by top brass. As a response, General Westmoreland, then Chief of Staff in the Army, called for a study to determine the moral and ethical climate of Army officers. The results were shocking. Officers widely reported they saw a "stark dichotomy between appearance and reality of the adherence of senior officers to the traditional standards of professionalism" (Brinsfield, 1997: 41). In response to claims that the system was morally bankrupt and rewarded "selfishness, incompetence, and dishonesty," Westmoreland and the Army War College instituted new ethics courses at West Point and the Army War College itself, positioning military chaplains as key faculty. While this new course did not correct every issue, particularly as the military moved to an all-volunteer force, the 1980s saw an "intellectual" and "ethical renaissance," which "culminated with the formal codification of the seven Army Values" as well as the eventual Army Ethic in the late 1990s (Wilson, 2008: 33). This period marks the establishment of much of ethics education in the Army that would come to influence post-9/11 veterans.

However, it was not quite so simple as the Army correcting issues among its officers in the wake of Vietnam and Westmoreland's study. The

Navy had its share of public problems as well. Two major incidents spurred the initiation of ethics education at the Naval Academy and their eventual adoption of Core Values. First, retired Lieut. Col. Oliver North—the current President of the NRA—came under public scrutiny for his involvement in the Iran-Contra affair of the late-Reagan era. North had developed the second part of the plan, which was to use funds from the illegal sale of weapons to Iranians in exchange for hostages to support Contra rebels, an anti-socialism insurgency group, in Nicaragua. When news of the scandal broke, North testified before Congress and was convicted of three felony charges. The scandal reflected poorly on the Naval Academy, North's alma mater, and a Congressional committee mandated an ethics course at every military academy, now cynically referred to as "the Ollie North course" (Wertheimer, 2010: 1). While new to Annapolis, the new ethics course was similar to those already at West Point and the Air Force Academy.

Second, there was a major cheating scandal among Naval Academy cadets in 1992 on a fall semester final exam. One hundred and thirty-three students were eventually implicated in a scheme to steal an electrical engineering exam, cheat on it, and cover it up. The scandal was the straw that broke the back of the Naval Academy's deficient ethics efforts. Not only had the North scandal shaken confidence, but in 1991, the Tailhook scandal brought allegations that Navy and Marine Corps officers had sexually assaulted eighty-three women and seven men at a symposium in Las Vegas (Winerip, 2013). The Naval Academy brought in a superintendent and four-star admiral Charles Larson to correct the situation. In addition to disciplinary actions, Larson updated the more than a century old Honor Code, expanded the power of the student Honor Council, and expanded the number of ethics courses to take place over multiple semesters rather than only one semester as had been the case (Argetsinger, 1996). In response to these scandals and the moves made by West Point, the Air Force Academy quietly implemented a new Core Values Program along with the newly mandated ethics course as well (Dierker, 1997: 110–1).

The result of various scandals and shakeups was the implementation of mandatory ethics curricula, depending on the academy or program, for officers, and explicit rules-based moral training for enlisted. It also led to the development of Core Values for each of the military branches and influenced the Code of Conduct, Honor Codes, Resilience Training, expanding ethics education and courses throughout a military career. The expansion of ethics education and moral training on values also changed who developed and taught military personnel. Once exclusively the realm of military chaplains, now civilian and military ethics philosophers and educators, high-ranking officers, and JAG lawyers fill these roles alongside chaplains at various points in a service member's career from basic training to professional schools to ROTC to specialized programs like the National Character and Leadership Conference (Wilson, 2008; Cook, 2008; Wead, 2014). Ethics education and moral training has remained a central part of military training since the 1990s, yet ethics issues continue to spring up. There is variation in consistency between various instructors and training sites and a large gap between the ethics education of officers and that of enlisted.

The Aspirational Versus Functional Divide in Ethics Education

Army Special Forces Sgt. (MOS 18F) Dean Chamois took a moment to answer whether he received any moral training. After getting some clarification on what I meant, he explained, "I think that's more in the officer realm than it is the enlisted realm. … If you think of management, I would say that officers are your managers, where they own accountability. … As an enlisted person, you're not taught these things. You don't go to these schools where they teach you. You're not going to officer candidate school; you're not going to career development school." Despite receiving some advanced training and being a highly decorated Sgt in the Special Forces, Chamois could not recall receiving much at all in the way of ethics education or moral training. He spoke of his own "responsibility" as a high-ranking enlisted Intelligence Sgt, yet he had received a different sort of training than officers, who he described as needing the training because "officers ultimately make the decisions because they're accountable."

This division between participants who felt they had received explicit moral training during their careers and those who did not fell in much the same way as Chamois described. Only twenty-three participants reported having such training, and they included all but one of the eleven officers with whom I spoke. That one claimed his ROTC program and later training had not included any moral training. This meant that over half of the participants claimed they had not received moral training. The difference tended to be between enlisted service members and officers. Enlisted service members tended to report not having such training at all. Only thirteen of the thirty-six enlisted service members recalled receiving it. Among those thirteen, some equated behavioral prescriptions and rules of conduct in war as moral training. Their training was simply of a different kind.

From the enlisted perspective, then, Army SGM Sam Griffin captured the situation. As he put it, "No, we never talked about that kind of crap. We talked about how to fight and win." His emphasis was clearly on the need to focus on how to be strategic and to fight enemy combatants effectively while keeping fellow service members safe. Putting it a little less bluntly, National Guardsman George McClintock said, "Not really. At Fort Benning they trained us to kill and kill before you are killed …, but at the same time you don't fire on anyone until fired upon, so that kind of aspect." In other words, ROE were certainly explicit, but this was not a lesson in just war theory or in learning to reason through the morality of and in war. It was a 50-minute presentation on Army Values during the "red phase" of basic (Recruit Sustainment Program, 2018). Although some enlisted service members did understand their ROE, Code of Conduct, and Core Values as moral training, most felt that they had received no moral training of any kind. What training they received was different in kind to officer training, even if there was some overlap in content.

The discrepancy between officers and enlisted is emblematic of an ongoing debate about ethics education in the US Armed Forces and of the reality that programs are "still overwhelmingly biased towards the production of (good) officers" (Carrick, 2008: 191). It is a debate about a presumed trickle-down effect of just conduct in war. When officers make ethical decisions, does that affect the reality among the enlisted who are overwhelmingly the boots on the ground in the theater of war? Ideally, both officers and enlisted service members ought to receive ethics education and moral training. When the stakes are truly life or death for them, enemy combatants, civilians, and the whole network of people connected to their lives—not to mention the American public—ethics education is a crucial part of training. The emphasis on officers receiving more ethics education than enlisted service members is both a significant reaction to the moral shortcomings of the Vietnam War and a continuation of the persistent organizational framework of the military that assumes officers are exceptional, and enlisted personnel simply obey orders.

Both officers and enlisted receive moral training and ethics education during training, but they are of a different kind, method, and aim. This distinction is one between a "functional view" of ethics education and an "aspirational view" of it (Wolfendale, 2008: 165). Put more simply, they are "rules-based" and "values-based" respectively (Rowell IV, 2013: 12). That is, the functional view is one that emphasizes rules that govern behavior, instills specific habits, and promotes strict adherence for the smooth functioning of the military. By contrast, the aspirational view of ethics education emphasizes moral growth, moral role models, and explicit ethics education on morality in war. This usually takes the form of a formal course (Wolfendale, 2008: 165–169). Rules-based ethics education focuses on military efficiency. Values-based ethics education focuses on moral character (Rowell IV, 2013; Wolfendale, 2008). In practice, while officers certainly learn rules and habits, they must strictly adhere to an Honor Code while at a military academy, and have significant punishments for violations, the approach to ethics education for officers is largely values-based. They have at least one sanctioned ethics course (Wertheimer, 2010) if not many spread out over their time at the academy and at later professional schools during their careers. Enlisted service members and NCOs, on the other hand, receive much more training on conduct and misconduct with little if any attention to the morality of war (Rowell IV, 2013: 13; Wolfendale, 2008: 167). It is this distinction, I argue, that led to such a large number of enlisted service member participants claiming they had received no moral training; when the moral training was all rules and conduct, questions of morality were not present at all.

This all raises the question of why there is a persistent difference between moral training and ethics education for officers and what enlisted service members receive. Officers, of course, have years in training—in a military academy, ROTC, or other War College and special programs—during which ethics education can take place. Enlisted, by contrast, go to basic training and some form of professional training and then begin their careers in earnest. However, the more troubling answer is "a reluctance to admit that the ordinary footslogger has the intellectual capacity to be ethically educated in the first place" (Carrick, 2008: 192). The history of ethics education in the military is one that emphasized moral values in enlisted men, like integrity and trustworthiness, with guidance from military chaplains (Brinsfield, 1997). Officers were presumed to be gentlemen, meaning they had a good education already. While Core Values are a part of ethics education for both enlisted and officers in the various branches, the insistence that enlisted service members cannot or should not learn more complex ethical theories remains.

This insistence is baked into the culture of the military. A retired veteran and former professor at a military academy, Ben Coker,[2] explained to me that the Army had begun to develop training for enlisted service members on the morality of killing. However, he revealed, "JAGs wouldn't let it be released because they said, 'Anything more to give a soldier than rules of engagement will just confuse them and lead to ill-discipline.'" The military wants to and needs to be an efficient machine; having service members who think too long over the basis of the morality of killing slows the well-oiled military machine. The technologies of killing must be left to JAG or CO purview, not individual moral discernment. As Prof. Don Carrick postulates concerning the potential for forcing a burden of ethics education on enlisted, "Plunging headlong into an ethics education and development programme ... has an inherent risk of producing soldiers from whom *too much* thinking and *too much* decision making was demanded" (Carrick, 2008: 192). Service members, particularly those in combat roles, must make decisions quickly. In the view of many in the military, too much moral deliberation is a real threat to efficiency and the successful completion of strategic aims. Emphasizing moral education among the enlisted is, for some, needless if not dangerous.

Moreover, military culture is skeptical of "too much" deliberation. Prof. Coker explained, "There's definitely a theme, you know, a part of the culture, especially from those who don't really get good academic degrees, and their background is, 'Let's not think too deeply about these things.'" The culture in the military was one that emphasized a high-operational tempo and obedience to authority (Wood, 2016). Coker continued, "It's almost a willful ignorance at the individual level, and there's also a concern that, 'Hey, a little bit of knowledge is dangerous. Let's just tell them what they should do and not do and not have them thinking too much.'" Again, if moral deliberation would hurt combat efficiency or lead to a breakdown in the strict hierarchical system in the military, then such an educational emphasis would be harmful to military operations. As Ch.(Maj.) John Williams explained to me:

> The Army's a blue-collar institution. It's like working with a construction company or something. I worked in construction. They would talk about roof slopes at lunch. They would talk about different kinds of wood, and,

[2] Like the other service members and chaplains, I assigned a pseudonym to the professor for the sake of confidentiality.

> once a while, they'd say something about the government or something. Like, we did not have philosophical discussions about the nature of goodness. The military is very much like that for most of its participants. The way the culture is, you're not really supposed to think too much about most things.

Even if the military were to implement more rigorous ethics education among enlisted personnel, there is a persistent organizational framework that makes reflection, particularly moral reflection, not only infrequent but potentially dangerous and worthy of skepticism.

The dividing line between ethics education for officers and enlisted service members is truly one between aspirational and functional approaches. This distinction is culturally reinforced and embedded in the history of ethics education in the US military. It finds expression today in the continued lack of extensive ethics education for enlisted service members, while officers receive training over the entire course of their careers. In a "hierarchical institution such as the military, it might appear more important to ensure that those giving the orders are of good moral character than it is to make sure enlisted personnel are morally upright people" (Wolfendale, 2008: 168). In effect, they are aiming enlisted personnel at strategic ends and requiring obedience. Given that the "just following orders" defense does not hold water and given the reality of battlefield experience,[3] such a self-serving organizational framework is likely a crucial source of moral trauma, as we will see in Chap. 5.

The Teachers and Contents of Ethics Education and Moral Training

Prof. Coker's explanation of Judge Advocate General's Corps (JAG) lawyers shooting down the idea of more robust ethics education for enlisted personnel raises some interesting questions. Who oversees ethics education in the military? Who teaches it? In brief, the answer is, perhaps not surprisingly, that it depends.

[3] See for instance *Operational Law Handbook* 2010, p. 38, that calls out and condemns a "just following orders" defense—likely as a specific response to situations like the My Lai Massacre or more recent atrocities like the Abu Ghraib torture and prisoner abuse crimes in the early years of the Global War on Terror.

In the early days of ethics education, particularly as it developed in the 1970s in the Army, high-ranking officers felt "the chaplaincy, because of its professional training, should be the proponent for ethics" (Brinsfield 66). Military chaplains were, after all, the experts in ethics and had represented the moral sphere within the military to that point. Further, they already held positions at military academies and professional schools along with their regular duties as spiritual advisors to enlisted and officers alike. However, Chaplain Orris E. Kelly, who became the 14th Army Chief of Chaplains in 1975, resisted the notion and eventually outright declined. He believed that ethics education housed in the Chaplain Corps would be just another chaplain program that would have no "real impact" on the Army (Brinsfield 67). Ethics education became the responsibility of commanding officers instead, spread out across different components and with the Chaplain Corps supporting their efforts. The result is that as ethics education developed through the late 1970s until today, material has been developed and courses have been taught by commanding officers, chaplains (at the behest of commanding officers or with positions at academies and schools), staff judge advocates, and supplemented by various visiting faculty positions for civilian ethics professionals—including a temporary Distinguished Chair in Ethics position at Annapolis for example (Wertheimer, 2010).

With responsibility for ethics education falling to various commanding officers, there is wide variation in who produces content for service members at any level. The Office of the Deputy Chief of Staff for Personnel (G-1), for example, develops Army Core Values, a key part of moral training for both officers and enlisted. The Army's Training and Doctrine Command (TRADOC) oversees a number of organizations within the military that have all developed their own ethics education material, like the Center of Army Leadership, or co-sponsored programs like Comprehensive Soldier Fitness and Resilience Training that focus on character, good habits, and behavior (Wead, 2014). In addition to all these programs and resources, officers also take the required Philosophy course at military academies, which are four-year undergraduate programs (Wilson, 2008; Cook, 2008). Those that attend the various branches' War Colleges, usually later in their careers or as post-graduates, also have six to nine ethics contact hours in leadership classes, although they primarily employ an "ethics across the curriculum approach" (Behn, 2018: 10).

Interestingly, those attending Officer Candidate School (OCS) or ROTC programs receive fewer contact hours of ethics education, but they still have some explicit moral training. Prof. Coker told me, “people going into Officer Candidate School are just getting required Army training, and it was rules of engagement. They get nothing like just war theory. Those in ROTC don’t get any kind of just war theory. They just get Army Values. They’ll get a Law of Land Warfare class—like a 60-minute thing—but, in terms of thinking philosophically about ethics applied to war in terms of just war theory, ROTC doesn’t get that.” Even among officers, there was significant variation in access to ethics education. In addition to all these resources, there are, again, Honor Codes at the academies, ROE, Codes of Conduct, and Core Values training for all service members with some variation across each branch of service. Staff judge advocates bolster this training by instructing officers and enlisted service members on LOAC, operational law, and the like, but these rules and laws are usually absent of moral philosophy despite having roots in ethical theories like the just war tradition.

While the Chaplain Corps is not the primary player in ethics education, they remain significantly involved. As we have seen, religion has, in many respects, taken a backseat in moral training and ethics education due to the secularization of just war theory. In addition, there has been renewed emphasis on pluralism, the establishment clause, and the promotion of the American civil religion over the past few decades. Still, some chaplains hold faculty positions at academies or lead classes at professional schools. Military chaplains are specifically tasked with providing moral leadership training across all levels, particularly among officers and higher-ranking NCOs. As Ch. (Col.) Thomas Sandberg explained to me, “[A]t the unit level, ethics is actually taught by the lawyers. In the schools throughout the Army, it’s taught by a chaplain.” To illustrate, for example, there are 22 chaplains deemed “ethics subject matter experts” that are located at different TRADOC facilities around the US providing instruction and developing ethics education programming (Wead, 2014: 5). Modern ethics education has significant theoretical roots in Christianity, and there is historical precedent for religious involvement, but the role of religion has shifted. Despite this, religion does continue to play an important part in ethics education because of the role of chaplains.

There is a good deal of variation in how the chaplains approach ethics instruction. Ch. (Col.) Thomas Sandberg taught ethics education during his career but approached it differently from his peers. “There is not a central curriculum that these chaplains teach on, believe it or not,” he explained. “So, in one place, if someone’s influenced more by C.S. Lewis, you're going to get ethics according to C.S. Lewis. And, in another place, you're going to get ethics according to however that chaplain sees fit to teach that block of instruction." Ethics education for officers and higher-ranking NCOs, then, was a matter of instructors' taste.

Among the chaplains with whom I spoke, teaching just war theory to officers was by no means uniform. There was a more formalized approach taken by Ch. (LTC) Luke Fischer, who had done explicit ethics training for officers, enlisted, and the larger public at various times in his more than three-decade career. He shared a "representative" presentation[4] with me from his days working at the Western Hemisphere Institute for Security Cooperation (WHINSEC)[5] where he gave many of his lectures. Interestingly, he introduced just war theory by contrasting it with "government ethics," or the ethics content provided by JAGs, as opposed to "moral ethics," which he situated as the content provided by chaplains. Already this foundation placed the just war tradition and questions of morality explicitly in the realm of religion. He then introduced the idea of three competing normative—what he calls "popular"—ethical theories: utilitarianism, deontology, and virtue ethics. He called the ethics of the military "virtue ethics." Virtue ethics is the Aristotelean ethical system prescribing norms of behavior lying in a mean between excess and deficiency and governed by reason. Importantly, however, his nominal use of an Aristotelean view of ethics is one heavily influenced by Christian theology. He linked the Core Values of different branches to this normative system.

After discussing what ethical failures look like and reviewing the "military ethical decision-making process"—a cycle of identifying a problem, knowing rules and regulations, and then committing to an action—he spoke of moral foundations and housed these in the Ten Commandments along with Jesus' ministry, John the Baptist's interactions with soldiers, and the Apostle Paul's letter to the Romans. He then introduced just war theory as the "moderating balance" between "Crusader/Jihad Ethics" and "Pacifist Ethics." This position reflected the Aristotelian mean between two extremes, but, by his situating it in the Christian tradition

[4] Ch. Fischer requested that his presentation not be reproduced, so what follows is a description of his approach instead.

[5] WHINSEC is a DoD educational institute overseen by the US Army. In addition to US military officer training, the institute also provides training for over thirty countries of the Western Hemisphere.

and introducing Augustine of Hippo and Thomas Aquinas, he also gave it religious authority.

He then went into specific just war theory concepts like the *jus ad bellum* and *jus in bello* distinctions, major concepts within each, and more sophisticated concepts like *just post bellum*, as well as various arguments against the tradition. In his conclusion, he posed the question of whether just war theory was still valid, answering that the world is a safer place for it undergirding modern restraint in warfare. He linked the spirit of just war theory to the motto of the US Army War College, "Not to promote war, but to preserve the peace." Ch. Fischer's presentation was, in his estimation, representative of how just war theory was widely presented to service members in presentations (outside the Philosophy classrooms at military academies).

When his lectures turned to specific ethical questions in war—like the act of killing—he provided a sophisticated rationale. Calling such ethical discussions "foundational for young officers," he explained the killing versus murder distinction by first explicating the Sixth Commandment's original Hebrew. The root radicals in Hebrew for "kill"—as he explicated in his presentation—emphasized "death by deceit" or "ruthless violence," suggesting that the commandment did not include justified killing. He then brought in LTC Dave Grossman's book *On Killing* to further explain this distinction. Grossman (1996: 342) goes into some depth on the murder versus killing distinction stating, "[T]he Sixth Commandment refers to killing for your own personal gain; it has nothing to do with killing under authority." He then cites examples throughout the Bible where killing and the role of soldiers are shown to be honorable and acceptable. This was a common justification among my participants. They often referred to *On Killing* by name and offered similar understandings of justified killing in war. Ethics education in officer training and professional schools evidently goes beyond purely just war tradition principles. This grounding in Abrahamic religious tradition reinforced the pervasive presence of religion in the moral realm of the military.

Ch. Sandberg, by contrast, taught ethics at the Sergeant Major Academy and the National Defense University where he was also a pastor. Working with high-ranking NCOs and officers, he disagreed with Ch. Fischer that there was a formalized way of teaching ethics. Sandberg's approach emphasized "moral reasoning" at the individual level instead. He explained, "We all operate under some kind of a moral operating system. What I always thought of instruction being is helping people understand the moral base that they're using to reason through different problems in their professional context." By contrast to Ch. Fischer's approach that relied heavily upon an explicit lecture on the just war tradition, Sandberg felt that the "just war tradition is just one of the sources we use."

My participants mostly encountered ethics presentations and courses taught by chaplains at professional schools, war colleges, and other facilities that largely provided education to higher-ranking officers and NCOs. Military academies, by contrast, have their own faculty to teach the requisite Philosophy course that cadets must take that has many more contact hours of ethics instruction. Taken in their second year at West Point, the course "grounds the cadet in basic logic, major ethical theories in Western philosophy, and the Just War Tradition" (Wilson, 2008: 38). Prof. Coker, who I interviewed, taught such a Philosophy course at a military academy. He explained, "Roughly half the course is just war theory, and everyone reads either Brian Orend's *The Morality of War* or Michael Walzer's *Just and Unjust Wars*. Each has been used, one of those two texts, and they give it a good treatment, a better treatment than anywhere else in an Army institution." Written about three decades apart, both texts cover the just war tradition in depth, although Orend's text speaks more to the post-9/11 climate. They connect just war theory with historical and modern examples with some attention given to "realist" and "pacifist" views situated as extremes between which just war theory is the mean. He explained he supplemented that main reading with explorations of philosophical ethics from Kant, Mill, and Aristotle. The second half of the course is on "how these things are applied to war because a lot of the rules of war are combinations like in our Constitution, the combination of utilitarian rules with the etiological limits on behaviors."

The key differences among these organizational approaches are focus, time spent with the material, and depth. Various training schools included just war theory in their curriculum as an aid to practical moral decision-making or, in Ch. Sandberg's case, "moral reasoning" skills, but the Philosophy courses at military academies were able to spend a whole semester with ethics philosophy and the just war tradition alongside practical realities. Cadets wrote papers and took exams on the subject. Moreover, as Prof. Coker proposed, "Probably the biggest thing is instructors, right?" He felt that his advanced degree and those of his peer "ethics cadre" had appropriately prepared them to teach ethics and the just war tradition to cadets. Conversely, instructors of "typical Army ethics" at other training sites taught important ethics education like "'You're allowed to do this, but don't do that.' Right? It's very rule-based. It just is. And that doesn't take time, and it doesn't require any expertise. … Generally, when I see people who haven't taken several courses in just war theory try to teach it, they mess it up." He suggested the military needed to do additional resourcing to have just war theory training reach a larger part of the military.

This difference in approach to instruction and time spent with the material is not without potential effects. Only about 20% of new officers come from academies (Beauchamp, 2015); the majority come from ROTC and OCS that do not have such a robust ethics education programs; and Bell (2014) shows a disparity between academy graduates and ROTC officers. On the one hand, the ethics education of cadets from both programs led to an "increase in sensitivity toward civilians in [their] proportionality calculations in balancing military necessity and humanity for high-value objectives." However, there was much more variation in questions regarding distinction, obedience to ROE, the assumption of risk and the like, particularly in difficult ethical scenarios. Military academy training, compared to ROTC, correlated with a "significant shift of cadet norms" in more difficult scenarios—like "using force to protect fellow soldiers." This indicates that sustained ethics education from academic instructors could play a significant role in managing civilian casualties.

Not only do cadets at military academies have a more prolonged and explicit instruction in ethics at the academy, but officers also receive additional ethics education throughout their careers. Marine Col. Owen Gray, for instance, recalled receiving moral training as he advanced in the ranks or took on new positions. "As an officer, we get more training at a higher level once we get into the Basic School," he said. "The Basic School for the Marines is a six- month course for every Marine officer where they really go into everything, and the law of war and ethics and morality are brought out far more extensively there. It's expected that as officers, we will impose those types of ideals and those types of thoughts and those ethics on our Marines." Regardless of whether the just war tradition remained explicit in officer training or how long the courses lasted, reminders of just conduct in war, moral decision-making, and methods for instilling good behavior in subordinates continued throughout an officer's career.

In the larger picture, however, ethics education is an inconsistent and sporadic part of military training, and its links with religion are varied. Where chaplains taught the just war tradition, they made explicit links to

Christianity and religious resources. By contrast, those who had non-chaplain instructors—like JAGs—and who received more training on the law of war rather than the ethical concepts supporting them tended to say, like Navy LCDR Ian Davison, ethics education was not presented "as a Christian tradition." During officer training at a War College later in his career, Davison explained that ethics education was largely devoid of explicit religious connections.

Ethics education is not only about providing avenues for justifying war and actions in war; it also functions as moral character development, shaping officers through habituated behaviors. Beyond ethics education instruction through lectures and courses, officers also received professional character training. Both Wilson (2008) and Cook (2008) speak of military academy emphasis on character development among officers. Citing the *Cadet Leadership Development System*, Wilson (2008: 35) described West Point's commitment to transforming its cadets into officers that can be a "person who will set 'the professional example by personifying' character that displays 'an awareness of and commitment to something bigger than [one's] self.'" Cook (2008: 58) links this sort of character-building ethics education to habit formation qua Aristotelian virtue ethics, which is meant to result in "consistent reliable patterns of behaviour ... believed to be essential for a well-disciplined and reliable officer corps." While the Philosophy courses, just war theory lectures, and lessons on moral decision-making contribute to this habit formation in part, the emphasis on character development comes in the form of Core Values, Codes of Conduct, and Honor Codes.

Importantly, apart from the Honor Code, character development is not unique to the experience of officers. Core Values and the Code of Conduct of each military branch were the most cited sources of moral training among enlisted. Where enlisted service members did not have extensive ethics education and often did not know what I meant by "just war theory," they did have instruction on Core Values and the Code of Conduct—along with the explicit instruction on ROE and LOAC—particularly regarding their specific roles. Each branch of the military has their own values and codes of conduct, but to illustrate, consider the Army Core Values, which are loyalty, duty, respect, selfless service, honor, integrity, and personal courage (US Army). They represent virtues and highlight the Aristotelean virtue ethics approach of the military, emphasizing habit formation in training. These virtues are consistently reinforced by commanding officers and military chaplains.

Similarly, an emphasis on good moral habits came through among participants who felt the Core Values were the extent of their ethics education. Air Force Maj. Robert Derry, a late career officer who had gone through enlisted basic training earlier in his career, for example, explained, "All of [the branches] basically had Core Values that they were instilling, and then you do things the way you're supposed to do things. There's a reason we have you do these things. You don't have to ask why. You just need to do it." This sentiment that moral training instilled good habits so that active moral deliberation was unnecessary in the field was relatively common among enlisted participants. Special Ops Sgt Edward Roberts echoed the sentiment that other branches were "very keen on instilling the values of the institution"; however, "in terms of big picture, broad strokes questioning the morality of conflict, that's not really something we ever talked about because it's not really important to the job. The job of the Army is to fight and win." The Core Values, Code of Conduct, and related materials ensured that service members were habituated to be good people who knew what to and not to do in war. Philosophical discussions of morality in and of war were beside the point.

That enlisted service members have little ethics education compared with officers should now be readily apparent. They do have Core Values; learn about ROE, LOAC, and the Hague and Geneva Conventions; and have access to moral development support from military chaplains and other religious resources. They learn the rules and regulations relevant to their specific role in the military, yet they do not receive new moral reasoning resources that would allow them to consider the justness of their actions or to think critically about the moral quandaries they will likely face during their careers. Moreover, they mostly say that those questions are beside the point compared to achieving strategic goals and protecting those around them. It is no wonder, then, that the majority of enlisted responded to my questions about moral training with a "no" or "not really" or "I don't remember anything like that." The functional ethics education of enlisted that relies on checking off boxes as modules to be completed is vastly different from the aspirational ethics education of officers—particularly those at academies—who can spend more time engaging with ethical deliberation with the guidance of instructors. The military framework, then, is one of assuming that the moral character and ethical deliberative capacities of officers aiming the spear will trickle down to those at the tip.

Conclusions

That the gap between ethics education in officer training—even between officers in different training programs—and enlisted is so large ought to worry us. The absence of moral guidance and deliberation among enlisted can explain the troubling joke about obliterating an enemy combatant that opened this chapter. More seriously, it can explain reports like that from Castro and McGurk (2007: 29–30) that found that among US soldiers and Marines fighting in Operation Iraqi Freedom,

> Less than half of soldiers and marines believed that noncombatants should be treated with dignity and respect, and well over a third believed that torture should be allowed to save the life of a fellow team member. About 10% of soldiers and marines reported mistreating an Iraqi noncombatant when it wasn't necessary, either by destroying their private property or by hitting or kicking them. Less than half of soldiers or marines would report a team member for unethical behavior, instead preferring to handle it themselves at the team level. Although they reported receiving ethical training, nearly a third of soldiers and marines reported encountering ethical situations in Iraq in which they didn't know how to respond.

These troubling findings would make anyone question if ethics education makes a difference at all. Can overhauling ethics education prevent future service members from having similarly shocking attitudes? It is a question of whether moral resources precede action in either habit (Dewey, 1922) or moral deliberation (Swidler, 1986). Bell's research (2014) has shown that ethics education does have an impact, particularly when it is applied with consistent content, intensity, and using a scenario-based ethics training method. However, some, like journalist David Wood (2016), have suggested that military training creates dissonance by habituating the ability to kill alongside honoring moral excellence. The fact is that "higher levels of stress" and "psychological conflict and suffering" within the military experience likely add to the formation of these attitudes (Thompson & Jetly, 2018: 8–3), and a lack of appropriate ethics education that could form preemptive strategies for moral dilemmas endemic of military experience may have impact.

However, this raises important questions about what "effective" moral training and ethics education would look like. There is a persistent disconnect between the ethics and moral commitments supplied by this training and the ethos of military culture that aims and re-aims service members at military strategic ends. However, correcting these disconnects may not actually solve the moral problem. Built-in justifications that absolve the perceived sin of killing—perhaps the primary focus of ethics education—may still be damaging in the long run. Consider the popularity of Dave Grossman's (1996: 343) *On Killing*. In it, he writes powerfully, "'Thou shall not kill' is a poor translation taken grossly out of context and … this has been responsible for doing great emotional harm to our veterans." Making the murder versus killing distinction a guiding framework for service members allows them to manage the reality of perpetrating violence more effectively, but that same framework is the one that keeps them fighting—that sets them up for potential moral trauma later. It socializes them to the professional warrior identity and frames their future work as essentially good (Lifton & Markusen, 1990), even if it has the capacity to do harm. It supplies them with a distinct set of moral principles and expectations that represent a process of what psychiatrist Robert Lifton calls "derealization," wherein service members divest themselves of the reality of what they are doing (Lifton, 1986: 442). Military culture and religion supply explicit and implicit tools that can preempt trauma and promote resilience; that does not mean they are not destructive.

Nevertheless, making ethics education more consistent and widely available to enlisted personnel remains important, particularly for the modern context where strained tensions with the local population play a significant factor in military operations. The modern context, however, is one where these tensions are coupled with consistent attempts by enemy combatants to "provoke disproportionate retaliation from Western forces" by playing against our ethical norms and values, and by evading identification as combatants. Hiding among civilians, not wearing uniforms, and using women and children in attacks obfuscate role clarity and increase the number of ethical dilemmas service members face (Thompson & Jetly, 2018: 8–1). They also very clearly lead to hateful attitudes toward the local population and a dehumanization of the enemy (Castro & McGurk, 2007). The absence of consistent ethics education that takes this modern context into account makes the "joke" of disproportionate force one that lands and is winkingly internalized.

The problem is that to correct ethics education would mean taking on certain organizational frames the US military has internalized for decades—if not most of its history—that enlisted service members need to learn only those rules and regulations that affect their role. The organization assumes they lack the intellectual capacities or interest to learn or to habituate moral deliberation. Moreover, such deliberation could put the hierarchical structure of the military that places its confidence in officers making ethical decisions into question. These damaging assumptions relegate the moral domain to officers despite the consequences of potentially immoral action falling to enlisted personnel. Of course, changing these organizational frames would prove difficult. It is what Crawford (2013: 317) refers to as the "problem of 'many hands'" since no person can alter the cultural frameworks of an organization alone. Changing institutionalized beliefs like the need for moral deliberation among enlisted service members would be extremely difficult, particularly in an organization that favors conformity and obedience.

In addition to the more shocking organizational frameworks that need to change, this chapter also brings to light the significance of religion in ethics education overall. Religion—Christianity in particular—implicitly and explicitly shapes ethics education. Whether the just war tradition is a major part of study or whether the instructor draws attention to the theory's Christian roots, the tradition is inextricably linked to ROE and LOAC. The American way of waging war is one that is rooted in Christian tradition. That religion appears in more explicit ways like moral instruction from chaplains or explicit religious justifications showing up in classrooms and lectures only adds to its significance. Religion, then, provides a major toolkit that service members draw upon regardless of whether they make an explicit connection to it. Importantly, however, this religion is one that mixes Christian traditions with military beliefs and strategic aims. Having established the role and function of military chaplains and the ethics training that is reinforced and often taught by chaplains, we can look at how service members interact with religion in the military in institutional, communal, symbolic, and private ways.

Bibliography

Argetsinger, A. (1996, April 14). Naval Academy Charts New Moral Course. *The Washington Post*. Retrieved from https://www.washingtonpost.com/archive/local/1996/04/14/naval-academy-charts-new-moral-course/6558aa47-4f63-4bf2-a704-941aa843fb65/

Augustine of Hippo. (1984). *Concerning the City of God Against the Pagans* (H. Bettenson, Trans.). Penguin.

Beauchamp, S. (2015, January 23). Abolish West Point -- and the Other Service Academies, Too. *The Washington Post*. Retrieved from https://www.washingtonpost.com/opinions/why-we-dont-need-west-point/2015/01/23/

fa1e1488-a1ef-11e4-9f89-561284a573f8_story.html#:~:text=But%20graduates%20of%20the%20academies,who%20want%20an%20officer's%20commission.

Behn, B. A. (2018). *The Stakes Are High: Ethics Education at US War Colleges.* Air University Press.

Bell, A. (2014). Leashing the "Dogs of War": Examining the Effects of LOAC Training at the U.S. Military Academy and in Army ROTC. *Proceedings of the Annual Meeting (American Society of International Law), 108*, 370–373.

Brinsfield, J. W. (1997). *Encouraging Faith, Serving Soldiers: A History of the U.S. Army Chaplaincy, 1975–1995.* Office of the Chief of Chaplains, Dept. of the Army.

Carrick, D. (2008). The Future of Ethics Education in the Military: A Comparative Analysis. In P. Robinson, N. D. Lee, & D. Carrick (Eds.), *Ethics Education in the Military* (pp. 187–198). Ashgate Pub. Company.

Castro, C. A., & McGurk, D. (2007). Battlefield Ethics. *Traumatology, 13*(4), 24–31.

Clark, T. M. (2004). *Moral Development at the United States Naval Academy: The Midshipman's Perspective* (Doctoral dissertation, Naval Postgraduate School, September 2004). Dudley Knox Library.

Cook, M. L. (2008). Ethics Education, Ethics Training, and Character Development: Who 'Owns' Ethics in the US Air Force Academy? In P. Robinson, N. D. Lee, & D. Carrick (Eds.), *Ethics Education in the Military* (pp. 57–65). Ashgate Pub. Company.

Cooper, H., & Schmitt, E. (2021, February 25). U.S. Attacks in Syria Target Iran-Backed Militias That Rocketed American Troops in Iraq. *The New York Times.* Retrieved from https://www.nytimes.com/2021/02/25/us/politics/biden-syria-airstrike-iran.html

Crawford, N. C. (2003). Just War Theory and the U.S. Counterterror War. *Perspectives on Politics, 1*(1), 5–25.

Crawford, N. C. (2013). *Accountability for Killing: Moral Responsibility for Collateral Damage in America's Post-9/11 Wars.* Oxford University Press.

Dewey, J. (1922). *Human Nature and Conduct: An Introduction to Social Psychology.* Henry Holt & Company.

Dierker, G. J. (1997). *Core Values: A History of Values-Related Initiatives in the Air Force* (Doctoral dissertation, Air University, September 1997). Defense Technical Information Center.

Finnis, J. (1996). Catholic Natural Law Tradition. In T. Nardin (Ed.), *The Ethics of War and Peace* (pp. 15–39). Princeton University Press.

Forde, S. (1998). Hugo Grotius on Ethics and War. *The American Political Science Review, 92*, 639–648.

Forell, G. W., & Childs, J. M. (2013). *Christian Social Teachings: A Reader in Christian Social Ethics from the Bible to the Present.* Fortress Press.

Grossman, D. (1996). *On Killing: The Psychological Cost of Learning to Kill in War and Society*. Little, Brown.
Hartle, A. E. (2004). *Moral Issues in Military Decision Making*. University Press of Kansas.
Lifton, R. J. (1986). *The Nazi Doctors: Medical Killing and the Psychology of Genocide*. Basic Books.
Lifton, R. J., & Markusen, E. (1990). *Genocidal Mentality: Nazi Holocaust and Nuclear Threat*. Basic Books.
MacIntyre, A. (2007). *After Virtue* (3rd ed.). University of Notre Dame Press.
McMahan, J. (2009). *Killing in War*. Oxford University Press.
Orend, B. (2006). *The Morality of War*. Broadview Press.
Rowell, G. B., IV. (2013). *Marine Corps Values-Based Ethics Training: A Recipe to Reduce Misconduct* (Master's thesis, U.S. Army War College, 2013). Strategy Research Project.
Scott, W. (1847). Imprenta de la Calle de la Carniceria. *General Order, 20*.
Simon, H. (2018). The Myth of Liberum Ius ad Bellum: Justifying War in 19th-Century Legal Theory and Political Practice. *The European Journal of International Law, 29*(1), 113–136.
Swidler, A. (1986, April). Culture in Action: Symbols and Strategies. *American Sociological Review, 51*(2), 273–286.
Taylor, T. (1973). Foreword. In L. Friedman (Ed.), *The Law of War: A Documentary History*. Random House.
Thompson, M. M., & Jetly, R. (2018). Battlefield Ethics Training: Integrating Ethical Scenarios in High-Intensity Field Exercises. In *Moral Decisions and Military Mental Health* (Vol. STO-TR-HFM-179, pp. 8-1–8-15). NATO Science and Technology Organization.
Tuck, R. (2001). *The Rights of War and Peace: Political Thought and the International Order from Grotius to Kant*. Oxford University Press.
Waggoner, E. (2014, September). Taking Religion Seriously in the U.S. Military: The Chaplaincy as a National Strategic Asset. *Journal of the American Academy of Religion, 82*(3), 702–735.
Walzer, M. (2006). *Just and Unjust Wars: A Moral Argument with Historical Illustrations* (4th ed.). Basic Books.
Walzer, M. (2010). The Triumph of Just War Theory (and the Dangers of Success). In R. Wertheimer (Ed.), *Empowering Our Military Conscience: Transforming Just War Theory and Military Moral Education* (pp. 15–32). Taylor & Francis Group.
Wead, S. (2014). *The Evolution of Military Ethics in the United States Army*. Retrieved from https://www.cgscfoundation.org/wp-content/uploads/2014/04/Wead-EvolutionofMilitaryEthics.pdf

Wertheimer, R. (2010). Introduction: A Great Awakening. In R. Wertheimer (Ed.), *Empowering Our Military Conscience: Transforming Just War Theory and Military Moral Education* (pp. 1–11). Taylor & Francis Group.
Williams, H. (1995). Judgments on War: A Response. In H. Robinson (Ed.), *Proceedings of the Eighth International Kant Congress* (Vol. 1, Part 3, p. 1393). Marquette University Press.
Wilson, J. (2008). An Ethics Curriculum for an Evolving Army. In P. Robinson, N. De Lee, & D. Carrick (Eds.), *Ethics Education in the Military* (pp. 31–41). Ashgate Pub. Company.
Winerip, M. (2013, May 13). Revisiting the Military's Tailhook Scandal. *The New York Times*. Retrieved from https://www.nytimes.com/2013/05/13/booming/revisiting-the-militarys-tailhook-scandal-video.html
Wogaman, J. P. (1993). *Christian Ethics: A Historical Introduction*. Westminster John Knox Press.
Wolfendale, J. (2008). What Is the Point of Teaching Ethics in the Military. In P. Robinson, N. D. Lee, & D. Carrick (Eds.), *Ethics Education in the Military* (pp. 161–174). Ashgate Pub. Company.
Wood, D. B. (2016). *What Have We Done: The Moral Injury of Our Longest Wars*. Little, Brown and Company.

CHAPTER 4

The Religious Life of the US Military

With about 65% of the US military claiming some form of Christian affiliation (Hunter & Smith, 2010), it is easy to conjure up an image of service members participating in Christian services before an impassioned chaplain. National Guardsman John Ashman was quick to dispel that thought. "People have this image of soldiers kneeling and being religious. Well, not so much really," he said. "They're more interested in partying and having a good time than they are about listening to God." He recalled a Christmas service at a forward operating base (FOB), Waza Khwa, with about 200 troops stationed there in 2007; only six service members showed up, despite a chaplain flying in by helicopter to lead it. If the typical sorts of organized religion are not such a draw, where then does religion happen in the military?

The answer is that it varies by location and role. Nor can religion be defined only by organizational religious engagement, even if organizational practices do happen. Religion in the military is, like an individual's identity, always many things at once. It is both formal and informal, official and lived. Service members bowing their heads and praying *did* occur. Sgt. Paul Callaghan recalled chaplains praying with combat troops before every mission, even when he did not believe in God at the time. Others widely reported attending religious services when, like public affairs NCO Cordell, "they made an effort to go." However, it was clear that religion

T. H. Suitt, III, *Narratives of Trauma and Moral Agency among Christian Post-9/11 Veterans*,
https://doi.org/10.1007/978-3-031-31082-9_4

included much more than services and chaplains. Navy LCDR. Ian Davison stated it clearly, "I just don't think chaps are really where a lot of people work [out their faith]. There can be crisis moments where chaps are involved, but religion gets worked out in a lot of other settings for people in the military." Some expressed their faith through formal religious activities like worship bands while others took a more private approach. Air Force engineer Hailey Freeman related, "I didn't really have any connections to religion except for reading [a] devotional every day and reading the little verse that went with it." For her and others, private prayer and meditation were the only ways they expressed their faith. Still others found comfort in religious symbols like cross necklaces and pocket Bibles but rarely participated in formal religious activities or even prayer. And there were many combinations of all these besides.

Underlying these activities, practices, and symbols were also meaning-making systems, values, beliefs, and coping tools that allowed service members to make sense of their military experience. These varied as well. For example, Freeman recalled believing "God had [her] in the military for a reason." Sgt. Thompson believed that because he was part of the "one percent of our nation that put the uniform on and even a smaller percent that would actually go into direct battle, that surely God [was] going to look upon [him] with mercy no matter what." Navy cryptologist Justin Page explained that religion "helped [him] have a reason for why things were happening." Amid trauma or the stresses of everyday life, religion was often a producer of beliefs, values, meaning, and understanding in post-9/11 service members' lives, regardless of whether those were outward or internal expressions of faith.

All these diverse activities, beliefs, and ways of viewing the world represent what I refer to as religious resources. They express the significant relationships that can exist between an individual and the divine in public and private. Indeed, while organizational activities, practices, and interactions with chaplains are significant indicators of religion, they do not signal the entire sweep of what constitutes religious practice. The military's religious resource toolkit is not monolithic, and service members interact with multiple religious toolkits throughout their careers. Moreover, the cultural package that "religious resources" represents is just one toolkit of many that service members must choose from to find strategies for action amid different cultural spheres that each have their expectations (Swidler, 1986; C. Smith, 2003).

There is a varied and deeply embedded religiosity within the US military.[1] It has diverse roots and characteristics, representing both institutional and lived religious expressions and beliefs. The breadth of the research is limited, however, meaning that the origins, characteristics, and outcomes of the religious resources in a service member's typical life narrative are far from clear. This chapter explores different aspects of religion in the military through the ongoing religious military narratives of post-9/11 veterans. It will examine both organizational and non-organizational religious life, both formal and lived religious contexts that span their careers. In doing so, this chapter explores a complex dynamic between religious resources brought to the military and those produced by the military, showing the consequences of where and when religious cultural packages and strategies for action enter service members' lives. This dynamic paints a picture of religion in their lives as one of confluence and competition between imbricated social and cultural spheres where civilian religion meets military religion (and non-religion) before, during, and after service.

Religious Resources Brought to the Military

Enlisted privates, airmen, seamen, and officers interact with a complex set of military religious resources upon beginning their service; however, they also bring with them different sets of civilian religious resources that, up to that moment in their lives, had provided many of them with cultural toolkits, moral scripts, and expectations. In fact, despite having significant variation in religiosity at the time of joining, forty-one of the forty-seven veteran and reservist participants reported feeling that religion had shaped their upbringing somehow. That is, even if they claimed religion played little or no role in their day to day lives growing up, the majority of participants did link it with shaping their identity, sense of morality, or family lives in some way.

The religious traditions from which they came were varied. Fourteen participants identified with a Mainline Protestant denomination (American Baptist (1), Presbyterian (4), Methodist (5), Lutheran (1), and Episcopal (3)). Fourteen identified as Catholic. Ten identified as Evangelical, including Southern Baptist, evangelical, and non-denominational. Two identified as Church of Latter-Day Saints (LDS). Six claimed no preference at

[1] See, for instance, Ron Hassner's (2016a) literature review of religion in the military.

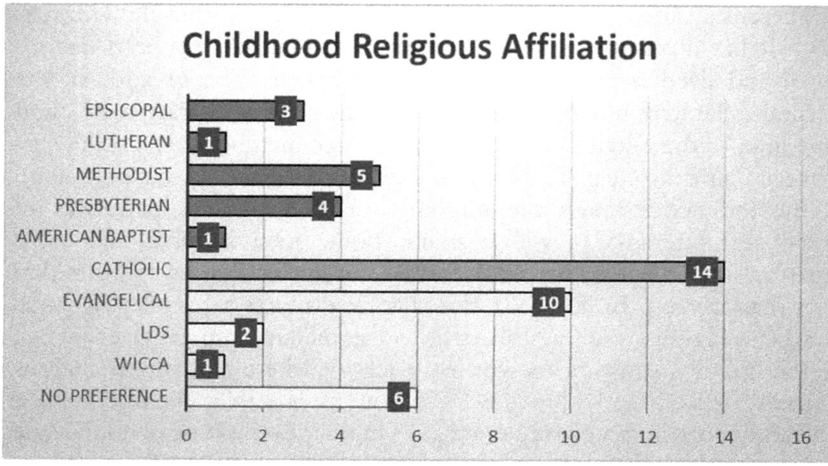

Fig. 4.1 Childhood religious affiliation

the time of joining. Finally, one identified as Wicca (See Fig. 4.1). However, twelve participants across Protestant, Catholic, and Evangelical traditions reported low religiosity at the time of joining. They claimed a religious affiliation without participating in formal religious practices or reporting intrinsic religious beliefs. The diverse and complex backgrounds of these different denominations are not the topic of this project; nonetheless, it is crucial to investigate patterns in the types of religious cultural toolkits that service members bring to military service.

Service members who brought religious resources with them to the military might have toolkits that could naturally complement the religious resources they would be exposed to while in the Armed Forces, or their religious resources might set them up for dissonance—a feeling of a psychologically distressing mismatch between two cognitions—namely between moral expectations and military experience (Harmon-Jones & Mills, 2019: 3). There were two common religious cultural toolkits among those who brought religion to their military career. The first tended to lean toward conservative ideologies, especially among evangelical and LDS interlocutors, where religion tended to have more explicit centrality in their self-identity. While not necessarily ideologically liberal, the other tended to have less reported outward expression and emphasized doing good and participating in acts of service. They placed a big emphasis on

"Christ's love commandment" or "the Golden Rule," for instance, but were otherwise motivated to action by other non-religious commitments.

The lines between these religious cultural groups are messy. There were instances of overlap and outliers, as well as six service members who entered the military with no religious resources to speak of. But the overarching narratives brought these two trends to the fore. The conservative package tended to give religious issues some importance. Often visible when participants talked about specific religious beliefs connected to military service (e.g., justifications for the perceived sin of killing), those with this religious cultural package approached their service with more explicit religious motives and rationalizations. Conversely, those who did not have such evident religious identity centrality focused on a general desire to serve, not necessarily drawing the link between a commitment to serve and their religious commitments and beliefs. Finally, there were participants in both conservative and liberal communities whose beliefs and moral expectations were held uncritically and were not activated until dissonance occurred, if at all.

Resonant Beliefs, Conservative Communities, and Religious Centrality

Most participants did report feeling that religion played some role in shaping their identity, but there were different degrees of reported influence. Those with high religiosity, particularly those from more conservative religious communities, claimed religion was central to their identity. Army linguist Walter Keller, for example, affiliated with the Christian Reformed Church, a conservative Dutch Presbyterian denomination. He explained that his "church community was central to everything" and "was very significant" in shaping his identity, sense of morality, and reason for joining the military. And he was not alone. Many others also claimed religion "absolutely" shaped their identity and sense of morality, and they brought particular religious frames, especially moral beliefs and expectations, with them to military service. These commitments usually played out in more formal religious engagement over their careers, but the unifying factor appeared to be rooted in ideological conservatism.

Conservatism itself had varying degrees of representation among the participants. For instance, Keller viewed himself as a conservative but stated, "I know very well mine are not the only views, and I'm not going to weaponize my experience or views against people that don't agree."

Keller was a self-described conservative but also emphasized open-mindedness. By contrast, MSG Mike Thompson, who had low religiosity upon joining the military but was raised evangelical, spoke at length about his conservative beliefs. Explaining he was a "believer but not a good follower," he felt his Pentecostal church ultimately shaped his morality, saying, "you are always led by the Holy Spirit to the point of, well, you know the difference between right and wrong. You know if it's something that you shouldn't do." He had strong opinions on what he believed were modern social moral issues like homosexuality and drug use. "It's all pure evil," he said. Although his participation in organizational and non-organizational religion was low during his childhood and upon joining the military, his religious beliefs influenced how he saw the world and his role in it, nonetheless.

Along with this conservativism came a sense of patriotic duty, bundled with the religious commitments. For someone like Air Force officer Robert Derry, a Southern Baptist, religion did play a significant role in his decision to join. "It was another moral thing to do," he explained; moreover, the military fit his understanding of the moral world. He felt the military was "naturally like a religion where there are rules that you don't break and things that you do and don't do." Similarly, CWO-2 Greg Bush, who grew up LDS, explained, "In my faith, the light of Christ or the spirit guides us in our lives, helps us make decisions and everything, so I've kind of gone with that—not just my gut feeling but the way I feel that I should be, things I should be doing in my life." In these cases, the decision to join the military, down to the moral expectations of military service and expectations about military life, was one that coincided with religious belief and practice in their respective conservative Christian denominations.

There is a reason this broad picture of religious and cultural conservativism readily aligns with military service. Part of what makes evangelicalism, and arguably conservative Christian denominations broadly, well-suited for motivating participation in the US military is the broad support for military service as a Christian duty. For example, Anne Loveland (1996: 4–5) points to evangelical philosopher Gordon H. Clark who claimed, "the New Testament, as well as the Old, authorizes the waging of war." Evangelicals "insisted that killing the enemy in combat was not murder and therefore did not violate the Sixth Commandment. They believed that the use of force by government was sanctioned by God as a means of protecting the rights of individuals and maintaining order."

Service members were acting as police, carrying out their divine duties to the state. With explicit built-in justifications for participating in war and for acts of killing in war, it makes sense that military service would fit into the cultural frames of certain conservative denominations.

The link between evangelicalism and the military likely increased in the post-conscription era. In addition to reflecting the everyday demands of military life, it also readily appeals to conservative ideologues, who are more likely to sign up. By "conservative ideologue," I am referring to James Griffith's (2009) identification of a common identity among conscripts from the Gulf War through the Bush administration marked by, among other attributes, conservativism, support for the Republican Party, and patriotism. As John Hamre, Deputy Secretary of Defense from 1997 to 2000, told sociologist Michael Lindsay (2007: 165), when the military shifted to an all-volunteer force, new service members increasingly came from "a segment of society that had strong cultural affinity to the military lifestyle and the values that are enshrined in the military community. So, over the last twenty-five years, the military has become far more evangelical [as well as] more Southern, more rural, more conservative." Recruiting patterns draw from parts of the US with a higher density of evangelicals, and these communities have significant built-in cultural frames that support military service.

The Significance of Service and Golden Rule Christians

Other veterans felt that religion had little to do with their decision to join the military. Despite believing religion had shaped their lives in some way, it had not shaped their careers. They brought religious resources to the service, but they did not tend to have high organizational religious participation or hold religion as explicitly central to their identity. Not to say that religion was not important to their lives; instead, they reported holding religious beliefs that quietly inspired their commitments. They tended to say that they did not let religion influence their interactions with others as they "did not want to proselytize." Army officer and Presbyterian Scott Michaels explained that his "sense of morality was always about how do we treat people." He recalled his "mom would always talk about the Golden Rule of do unto others as you would have done unto you." This emphasis on the Golden Rule above evangelism or even specific theological belief is emblematic of what Ammerman (1997a: 196) calls "Golden Rule Christianity."

According to Ammerman (1997a: 212), Golden Rule Christians are ones who favor service to each other and the community over any coherent theological belief system or the need for evangelism. Their religion is one that "emphasizes relationships and caring," doing good deeds, and helping. They want to improve the world and are often part of many different communities, even while their religious commitment to the Golden Rule quietly influences their other actions. To illustrate, consider Michaels' explanation for wanting to join the military. After the events of 9/11, "that inspired me to do some sort of service, and the service that interested me the most at the time was military service. I feel like that was directly linked to being able to make the world right." Interestingly, Michaels did not link his desire to "serve" and "make the world right" with his religious beliefs. Instead, he claimed religion played little part in his decision to go to West Point.

However, I argue that religious belief did generate this explicit commitment to service and motivated his decision to join the military after the 9/11 attacks activated this motivation in him. It made religious convictions of service significant for him even if he did not necessarily make that connection. While more evangelical-leaning or Mormon counterparts *were* more explicit in linking religion's role with their decision to join, Golden Rule Christians tended to keep explicit religious action and military service separate. The Golden Rule emphasis and desire for improving the world are rooted in religious frameworks, motivating service, but religious belief and organizational attendance were not otherwise a priority. Patriotic duty certainly played a part; however, Michaels and others worked out the dissonance of 9/11 using a Golden Rule religious moral frame.

Religious Resources Among Those with Low Religiosity

Conservative ideologues with high religious identity centrality and high religiosity tended to bring religious resources to the service that were consistent with religious military culture. Comparatively, Golden Rule Christians tended to have less organizational religious engagement, although religion was still important for moral guidance and comfort. But what of service members who came to the military with low religiosity? What did their religious resources look like?

There were those, for example, like National Guard Special Operations Sgt. Jaime O'Sullivan, who explained, "[My religious community] helped me develop as a person and kind of understand my religion and how I pray and stuff," but Christian faith only influenced his life "a little bit." His Catholic faith was not explicitly central to his identity, nor did it appear to directly impact his decision to join the military or lead to high participation in military religion upon joining. This lack of explicit engagement with his faith did not preclude him from finding comfort in practices like prayer. But in the absence of significant dissonance that would spur the activation of religious resources more overtly, he generally maintained his faith.

Some entered the military with minimal religious resources that provided a baseline for their moral attitudes and beliefs, but they then experienced a feeling of being "saved" after joining a new religious community or following major trauma. They had maintained a low level of religiosity until some inciting event occurred. Company Commander Will Berger, for instance, was raised Roman Catholic. He mostly only engaged when his family forced him, yet it still influenced his sense of morality. In his words, "I think it helped give me a perspective on values, and how to treat other people, and a bigger picture of a lot of things in life." Still, for him, religion "ebbed and flowed in and out." It was not until he joined a community while stationed in Hawaii with his wife that he was "saved" and "the spirit moved [him]." Religion did not appear to play much of a role in Berger's daily life until a significant moment activated the importance of religious beliefs and questions within him. In his case, it was a conversion to an evangelical tradition.

Looking at the overall picture of religious resources brought to the military, both the level and type of individual religiosity shaped experience. For some, religion was only minimally relevant, but for others, two broad religious cultural streams were apparent. Evangelical religious resources encouraged enlistment and neatly meshed with military culture. Golden Rule Christians were motivated by service but downplayed any overt connections between their religious commitments and their military experience. As was apparent in the role of chaplains and in patterns of moral training, religious resources found in the military are incredibly complex. In this chapter, it will become clear that there is not one monolithic religious experience in the military. Whether and how religious resources brought to the military interact with those found in the military depends on the job of the service member, the resources they have access to, and their ideological commitments.

Lived Religion: Meaning, Practice, and Presence

Recall LCDR Davison posited that much of the military religion does not happen where chaplains interact with service members. If one were to check off boxes for service attendance and whether service members adhere to a strict set of Christian beliefs, it would appear that military religious life is waning and would lead people, like National Guardsman John Ashman to believe, as he said, "I'll say this. Most people in uniform are not religious, no, not at all." However, service members *are* religious to varying degrees, but they have differences in how they interact with the sacred or rely upon religious resources. Alongside an established history of religious resources in the US military and the dynamic relationship between service members and chaplains, there is a broader picture of how service members practice religion. Setting aside religion as a rigidly normative category, we can understand religious life by seeing how service members live it.

This "lived religion" is messy; it blurs the lines between the sacred and the profane, even the religious and the mythic. However, it illuminates the ways service members dramatize their religious cultural commitments to the moral order by acting on their relationship to the sacred publicly and privately. While I have so far emphasized the role of chaplains and the religion the military provides on paper, in this chapter, I will emphasize the laity within the military to uncover their idiosyncratic ways of interacting with the sacred collectively and individually.

The study of lived religion is a relatively new approach to religious studies, coming into its own in the mid-1990s. Using ethnographic and sociological approaches, lived religion scholars emphasize religion as "the everyday thinking and doing of lay men and women" or "the *social* realities of everyday religious life" (Hall, 1997: vii; Ammerman, 2007), rather than only the sorts of religious resources that one could check off an itemized list of formal activities and beliefs. Also called folk religion, it is what Charles Lippy (1994: viii) describes as "the ways ordinary folks go about their business of making sense of the world, regardless of connections to movements or institutions." That is, it goes beyond religion as it is written in official doctrines or preached from the pulpit. Religious studies had long privileged masculine, heteronormative, Mainline concerns, but lived religion emerged at the margins. It expanded the field to include the voices of people whose everyday life experiences defied preconceived understandings. This new subject of inquiry challenged and continues to challenge our understanding of what religion is in the world. If Weber saw in formal religion the "locus of sacredness … removed from the rooftrees, graveyards, and road-crossings of everyday life," everyday religion is evidence of its dispersal back to mundane realms, still rationalized but not institutionally defined (Geertz, 1973: 174).

If there is relatively little scholarship in religion in the military, apart from chaplains' roles, there is even less on lived religion in the US military. Much of military lived religion research focuses on historical accounts during World War II (Walters, 2013) or through chaplain memoirs (Carter, 2004). Walters (2013) shows the importance of military religious expression shaping religion in the US post-war. The research focused on the modern context emphasizes the need for chaplains to integrate lived religious language into their growing repertoire of resources to accommodate the difficult transitions of service members back to civilian life (Grimell, 2018a, b). Still others provide a charitable exposition of lived religion in the military in modern and historical contexts. Ron Hassner (2016b: 137) explores what he refers to as "sacred" time, space, and authority on the battlefield in Iraq between US and enemy forces where belief and practice interact with warfare in novel ways. His emphasis, however, is on implications for future religious intelligence agents and policy and omits the importance of discourse, narrativity, and religious identity in modern military settings.

Still, despite this relative gap in the literature, there are frameworks useful in my approach to what I found. For example, Carter (2004: 180) describes the phenomenon of lived religion in the military as "combat religiosity" or "foxhole faith" that is a form of "popular religious expression" among service members in combat situations. This is an amalgamation of religious practices and beliefs shaped in institutional settings but lived out in diverse ways in "the spaces between official or learned Christianity and profane (or 'pagan') culture" (Hall, 1997: viii). While certainly shaped in combat, it does not only develop out of combat experiences. The occasions that motivate informal religious beliefs, practices, and symbols can appear in classrooms, domestic operating bases, or in the lives of those in support roles.

This section will address some of the challenges facing the study of lived religion cited in Ammerman (2016). By drawing the line from formal military religious resources available to service members to informal participation, I hope to avoid the issue of placing lived religion in strict opposition to "official" religion. The answer to what religion looks like in the military must include both the institutional and the everyday. As Ammerman (2016: 16) contends, "we may learn more by putting those 'outside the box' insights into dialogue with a similar set of questions addressed to the settings in which societies have institutionalized religion." Furthermore, as a pushback to scholarship that has mostly underlined individual agency and practice, I will emphasize the importance of communities and contexts in producing and reinforcing practices, symbols, and even folkloric myth. If there is a mystery to be solved to connect the dots between those claiming religion is on its way out in the military and those claiming religion and belief influence the majority of service members' lives in some fashion, an investigation of formal and informal religion in the US military can begin to resolve it.

Organizational Participation in Official Religion

Before diving into the unofficial and non-organizational religious activities that make up the broader category of lived religion, I will first investigate the organizational activities that are what we usually think of when describing "religion in the US military." As shown above, the military produces its own religious culture, albeit one divided. On the one hand, there is the evangelical-leaning, proselytizing-heavy religious culture. On the other, there is a religious culture strongly advocating non-establishment and providing accommodation for diverse religious expression. Both must work amidst the generically Christian civil religious culture the military produces with its gatherings, events, symbols, and practices. The various cultural packages compete within the various Chaplain Corps personnel and certain military positions like chaplains' assistants. Despite this cultural competition, the military offers a broad range of institutional religious resources of which Armed Forces personnel take part.

The most obvious location of organizational religion in the military would have to be religious services, but, as I have suggested, many service members felt that hardly anyone attended services during their careers. Service members do have a wide variety of official organizational religious activities to choose from—at least while training and while at large bases—but attendance appeared to drop depending on the type of religious service offered. This was a major concern for Ch. Sandberg, who remained worried about the drop in attendance at chapel services and gatherings, particularly at Mainline Protestant services. "Very few people would come to them," he said. Despite his and others' opinion that attendance was down, the vast majority of service members reported attending chapel services during basic training, regardless of their level of religiosity at the time. By contrast, attendance dropped during deployments, but it depended on the type of services offered. In addition, there were often other ways of participating in organizational religion outside of regular service attendance. Finally, many service members spent much of their careers outside of the warzone and would often find local churches with military outreach programs or would go with family and friends regardless of offerings on base. These activities were often not aimed at service member needs specifically.

From new enlistees to officers in training at OCS and military academies, organized religion in the military is first encountered in the form of Sunday chapel services. While officers in training, at West Point and elsewhere, reported varied attendance at chapel services, trainees at boot camp characterized Sunday chapel as a central and formative part of their training experience. Ch. Sandberg explained that recruits find out early on about access to chaplains and religious accommodation, which provides anything from Roman Catholic to Hindu services for them. However, he noted, "There's usually some kind of a free-flowing Protestant chapel, which the majority of them will attend, whether they believe or if they don't believe or whatever. They will come to it voluntarily." That was a point echoed by forty of the interviewed participants; almost everyone made the effort to go to chapel services during boot camp.

There appeared to be two main reasons for such widespread attendance. Surprisingly, the primary reason for over half of them was *not* a faith commitment; instead, Sunday chapel was an escape from the rigors of boot camp, a break from chores and yelling. As Army Public Affairs Specialist Jennifer Cordell, who largely maintained her faith through her whole career, put it, "I kind of hate to say this, but it was kind of an opportunity to go to church and not be around the drill sergeants and not have to be as formal." Those who did not attend reported being left to do chores or take on other duties.

Even if attending was not an escape from a drill sergeant, it was often an escape of some kind, a time to meditate and even make an emotional connection with the newfound community of the military. For example, Air Force Honor Guardsman Ryan McDonald felt that the services offered much more than just an escape:

> I think everybody that chooses to go is surprised at, again, their reaction, emotional reaction to going to church or to a service. You get there and you sit according to where you are in your training, so the newbies who we call Rainbows, they are all the way at the back, and they've got the least amount of hair because you just got your head shaved. We're in sneakers, we haven't gotten our uniforms yet, and we're all in the back and everybody's just passing tissues around because, for the first time since you arrived, it's quiet, it's peaceful, there's music and nobody's yelling at you, and you're just overcome. And I think it also has the effect of, I guess, giving kind of an adrenaline shot to your faith.

It was not just that it was a readily available place to escape yelling and extra work; it was a time to build community, to reflect, and to find comfort.

During training, beyond chaplain interactions and Sunday services, some participants reported having access to activities like fellowships and Bible Studies. These tended to be specific to those in ROTC, at OCS, or at other military academies like West Point, however. The reason for having more access to a broader range of religious resources for future officers appeared to be simply that those candidates were typically at educational facilities like universities where extracurricular faith groups were more widespread and readily available. Moreover, the groups officers mentioned, like Officers' Christian Fellowship, were lay led, not part of the military organization, and lacked any official denominational affiliation or backing. They will be discussed further when we turn to "unofficial" religious activities.

As recruits and young officers moved from training into their careers, the kinds of resources and levels of participation changed considerably. A little over half (26) of the veterans reported being involved in a specific religious community or attending services during their careers when and if available. Some FOBs, however, were in such remote areas that religious services, or even access to chaplains, were impossible. Of those twenty-six, three stopped attending during their careers as they lost faith, while six only began to attend services or participate in communities after a significant event or interaction with a religious community spurred their involvement. The remaining twenty-one did not participate in any organizational religious activities while in the service, though this did not necessarily have a bearing on the individual's non-organizational religious activities or intrinsic religiosity.

The kinds of services ranged largely across the Christian traditions. Special Forces Medic Thompson remembered that, at various schools and posts, he usually had access to either Catholic or a generic Protestant service. In his words, "If you're Catholic, you could go to a Catholic service. Or Protestant, Pentecostal, or Nondenominational. They group those all together." Many others mentioned a more generic inter-denominational worship service as well. LCDR Ian Davison claimed it "tended towards the vanilla flavor" for instance, and SSgt Edgar Jansen, who grew up Episcopalian, recalled the services were explicitly divided into general Protestant and Catholic services. This was a point echoed by Ch. Sandberg. "We will do church services down range," he said; "we'll do more of a Generation X type service, which draws more. … And, of course, we'll provide for Roman Catholic coverage and that will do it. But those are organized chapel services and soldiers can come when those are available." Again, the Christian offerings tended to fall into either generically Protestant or Catholic services.

At times, more specific kinds of denominational services would become available. Jansen explained, "There was a period of about, I want to say, two or three weeks where they actually did have a separate Protestant service that was Episcopalian, and that was mainly just because an Episcopalian chaplain was available." Once the chaplain left, however, services were again limited to either Protestant, broadly conceived, or Catholic. LDS service members reported having access to chaplains during training, but apart from small group gatherings, services during deployments tended to be nondenominational. CWO-2 Greg Bush recalled, "I was in a really remote area of Afghanistan, so I don't even know if they had services. I'm sure they had some nondenominational things, but I was literally taking a shower with water bottles, and I had porta potties to go in. So, yeah, getting to church wasn't really an option." Unlike the wide access while stateside, the high operational tempo and the remoteness of some FOBs made service attendance difficult, particularly for more specific denominations. It was also these more specific denominational services that Ch. Sandberg felt were attended "less and less."

Interestingly, chaplains and service members both recalled the importance of having the sacraments—communion specifically—and explained that they took on special meaning within a military setting. Ch. (Maj.) Williams, for instance, explained that he "emphasized the sacraments a lot" and felt that communion clearly had the widest appeal among service members, regardless of denominational affiliation. "That's the weird thing about the military," he said. "When you go somewhere, the most low church Baptist who wants to preach a 48-minute sermon ... will celebrate communion for everybody." This did not appear to be specific to Williams either; he claimed, "every chaplain will offer communion in deployments like all the time because that's what the soldiers want more than anything." It simply resonated with service members, particularly those in more remote deployments. As Williams explained:

> I think there's something about the visible sign of God's love that is really compelling, whereas like preaching is like, "Oh, another officer talking to me about how I should be stronger and braver." But like the sacrament really just speaks. When you think about it, it's a dude that's about to die. ... Talk about compelling and timely stories for soldiers to think about and relate to in a very different way.

In his experience, regardless of whether service members would participate in a communion during regular services back in civilian life, communion as a ritual struck a chord with service members in times of duress. The very real threat of danger coupled with the offering of a sacred ritual provided them with opportunity for religious engagement, often importantly without the appearance of banal religious institutional frames, which put off some service members.

Much like the communions Ch. Williams described, Ch. Sandberg reported providing impromptu organizational activities whenever possible. Speaking about experiences traveling to FOBs in more remote locations or at places he could not stay for a long period of time, he described the need for improvisation. As he visited with service members in these locations, he would often, in his words, say, "Hey, we're going to have a spontaneous chapel service." Actual spaces designated for chapel services were not always available, so they would hold them in "their place of duty" instead. Williams explained, "You're going to find most of the unit shows up for those. Oftentimes, you'll offer prayers. Oftentimes, the prayers will reflect upon things that the soldiers have told you. And you'll just say, 'Hey, would you mind us offering a prayer for that?' I found soldiers are very receptive to those things. Oftentimes, those are the things that soldiers will talk about the most." He did talk about having one-on-one conversations with some service members who would approach him for spiritual dialogue or counseling, but he felt much more strongly that these impromptu services and prayers tended to draw in the most people and were more reflective of the kind of work he did that left an impact.

These more spontaneous religious offerings are perhaps illustrative of the phenomenon of "foxhole faith" and "combat religiosity" that early twentieth-century chaplains wrote about in memoirs of World War II (Carter, 2004). These moments tend to be unrehearsed, yet remain the most memorable, coming up again and again, with combat veterans especially, as their most common and meaningful interaction with a chaplain. The very nature of these moments often forces chaplains to go beyond their formal liturgies and prayers to create words and rituals that speak to the military experience. Like those chaplains in WWII, they must mix official religion with a vernacular one.

Non-Christian services are much rarer. Army Chaplain's Assistant Lindsay Becker added that they, of course, provided Jewish and Muslim services in addition to their more broadly Protestant and Catholic services, but her experience was largely stateside. In the one case of Wiccan practice, National Guardsman George McClintock reported that while he was stationed in Germany, the chaplain set him and his fellow Wiccan practitioners up with a meditation area where they could hold meetings. Upon deploying to Baghdad, McClintock said the chaplain "helped find a place where we were able to be active in our spirituality, so he kind of, he was more into the Bible, but at the same time he allowed us and helped us have the ability to sit down in our group of people" and was "more than willing to help." Accommodations were possible at least to provide, as Medic Thompson had suggested, a space to worship when military chaplains were not able to lead services themselves.

Beyond organized and impromptu services and rituals, there were yet other organizational religious activities available to service members during their careers. Being a part of the worship band or in a choir provided some service members with the opportunity to go beyond simply attending a service and allowed them to connect to their faith and to communities through a different medium—music. "Well, I've loved music ever since I was a little kid," reflected National Guardsman SSgt Trey Underwood. When his unit was deployed to Bosnia, Underwood joined the Protestant "praise team" available to the service members where he was stationed. He continued, "They needed volunteers, and I stepped up and joined that, and it was good because I got to make some other friends that had some similar values that I did. And we all shared a love for music, and it gave me an outlet." His faith provided comfort and community, allowing him to escape the rigors of being in communication MOS while deployed—not to mention his later deployments providing additional security to his battalion staff. In the liminal space of a deployment (Turner, 2008), a collective expression like a praise team band allowed his interaction with organizational religious activity to reinforce his religious community and his Christian identity (Lincoln, 2003).

Religious activity is supported by volunteers like Underwood, along with the official chaplains. But it is not just chaplains who join the military specifically to support and cultivate faith. Chaplain's Assistants, or Religious Affairs Specialists—56M, support military chaplains without the need to be endorsed by an endorsement agency or even to have earned a divinity or theology degree. Army specialist Lindsay Becker was one such Chaplain's Assistant. She was, in her words, "first and foremost the bodyguard of the chaplain." Since chaplains are not permitted to carry firearms—as this would make them a combatant—it was Becker's job to protect her chaplain should he come under fire. "So, if the worst should happen, I would be the one carrying the weapon and protecting both of us," she said. Seeing that military chaplains would largely—though certainly not always—avoid being in the line of fire despite often accompanying service members on their convoys, Becker's job more often comprised aiding the chaplain in services and providing religious accommodation and even peer counseling to other service members. Just like other service members, Becker had to go through training and learned to fire a weapon. The difference was that her MOS kept her involved in religious life, which was extremely important to her at the time of joining. Becker's job was an interesting one because it explicitly bonded her religious and her military identities; she was both fostering religious accommodation and ready to take violent action should the situation dictate.

Finally, it is important to note that organizational religious activities included in the narratives of service members did not necessarily have to take place on military bases. Many of the informants in this study explained that they often had opportunities to participate in religious activities in local communities. This happened most often when they were stationed domestically or not directly in the war zone or at isolated bases. It also happened in times when they were on leave or, as in the experiences of some reservists, when they were in their civilian sector roles. These communities tended to have specific military outreach programs or made more explicit efforts to invite or welcome military personnel into fellowship.

For example, Army Company Commander Will Berger explained the importance of finding a community while he was stationed in Hawaii. He claimed he had not been religious while in the military to that point in his career; however, his fiancée, also an active service member, was adamant they find a congregation together. "It just so happens the first one we found had a … good military outreach program." His fiancée soon had to leave for training out of state, but some military people at the church reached out to him and invited him to a Bible study at his house. "I think he tried to give me a community and people to talk to about stuff in life. They were the same age as us and had similar experience like I did in the military. … It was good to get away from the chaos of the military and the people I knew there." He reflected on how some in the military were bad influences on him, so the ability to go to off-base religious services, Bible studies, and even church gym sessions gave him some respite from military life. "I just felt valued and part of the community," he said, a sentiment shared by those who, like Berger, found a religious community during their careers. The military has a tremendous religious presence with thousands of military chaplains and clear efforts to provide religious accommodations for service members, yet the religious life of the military also includes religious communities and practices *outside* of the military.

Through all these offerings, from worship services to praise teams to local congregational outreach, the central importance of community, especially though not exclusively among those who found religion while serving, is clear. Community, particularly chosen voluntary communities, reinforces identity, gives service members social capital, and unifies people along lines of validating beliefs, ritual and celebration, and transcendence. In Ammerman's (1997b) investigation of congregations in nine communities in five US states, she found that modern congregational communities, though voluntary and chosen, reinforced identity through a sense of purposiveness and purchase in a particularistic moral group set apart. As service members choose to participate in these communities, they find social, moral, and spiritual capital and belonging but continue to feel set apart (Ammerman, 1997b).

Within the military, the aims of chaplains, rituals, and symbols are fixed upon force multipliers and reconciling faith with participation. Service members are set apart as exceptional even in local congregations. As Ch. (Maj.) Lopez explained to me, "Socially, a soldier is going to interact with his unit. That's usually where he has close friends. But, when he attends chapel, that becomes a new sort of social equity and that can be very meaningful to many soldiers, the community that forms out of faith." In his estimation, that faith community provided a space for service members to find reflection and shared belief, particularly while deployed "I think one of the things that [being deployed] does is it gets people to kind of think about what's important in life and what they're going to do. Sometimes, they do that by making a change of getting religious. I would say there's the church social aspect of it." This social equity, importantly, created a faith community that reinforced identity, which reinforces moral beliefs, narratives, and expectations as well. In other words, community was vital to the promotion and reinforcement of religion as a viable toolkit amid military experience.

Unlike the service members who participated in this array of organizational religious offerings inside and outside of the military, nearly half of the participants did not, even those who reported a Christian affiliation at the time. As noted, there was low attendance at services, and many claimed religion did not play a large role in the daily lives of service members. What then of accounts of chaplains claiming, as Ch. Williams did, that "they really were thinking about spirituality all the time. They just didn't feel compelled to always be part of an organized system of it?" Religion in the military extends beyond the confines of the chapel and exists in community among fellow service members. It exists in activities during rare moments of free time. It often remains in quiet conversations and private prayers, meditations, and reflections. However, it often takes place in more hidden places, in specific symbols and objects—a space where the lines between organizational and non-organizational religion, between formal and lived religion, blend as these symbols take on mythic meanings specific to the military institution.

A "Lucky Rabbit's Foot" and Other Religious Objects in the Military

Ch. (Col.) Mark Granger, an Episcopal chaplain, recalled a civilian, Jill Boyce, coming onto Fort Bragg back in 2003. "She wanted to ensure that everybody who deployed had a bandana with Psalm 91 on it. And so, she garnered money from across the nation and printed these bandanas up: [Army Combat Uniform] camouflage-colored bandanas with Psalm 91. Well, they became almost like a rabbit's foot, you know." Service members used these bandanas, among other religious objects like pocket Bibles or gold cross necklaces, as what Ryan Lamothe (1998: 165) calls vital objects, meaningful symbolic artifacts linked to a "shared experience of and belief in omnipotence." These shared beliefs often shape personal or shared narratives, which ascribe "shared attitudes, practices, hopes, expectations, and aspirations" around the object. If the vital object has, for instance, a printed psalm on it that concerns God's protection and a promise that "no evil shall befall you" even while "a thousand may fall at your side, ten thousand at your right hand," then the narrative surrounding the object will likely be one of a shared expectation of protection from harm (Psalm, 91: 7–10). This, of course, was the intent of the bandanas. Boyce herself said of her decision to create the bandanas, "I had a dream that I was in Iraq in the middle of fighting between our soldiers and Saddam Hussein's. The next day, I envisioned a bandana with Psalm 91 written down the middle. I researched and found out that Psalm 91 was the Soldier's Prayer and that many lives had been saved through it in previous wars" (Boyce).

The stories surrounding the psalm alone have taken on a mythic character. They recount how the commander of the 91st Brigade had his men read Psalm 91 before every battle they faced in World War I and suffered no casualties, despite being involved in three of the bloodiest battles of the war. The narrative of the bandana, the vital object, is one extending from the popular, though likely fictional, account of the brigade. The bandanas come with the expectation that they will, like the recitation of Psalm 91 during World War I, protect service members facing dangers in war.[2]

By extension, these vital objects take on a significant role in coping with stress. Religion and Psychology scholar Kenneth Pargament defines coping as "a search for significance in times of stress." For him, significance is a "phenomenological construct" that involves beliefs about what has value (Pargament, 1997: 90–92). This can come in the form of religious coping, which is how an individual uses their religious resources to manage the different stresses of life, and it can involve what Pargament calls an "object of significance," or what Lamothe refers to as a vital object, that is an extension of one's meaning-making system. Religion provides a specific path to seeking significance through the sacred. The Psalm 91 bandanas function as literal sacred objects that can, in the context of those wearing

[2] While the stories of the "91st Brigade" are widespread and bring great comfort to many, they are likely no more than fiction. There was no actual 91st Brigade among the American Expeditionary Forces during World War I, although there was a 91st Division that suffered heavy losses during the war, about 25% in fact. It is possible the brigade in question was nicknamed the "91st Brigade" for their use of the psalm, but there is no record of this. I do not wish to draw attention to the truth or fiction of the accounts; rather, pointing this out shows just how powerful the narratives around Psalm 91 are for service members, their families, and military religious culture.

them, provide protection from harm, the source of stress in service members' minds. They are simultaneously a vital object and the coping tool.

The bandanas and other vital objects also point to a larger persistent belief underlying military culture, that of presence. From miniature scriptures to tattoos, these relics and symbols represent the presence of the divine in a profane realm, the theater of war. This presence is the "realness of the gods in the company of men, women, and children, in the circumstances of their times" (Orsi, 2010: xxi). That is, these symbols are not *merely* symbols; they are the "really real" presence of the divine in a public sphere (Geertz, 1973: 112). That service members imbue these vital objects with such meaning is indicative of the importance of presence. The Christian service members to varying degrees place meaning in the symbols and objects because they bring with them expectations of divine presence in the world. This specific underlying belief that God will "show up" because these measures were taken (wearing bandanas) has the potential to upend moral expectations and cause a disconnect between two cognitions, or dissonance.

As vital objects themselves with significant shared narratives surrounding them and built-in coping tools for combat stress, it is no wonder the bandanas caught on among service members, particularly among those in combat roles. They took on a sort of magical quality because they were imbued with the power of God's protection. Ch. Granger recalled, "People who ... hadn't gone to church ever in their lives were clamoring for these bandanas, right. And it became like a rabbit's foot. And then chaplains began to pray this Psalm 91 for missions, before missions." The bandana's appeal to individuals who were not already particularly religious illuminates their power as vital objects. They were simultaneously good luck symbols and sacred objects embodying the "really real," beliefs that imbue religious symbols with their authority.

Granger added that service members who received a bandana took Psalm 91 very seriously and at face value. "Taken literally, it sounds like 'Hey, if I sign up for this, this God in Heaven is going to take care of me.'" This produced a problem, however. What happens when the bandana fails in offering protection? What happens if some service members wearing the bandana die while others live? The religious object had built-in mechanisms that could enhance stress should the expected narrative not play out. "Inevitably," Granger said, "men were killed who had signed up for Psalm 91. And [it] left those standing around to question what happened, how come this happened? We prayed this prayer, you know. There was this guarantee of Psalm 91 that nothing was going to happen. ... It challenged everybody's faith. It challenged everybody's." The failure of the bandanas to protect every service member who wore one led to the questioning of faith for service members with whom Granger worked, weakening the ability of the vital object to aid in coping with stress for those that remained. The expected narrative no longer held true.

The failure of the bandanas as vital objects appeared to challenge Granger as well. He admitted still having questions about Psalm 91 to this day and reflected on how he recently reached out to other clergy to make sense of it when it appeared in the lectionary. He asked them, "Is Psalm 91 a psalm for us today? Is Psalm 91 for the Messiah? Is Psalm 91, you know, what's it for? Is it literal? Is it metaphorical?" He has settled on it being less about literal present protections and more about eternal protections. "It's a deep spiritual understanding of who the God of the universe is and that our souls are going to be garnered and protected forever and ever. Because we're all going to die right? We're all going to die at some point and these clay pods that we occupy are going to go away. So, there's no way around it. Even Lazarus died the second time." What appeared to be important for Granger to understand—and what he has since shared with service members—is that Psalm 91 speaks to eternal salvation but not to a physical suit of armor. Belief in the object's literal story was not important; belief in the object's coping effects was. All the same, Jill Boyce continues to distribute the bandanas to whomever needs them, and while not as commonly worn today, they still likely provide comfort to some in times of stress.

The Psalm 91 bandanas were not the only religious objects that took on significance for service members. Miniature bibles served a similar function as vital objects in coping with stress by producing a feeling of protection. Ch. (Col.) Sandberg, the Lutheran military chaplain, recounted how one of his chaplain's assistants received miniature steel-plated New Testament Bibles that were given out to any of his soldiers who wanted one. They had "May the Lord Be with You" printed on their face and fit nicely into a service member's uniform's cargo pocket. "One soldier came in," Sandberg recalled, "and there was a bullet embedded in the Bible. He came into the aid station with that. And this chaplain immediately picked it up and wandered around preaching in the trauma room. 'The Word of God protects you. The Word of God stops the bullets.' All this other stuff, until the doctor finally said, 'That's an exit wound, you moron.' The bullet had gone through the soldier's body and the Bible had stopped it on the way out." While the doctor immediately attempted to nip the chaplain's assessment in the bud, Sandberg's story reveals that these bibles functioned much in the same way as the bandanas. They represented, in Ch. Sandberg's words, "this almost talisman version of what God is. And it's just like a lucky rabbit's foot or something else inside this very violent world these soldiers live." Like the bandanas, the steel-plated Bibles were manifestations of sacred protection from harm, and the folklore surrounding the object contributed to this feeling, which likely aided in coping with the stress of war.

Like the bandanas and the stories of the 91st Brigade, the pocket Bibles also had built-in legends around them. Since the Civil War, there have been numerous stories from American conflicts and wars telling of service members whose pocket Bibles stopped a bullet, saving their lives.[3] World War II was especially relevant for building the mythology around the pocket Bibles.

However, religious objects and symbols did not necessarily have to coincide with widely shared historical or folkloric narratives. Veterans also mentioned gold cross necklaces and religious tattoos that similarly brought a feeling of presence or protection even while they would likely be hidden from view, private to the individual. Special Forces Captain Russo recalled, "When I was a young platoon leader, I wore my gold cross around my neck … in the worst part of the Iraq War, where it was really, really awful, because I did have faith. I did hope that someone was out there protecting me and my guys, and that if I wore this cross, then maybe that would protect me." While the legends of the 91st Battalion and the history of pocket Bibles stopping bullets allowed other kinds of objects to catch on within the ranks, more traditional religious symbols like crosses and verse references tended to take the form of a protective talisman as well. Like the other objects, they maintained a narrative of protection, even if it was one more privately held to the individual.

Tattoos appeared to function similarly. Sgt. Damien McDaniel reflected on a tattoo he had before losing his faith and that he has since removed, "I had a tattoo at that time and it was Jesus over my heart and it was a reminder that he is going to give me strength, and I think I drew on that quite a bit during my initial training." Like the other objects, it gave him

[3] See "Saved by the Good Book," *Guideposts*, 19 December 2016, https://www.guideposts.org/inspiration/miracles/gods-grace/saved-by-the-good-book for just one set of examples of this phenomenon happening through modern history.

comfort and strength, allowing him to cope with military service stress. In addition to tying into military masculine culture and identity, such tattoos also "represent and honor relationships and create and inscribe solidarity. These men tattoo themselves into a narrative" (Maldonado-Estrada, 2020: 64). In this case, those relationships are one with God and one with the Christian community, and it places McDaniel and others with religious tattoos, again, in that overarching narrative of presence and protection. As sociologist and religious scholar Alyssa Maldonado-Estrada explains, "[W]earing a tattoo is a bodily practice that works to reaffirm a community identity." The objects and symbols Russo and McDaniel had were made meaningful by a personal narrative, distinct from the public narratives of the bandanas and pocket Bibles, but they function similarly as means of protection and coping amid the stress of war.

Tragically, like the bandanas, the expectations for these objects and symbols did not always match reality. Capt. Russo and Sgt. McDaniel both lost their faith during their careers when faced with the reality of God not showing up. Russo no longer wears his cross, and McDaniel has removed his tattoo—a process that symbolically removed him from the Christian community of which he once felt a part. The objects themselves did not appear to precipitate the loss of faith, but they surely added to the disillusionment, even betrayal, that service members like them felt. Like Ch. Granger, Ch. Sandberg and his fellow chaplains had difficulty knowing how to make sense of the pocket Bible not providing protection, and his theological reckoning led him to find God in suffering. Sandberg explained, "What you find that chaplains who care about these soldiers do is they actually help find the meaning or God's presence in their suffering or their struggles. And you find that God is a healing force in the exit wounds. I think that's the thing that tipped the balance." Instead of preaching about a God who would prevent those with faith from coming to harm, Sandberg realized that emphasizing a God who suffered with the individual, who helped him through the pain, was far more useful for veterans. It was a shift from preemption to post-trauma.

Beyond the scope of official religious gatherings or even one-on-one interactions with chaplains, these vital objects expand our understanding of where religion takes place in the military. It is both commonplace and hidden, depending on whom I asked. Deeply personal or ways of reinforcing community through shared myth, these objects were significant props in reinforcing one's identity as a Christian, even when the objects had mixed orthodox and unorthodox meanings. Mythic beliefs often support vital objects and religious symbols in the military with deep roots of historical significance to the US military. They take their place as pieces of the larger religious tapestry.

Roommates, Confidantes, and Community: Unofficial Religion in the Military

When service members enter the military, they have access to a large offering of military-produced organizational religious activities like denominational services, mandatory interactions with chaplains, and praise team participation. But as those "official" religious spaces lessen in popularity or attendance, religion is still present in a mix of symbols and mythic stories that are culturally produced inside and outside the military. This religious culture is reinforced through shared narratives and religious experience and often comes in the form of informal and unofficial religious offerings. Some are highly organized, like lay-led Christian fellowships, while other religious interaction is as simple as dialogue between roommates. These "everyday" religious activities reveal the permeability of social spheres, even within the military itself, bridging the apparent secular and religious divide. As Ammerman (2007: 9) puts it, "each domain colors the other." That is, LCDR Ian Davison's claim—"I just don't think chaps are really where a lot of people work [out their faith]"—is correct; religion in the military largely takes place in presumably neutral spaces, connecting religion to the military experience across explicitly religious spaces and military and civilian ones. We saw that first with symbols and vital objects, but it becomes even clearer when looking at informal communities, organized or spontaneous.

Informal religious community was a major part of the narratives among the participants of this study. While it is certainly an important feature of those who found faith post-trauma, it played a significant role for service members overall who were involved in fellowships, impromptu Bible studies, or who confronted questions of faith in general. As Ch. Sandberg explained to me, "It's not the going to church or going to a religious education class that plays the significant role, but it's those dialogues in the field." Those dialogues formed the basis for community, which reinforces identity (Lincoln, 2003), including attendant moral scripts (C. Taylor, 1989), through shared beliefs, stories, and experiences of liminality that make people feel they are part of something greater than themselves (Hill, 2000). "God is in every place or every encounter that we have," Ch. Sandberg continued, and it is those encounters that will be the focus of this section.

Unofficial religious activities reported among service members were often completely spontaneous and typically involved relatively few people. In addition to those informal practices, there were also participants who mentioned more formal, though non-institutional, groups they interacted with through training or during their careers. These lay-led fellowships had large organizational structures that facilitated the development and dissemination of literature, like pamphlets and magazines, to service members, veterans, their families, and anyone else who cared to participate. More importantly, Bible studies and retreats provided space for community. There are a number of Christian groups that provide resources for military personnel and their families; however, the two largest fellowships appear to be Officers' Christian Fellowship (OCF) and Christian Military Fellowship (CMF).

OCF was the most mentioned fellowship among the participants, particularly among those who attended West Point. Although explicitly a lay-led organization, meaning military chaplains did not assist in their activities, those leading the fellowship tended to be superior officers in the military. The organization provides resources for any officers—active, reserve, or retired—and their spouses, with tools for engaging in Christian fellowship. They facilitate a wide range of activities, from one-on-one conversations to Bible studies, to widely circulated publications like *COMMAND* magazine, to conferences (OCFUSA.org). The Bible studies and retreats were the major aspects of OCF service members engaged with the most, and these activities clearly provided a sense of lasting community among them. Navy officer Catherine Bakker, for instance, explained, "It was a nice community where we could do stuff. … I remember feeling very comfortable talking about issues and we would bring them up and I became extremely close to a fellow midshipman. And he and I, we'd go on the OCF retreats, and we're good friends to this day. His family and my family get together and do things to this day." Bakker emphasized that the fellowships allowed service members to connect their everyday experiences in the military with their faith, and they created a space where "it felt like he and I were in this together."

Among the most interesting offerings of that fellowship, however, is the opportunity for OCF superior officer members to conduct a special ceremony on graduation day for West Point (and other military academy) students who were commissioning. Referred to as a "spiritual commissioning ceremony," it is an opportunity for new officers to be "sent out in a dual calling—the privilege of serving God as His ambassadors in uniform" (OCF Communications, 2019: 10). Despite not being an official part of the military or even involving military chaplains, OCF has the ability to bring new officers to the chapel on or before graduation day to "have hands laid on them" that "symbolizes a spiritual 'sending forth' for a lifetime of service to Christ" (11). The ceremony has drawn some criticism for the way it "[contradicts] the extensive Officership training the cadets receive to support and defend the Constitution" (Anonymous retired Army colonel, 2019); however, it remains an option for newly commissioned officers. Only a select number of those in my sample were members of OCF and none partook in the ceremony; however, it is clear from interviews in OCF Communications (2019) that the ceremony was one designed to reinforce new service members' religious commitments and identity. As Ammerman (1997b: 354) argues, choosing a community entails making commitments that can come to shape our motivations and moral expectations.

Not all religious communities were so structured. Many were completely spontaneous activities between roommates or unit members. Army linguist Alan Bode, for example, discussed the importance of a Bible study he started while stationed domestically. It "reached out to half a dozen, a dozen young service members and their spouses," and he felt it allowed him to have a big influence on their lives. "I maintain some of those friendships to this day, so that was a nice privilege," he said. The Bible study established a Christian community among military personnel and their spouses that, while officially outside of the military, was one that was rooted in shared experience and identity, connecting military experience with Christian faith.

Even more informal, participants reported having a range of conversations about faith or even leading prayers for their units before missions, filling in times and spaces with religion where institutional symbols and facilitators were not present. On one end of the spectrum were conversations with a close friend or roommate, someone deeply trusted by the service member. Public Affairs officer Jennifer Cordell, for example, recalled having religious debates with her roommate who was from a Pentecostal background. One of the debates was whether members of different denominations would go to Heaven. "I don't know how we stated the conversation," she said, "but her family was a lot more strict ... [and]

she suddenly started to cry because I guess she had some Catholic members of her family or some members of her family that weren't Pentecostal, and she'd been told that they wouldn't go to Heaven." In response, Cordell told her roommate, "I don't think God's really keeping a list of how you pray as long as you were a decent person." Despite their different denominations and theological understandings of salvation, these conversations brought comfort to both and helped Cordell grow closer to her roommate and maintain her faith throughout her career. The point of concern between them was resolved by an idiosyncratic though deeply held belief about who God is and how God would treat those with different affiliations.

Everyday experiences often raised important issues that became the subject of religious conversation. For instance, Air Force Commander Robert Derry was a crew member with Missile Combat Command. He and his unit oversaw nuclear missiles and lived with the constant stress and weight of responsibility that they might have to fire them one day. Shockingly, Derry claimed he "ended up in custody of 30 of them, due to electronic problems with some of the other sites. [He] was actually the fifth largest nuclear power in the world at one point." The weight of that pressure brought up existential questions that laid the groundwork for religious community. He reflected:

> How can I really go downstairs, eight times a month, for four years, ready to turn the world into nuclear ash, if I didn't believe there was somebody that was greater, and more in charge? And half of us that were down there were reading Revelations at the same time going, "Gee. Some of the stuff they talk about in here, that could be the result of a nuclear bomb, or God using this in such a way, or one of the many plagues, and how do you wipe out one third of mankind?" "Well, I have no idea," said the man, with the keys that would launch 10 nuclear weapons.

Service members faced significant religious quandaries due to the military experience, creating spontaneous religious community through shared experience.

Of course, those conversations and close bonds tended to be reflective of the close bonds forged in military experience in general. Seventeen of the participants mentioned having extremely close bonds with their fellow service members, calling them "life-long brother love relationships" and "camaraderie I long for." As Ch. Williams explained to me, "I knew that the soldiers weren't that afraid of dying, they're really afraid of being alone and separated from their friends who were there with them." Along with the military camaraderie also came some degree of comfort in talking about more personal questions, including ones about faith. Special Forces CWO-2 Greg Bush, for instance, explained that he was known in his unit for "reading scriptures all the time and saying [his] prayers all the time" and people would come to him "with their problems and they'd have [him] pray with them." Although not formal in any way, their conversations were religious. They raised questions like "what's this life for and stuff like that, the purpose of life. Or they had faith in Christ and they just needed to be around someone else who had that same faith or could empathize with what they were feeling." Even without a military chaplain present, service members could themselves become spiritual guides and have religious dialogue and foster community. In informal ways, they also became religious ritual leaders. Special Forces Sgt. Mike Thompson, for instance, claimed that, although he largely came into his faith after a catastrophic injury, he would make his unit pray before every patrol. "I would pray the Lord's Prayer, and I would say Psalms 23. ... Always, always, always no matter what," he said. He credited the prayers with bringing feelings of comfort to his unit. Much like the bandanas and other religious objects, the rituals, whether performed by chaplains or simply religious service members, provided feelings of comfort and protection for service members and established religious community among them, even those who, like Thompson, said they were not particularly religious at the time.

More often than not, however, religious dialogue and community took place in quieter moments. Army National Guard LTC Ford Koval explained that his unit knew he was religious, but he tended to keep that part of his life to himself. But when time allowed for some reflection after a mission, his role as the default religious leader in the unit came into play. He reflected on how his fellow soldiers would come back from a mission saying, "Man, I killed that guy. All right, we got out. Blah, blah, blah. The mission was a success. I killed a couple Taliban." But, he explained, "once things died down, and we were behind closed doors, the reality of, 'I just killed somebody,' would set it. So, we had conversations about that, and, 'Am I going to go to hell,' and those types of things." Religious community often took the form of more private conversations where trust was built between "brothers" rather than found in the institutional power of superior officers or chaplains.

Hidden Religion and Private Practices

There were explicit religious activities and conversations and communities all over the military, yet the service members who said those were not important may well have been right. Right in the sense that those very public, official displays of religion were not necessarily where religion was happening. Instead, it takes place in quieter spaces and conversations—if not entirely privately. As Air Force Honor Guardsman Ryan McDonald explained to me, religion in the military simply happened more explicitly for those who were explicitly religious. "I had friends who were definitely more religious or more tied into their faith," he said, and "they tended to be Protestant or non-denominational. And I think because it was more in the forefront of their mind, it tended to be something that they were thinking about more often, and so we had plenty of conversations about it." He felt, by contrast, that religion would not come up for people who held their faith privately or who were not religious at all.

The question of when religion comes up is an important one. For service members whose religious identity was central, religion might come up often, in both formal religious participation and everyday action. For others it might remain personal and private without an explicit cause for dialogue or a disruptive incident. Ch. Williams picked up on this point as well; "everybody else was just like, 'When's lunch time, what do we have to do today?' They were very focused on the actual job that our unit was given." They were not asking deep religious questions or seeking the chaplain for religious counsel. Ch. Williams felt that "relational struggles" were much more common; service members were more likely to have issues back home that he needed to help them navigate than to come with questions of faith.

For many of these service members, in fact, everyday military action did not spur conversations about faith. Army National Guard Major Chris Herder put it bluntly. He discounted the talk of people in his unit who identified as Christian but rarely talked about it or explicitly practiced it. He felt that although they claimed to be religious, they tended to act in ways contrary to their faith, particularly when confronted with difficult decisions about the use of force. "They're infantry dudes; they just want to blow shit up and kill bad guys for the most part," he said. "They were all religious. They were all *very* religious, but at those moments … where they should have been in that deep pondering, it went out the window." Herder would ask them about it later, but they would respond, "Oh, now is not the time to think about this stuff. Now is the time to do stuff." In Herder's opinion, if they were as Christian as they claimed to be, their moral deliberation ought to have been more explicit. He explained, "In those critical moments, I saw the most religious people act the least religious." Even if they privately struggled or acted out their faith in other ways, what Herder saw was the compartmentalization typical of the military—a cultural frame trained into service members. It likely dampens the outward practice of religion and relegates religion to private practices and informal communities (Wood, 2016). Army infantryman Franklin Rivers, for example, explained, "We know there's going to be casualties. We know there's going to be instances where good people die. And again, a lot of the military has always been taught to suck it up and drive on. It's okay to talk to your buddy, but you still have a mission to complete. So, I would just say we were there for each other on that level, but we did not talk about [questions of faith]." In keeping with the machismo that overshadows military culture, openly talking about questions of faith was often frowned upon.

As a result, much of where religion happens in the military is entirely on the individual scale. For many service members, faith is, as Ch. Calvin Lopez described it, "something that is internal. It's how we sort through our actions." A reliance on private prayer and meditation was quite common. Like Army Intelligence officer Michaels who maintained that he relegated his religious practice to private prayer, many service members did not participate in any organizational religious activities or even small communities. Private prayers were the site of their only religious practice. Michaels explained, "Just for me, it was a very, very personal journey for me, and I didn't feel I could—like I didn't want to—share it with anybody. … I'm not searching for those opportunities to share it with anyone. It was just this is my personal journey." He adamantly wanted to keep that part of himself private, and he said he did not want to "proselytize or anything like that." Even though he kept his beliefs to himself, he still had religious thoughts and engaged in private religious practices. He would pray on deployments and would religiously read a daily devotional. "The pages are maybe six-inches high, just a few hundred words on every page, and you read it once a day. Every page is a day, and I remember reading that, and that would provide comfort."

Many others shared his perspective and had similar practices. With extremely long workdays or missions, religion happened in the moments between other duties or in their heads or in notes on their computer screens. These practices were no less significant than the practices of those who went to chapel services. Navy airman Ruth Hannon, for instance, explained, "I'd have to say I didn't do any extra, I didn't do any Bible studies, I didn't become a member of any parish. I didn't really attend a lot of church. I prayed. I've always prayed, not as much as I should have." Similarly, National Guard combat medic LTC Ford Koval, who would sometimes speak with his men, said he did largely maintain his faith personally. Private prayer was his main method of interacting with the sacred. He worked as a medic in a rural clinic in Afghanistan where he saw incredible suffering among civilian locals, including young children. "Faith came into play there. I prayed a lot for those people. I really did. There was nothing else I could do but pray. And so thinking back, those were some of the areas that God became really important to me, and praying, and hoping that He would help them."

As service members navigated the military experience, many found that they could not, or would not, participate in institutional religious activities. This did not, however, indicate that religion was absent. To the contrary, religion—Christianity specifically—is widespread. Where does religion in the military happen? It happens in formal religious offerings and in interactions with chaplains. It happens in the religious objects with which service members interact. It happens in fellowships and Bible studies. It happens in private conversations and in prayers before patrols and missions. It happens in the hearts and minds of service members worried about their families at home, their friends beside them, and the civilians in their care. These opportunities can provide communal experiences of the sacred and further the bonds between brothers in arms. However, those same formal and informal practices also reinforce military culture. Those participating in formal practices absorb civil religious narratives along with beliefs and moral expectations that reinforce and justify their participation in the military. Those participating in local communities or reading religious materials supplied to the military also receive an endless feedback loop of justifications and support for military culture. Even those praying privately and keeping religious beliefs and practices to themselves are enacting the military cultural framework of compartmentalization—that there is a separation between one's religious convictions and their military professional role. While religion plays out in many wonderful creative ways in the military, it is not always beneficent.

"My Beliefs Say I'm Supposed to Kill You": Lived Religious Intolerance

The sacred objects service members carry, the prayers they whisper privately, their meetings with chaplains, and the nighttime conversations with confidantes all reinforce their religious identity and their private cultural religious frameworks in explicit and implicit ways (Griswold, 2004). These symbols and experiences influence and strengthen deeply held beliefs and practices that maintain community—here the military Christian community—and affect the narrative sense of self (C. Taylor, 1989). This sense of community and shared identity as both Christians and warriors strengthens service members' commitments to both, validating their participation in the military (Settles, 2004). However, part of defining and reinforcing this identity may include an "othering" of those outside the group—a way to conceive of a group as "one's binary opposite" (Z. Smith, 2019: 6).

Post-9/11 conflicts have created two decades of unsettled times (Swidler, 1986) in the lives of service members and the American public at large. Wartime is itself a persistent interruption of our desire for peace, and a contentious and protracted war against an enemy defined in religious terms has provoked significant identity work. To be unsettled always activates our individual and communal "implicit sensibility about how [we] ought to live" (Guhin, 2016: 152). The increased importance of moral questions deeply entrenches our commitments to our identity. Those in the military find themselves reinforcing the warrior identity, the American identity, and, for some, the Christian identity. As war comes to test these identities and more firmly reinforces each, it also hardens distinctions between us and those in opposition to the resolution of persistent unsettledness—the enemy.

Othering in warfare is certainly not a new phenomenon, nor is othering of the enemy always along religious lines. Indeed, it is vital to the military experience and is part of training; dehumanization of enemy combatants makes participation in violence easier. It justifies aggression. Further, "contemptuous hatred of the enemy … is the obverse of the love of and loyalty to fellow soldiers that is called 'unit cohesion'" (Crawford, 2013: 248). Hatred of the enemy reinforces love of those who are not other. It "allows for acts of violence that would usually be forbidden to be celebrated" and "protect[s] our image of ourselves" (Steuter & Wills, 2008: 38). It creates an active moral framework that tells service members, "You are not a bad person because you are not like the enemy."

In a war whose enemy is primarily characterized in religious terms—radical *Islamic* terrorists—this othering often takes the form of religious intolerance, and it has played out in ways that have made headlines. For instance, American journalist Jeff Sharlet (2009) revealed that US Special Forces infantrymen were desecrating mosques and other Islamic sites with spray-painted crosses. Others wrote "Jesus killed Mohammed" in giant Arabic letters across the front of their Bradley Fighting Vehicles and had their interpreter shout the same from a bullhorn during an adhan, or one of the five daily calls to prayer. Other articles have highlighted a patch worn on uniforms depicting a crusader eating a ham hock that reads, "Pork Eating Crusader," in both English and Arabic (R. Johnson, 2012) and an incident with American NATO forces burning copies of the Qur'an in 2012 that incited a riot in Afghanistan (Rahimi & Rubin, 2012). These incidents seem to reveal rogue service members going off on their own and making hateful decisions; however, these events are natural extensions of a culture that—on an institutional level—dehumanizes the enemy.

While the dehumanization of the enemy in religious terms is not a pervasive characteristic of religion in the military, several participants reported interpretations that reflected religious othering. Army infantryman Roger Kettles, for instance, called Allah a "demonic thing" and a "djinn" and felt that the war was one of "spiritual warfare." Kettles believed that we could even blame enemy combatants for higher suicide rates among veterans and military personnel over the last two decades. "These people are so willing to kill themselves for their god," he said. "That's not how our god works, but now that we've gotten attacked by their beliefs and by their god, by all these demonic activities, hey, what do you know, now a lot of soldiers are killing themselves." His assessment of events—though not explicitly shared by other service members—revealed a process of mixing his faith with a folk understanding to reconcile the othering of enemy combatants. Similarly, but with a more direct path to religious texts, Special Forces CWO-2 Greg Bush explained the evilness of the enemy by comparing them with Gadianton robbers in the *Book of Mormon*. Characterized by their wickedness, he explained that Al Qaeda and the Taliban were akin to these robbers, "living up in the mountains [where] they grow strong and they come down and wipe out innocent people down in the lowlands and they always retreat up in the mountains. … That's what I attribute to Taliban and Al Qaeda and all these terrorist organizations that I was fighting. I equated that to the scriptures that I grew up with." In his estimation, opposition forces were embodiments of evil and threatened the safety of the world. "I've seen evil. I've listened to tortures, and I've seen just things that would give you nightmares because it gives me nightmares," he said. Islamic opposition forces were an existential threat to his religious worldview. "That's why I joined," he added.

In Kettles and Bush's descriptions of the enemy, the otherness of Islam was in direct opposition to their Christian identity. They maintained their own identification with moral goodness by placing the self in opposition to perceived immorality and evil. Their religious cultural frames further entrenched them in opposition to the enemy. The war was not just one fought on the battlefield or through political maneuvers; it was one of spiritual warfare as well. Their beneficent Christianity was placed in opposition to an Islam that was the embodiment of evil.

This mixed with American civil religious understanding as well. As National Guardsman Andrew Nelson put it, "I've read into American history and stuff and there's a reason why the Islamic faith in early American history was not present. It's because it wasn't allowed because they want to go in and take over and convert everybody, and whoever doesn't convert they want to kill." In a version of the US where Islam was not allowed, permissible Christianity is the religion of life and freedom by default. Islam, by its very nature (not for being terrorists or aggressors) is othered as barbaric and undemocratic. This broader othering can also have the unintended consequence of both widespread religious intolerance and othering fellow service members as well.

As a result, being Muslim in the military can be difficult. Both news stories (Gibbons-Neff, 2021) and scholarship (Sandhoff, 2017) capture this difficulty. A recent story described the experience of Army Sgt. Cesilia Valdovinos whose CO forced her to remove her hijab (Myers, 2019). Religious intolerance extends to other minority religions as well. For instance, Army National Guardsman George McClintock, a practicing Wiccan while in the military, reported harassment by his E6 sergeant for his Wiccan beliefs. Although chaplains had been accommodating for facilitating his practices, his NCO pulled him aside and privately threatened him. "You don't change your ways and start coming to church with me, I'm going to make your life a living hell. That's sorcery and my beliefs say I'm supposed to kill you." As his career progressed, the sergeant continued to abuse and threaten McClintock. "He'd take me between the trucks and the tanks where nobody would see. He would have me do pushups and all those different things in that heat and in the sand, and he'd kick me while I was doing the pushups, and he'd punch me and various different things like that," McClintock explained. The altercation with his sergeant gave way to threats from others. Three other assailants "started threatening to kick my ass," he recalled. Between these incidents and another where his life was directly threatened and left him with PTSD, McClintock felt persistently attacked for his faith. Such incidents illustrate how military and religious cultural frames can create pathways for intolerance, producing and reinforcing deeply held beliefs that promote the dehumanization and hatred of the other.

Although these examples paint a disturbing image of religious intolerance in the US military, this was far from universal among my participants. Most explicitly separated enemy opposition forces from civilians and did not make direct judgments about Islam broadly, even if there was general distrust or uncertainty surrounding locals, their customs—particularly around the treatment of women—and their loyalty to the US mission. In fact, despite encountering atrocities in war, some explicitly pushed back against such intolerant notions. Captain Lou Granger, an officer in the Army Medical Service Corps explained, "I think God loves us all. So, I remember really thinking a lot about those kind of things when I was there, and just kind of working through, you know, I'm not special ..., I'm obviously privileged, but these people, God probably loves them more. They're living in trash heaps." By contrast to the explanations above, her religious cultural frames allowed her to look at local life with compassion and empathy. She recalled speaking with her career-military father who had claimed, in her words, "We're at war against Islam." She replied, "I don't think we're at war against Islam. We're at war against poverty."

Conclusions

This chapter has set out to solve a persistent mystery of sorts. If over 65% of post-9/11 service members claim a Christian affiliation (Hunter & Smith, 2010), where are they? Why is chapel attendance at Mainline denominational services diminishing? Why did some service members, even religious ones, claim "most people in uniform are not religious"? The answer is clear, if complicated; religion takes place in varied locations, publicly and privately, and in formal, informal, and idiosyncratic ways, not to mention that people have different religious identity centrality and levels of religiosity. Service members act out their commitments to faith in diverse ways, which publicly and privately recommit them to the moral narratives and moral order of which they feel a part. Across these types of religiosity, there are both formal and everyday lived religious expressions, beliefs, practices, rituals, and symbols.

Religion was present in formal ways in organizational religious offerings and institutional symbols and rhetoric, often in ways that aimed service members toward the strategic aims of the military. Whether it is merely a way to get out of boot camp training for an hour on Sunday or subtly included in generically Protestant prayers at large military gatherings or practiced privately and unconsciously as part of one's larger self-identity, religion, Christianity specifically, is simply a part of the military narrative. Religiously infused ceremonies honored, supported, and motivated their service. These formal ways almost always involved a military chaplain, although there were also local congregations with military outreach programs. However, as often as not, these formal religious resources were spontaneously mixed with popular lived practices that could speak to the military context. Chaplains themselves participated in these hybrid interpretations. The military's religious resources are not monolithic; there is significant variation. Some have creative potential like Ch. Sandberg's emphasis on God's presence in the exit wounds; some are destructive.

The mixing of formal religion with folkloric myths and longstanding narratives shows how the lines between official and lived religion are permeable. There is little separating the stories of miniature Bibles from, say, the instances of wearing bandanas with Bible passages on them or even getting tattoos. They are examples of religion dispersing to the mundane realms of life. And the profane world in which they operate is one where religious and national identities are being intermingled. Religious objects and symbols can become secularized and then "resacralized as national." Zubrzycki (2006: 220) describes how, when Poland fell under Communist rule, religious objects and practices took on national identity as a way of fighting against the secular regime. Among the US veterans I interviewed, religious objects, often rooted in conservative ideologies (like the bandanas) or patriotic myths (like stories of Bibles stopping bullets for Allied soldiers), went through this same process. They are themselves religious objects that have then been mythologized as nationalistic and resacralized as religious. A sacred form of protection becomes a mark of national identity—God will protect the American combatant, for instance. Everyday military life is a space where formal and lived religion touch. They are sometimes found as props in formal settings, and they sometimes take on idiosyncratic expressions among the service members, mixing myth, faith, and comfort.

As religion in the military appears in informal settings or is brought into the military by extra-institutional groups like OCF, religious resources move more clearly into lived religious expression. They focus not on liturgy or formal belief so much as community, expression, and agency. Religion, here, takes place in quiet conversations between roommates or lay-led Bible studies. It comes with idiosyncratic rituals and practices that reinforce religious identity through community (Lincoln, 2003). Through shared or exchanged beliefs, stories, and experiences of liminality, service members experience a connection with the sacred, something greater than themselves. The conscious choice to be part of these conversations or communities reinforces religious identity. Even though they are not formal, they are no less important to service members' religious identities and mark their continued participation in the sacred even if they are not marked present at a formal chapel service. Furthermore, even when religious resources do not have an outward expression, it is clear that religion in the military still takes place privately in moments of both conscious deliberation and in general habits of faith that bring comfort but do not extend into formal religious participation.

Religion, then, is a large part of the military experience. Even those who entered the military as non-Christians had stories to share about the influence of religion and its relevance to fellow service members' lives. At the same time, there was considerable truth in Maj. Chris Herder claiming he "saw the most religious people act the least religious." In the post-9/11 conflicts, the narratives and expectations that service members hold about the enemy are inevitably shaped by religious identity and extend to other non-Christians working alongside them. Chapel attendance is dwindling, but religion and the cultural resources it produces and provides weave an intricate web throughout the military that influences post-9/11 service members' lives in explicit and implicit ways, influencing action, belief, and identity.

We can now see the full assembly of religious resources in the US military. From chaplains to ethics education to religious practice, the religious cultural toolkit of the military is one that is simultaneously good and bad, or rather, creative and destructive. Religious beliefs, narratives, and justificatory frames supply service members with pathways for participation in the military. The "successful" chaplains are those who share the military *habitus* and can counsel service members using frames that match their experience. The "successful" concepts in ethics education are those that allow service members to fight; they mock the concepts that do not. The "successful" religious practices are those that reinforce military community; otherwise, religious practice is private. Those "successes" form a creative alternative to a service member's inability to cope with and make meaning of experience. However, "success" may also be destructive when coping and justifying actions thrusts service members relentlessly and repeatedly toward potential moral trauma. This remembering of both the historical narratives of military religious culture and the stories of how service members interacted with them provide the first steps in retelling service members' stories and reimagining new theological and ethical frames. The following chapter will show how those religious beliefs and expectations brought from home or supplied by the military motivate action amid potential trauma.

Bibliography

Ammerman, N. T. (1997a). Golden Rule Christianity: Lived Religion in the American Mainstream. In D. D. Hall (Ed.), *Lived Religion in America: Toward a History of Practice* (pp. 196–216). Princeton University Press.

Ammerman, N. T. (1997b). *Congregation & Community*. Rutgers University Press.

Ammerman, N. T. (Ed.). (2007). *Everyday Religion: Observing Modern Religious Lives*. Oxford University Press.

Ammerman, N. T. (2016). Lived Religion as an Emerging Field: An Assessment of Its Contours and Frontiers. *Nordic Journal of Religion and Society, 29*(2), 83–99.

Anonymous Retired Army Colonel. (2019, November 14). OCF COMMAND Magazine Cover Photo, "Sent Out to Serve the Nation and the Lord" [Letter written November 13, 2019 to Mikey Weinstein & Members of the Military Religious Freedom Foundation (MRFF)]. In *Military Religious Freedom Foundation*. Retrieved from https://www.militaryreligiousfreedom.org/2019/11/ocf-command-magazine-cover-photo-sent-out-to-serve-the-nation-and-the-lord-2/

Carter, B. L. (2004). *"Reverence Helmeted and Armored": A Study of Twentieth-Century U.S. Military Chaplain Memoirs* (Unpublished doctoral dissertation). University of Kansas.

Crawford, N. C. (2013). *Accountability for Killing: Moral Responsibility for Collateral Damage in America's Post-9/11 Wars*. Oxford University Press.

Geertz, C. (1973). *The Interpretation of Cultures*. Basic Books.

Gibbons-Neff, T. (2021, October 27). *For Muslims in the U.S. Military, a Different U.S. than the One They Swore to Defend*. Washington Post. https://www.washingtonpost.com/news/checkpoint/wp/2015/12/09/for-muslims-in-the-us-military-a-different-u-s-than-the-one-they-swore-to-defend/

Griffith, J. (2009). Contradictory and Complementary Identities of U.S. Army Reservists: A Historical Perspective. *Armed Forces & Society, 37*(2), 261–283.
Grimell, J. (2018a). Advancing an Understanding of Selves in Transition: I-Positions as an Analytical Tool. *Culture & Psychology, 24*(2), 190–211.
Grimell, J. (2018b). Revisiting the Courage to Be to Understand Transition from a Military Life. *Practical Theology, 11*(5), 387–400.
Griswold, W. (2004). *Cultures and Societies in a Changing World.* Pine Forge Press.
Guhin, J. (2016). Why Worry about Evolution? Boundaries, Practices, and Moral Salience in Sunni and Evangelical High Schools. *Sociological Theory, 34*(2), 151–174.
Hall, D. D. (Ed.). (1997). *Lived Religion in America: Toward a History of Practice.* Princeton University Press.
Harmon-Jones, E., & Mills, J. (2019). An Introduction to Cognitive Dissonance Theory and an Overview of Current Perspectives on the Theory. In E. Harmon-Jones (Ed.), *Cognitive Dissonance: Reexamining a Pivotal Theory in Psychology* (pp. 3–24). American Psychological Association.
Hassner, R. E. (2016a). Hypotheses on Religion in the Military. *International Studies Review, 18*(2), 312–332.
Hassner, R. E. (2016b). *Religion on the Battlefield.* Cornell University Press.
Hill, J. (2000). A Rationale for the Integration of Spirituality into Community Psychology. *Journal of Community Psychology, 28*(2), 139–149.
Hunter, C., & Smith, L. (2010). Military Leadership and Education & Religion's Role in the U.S. Military Mission. *Defense Equal Opportunity Management Institute Research Directorate*, 2–18.
Johnson, R. (2012, March 16). *The Pork Eating Crusader Patch Is a Huge Hit with Troops in Afghanistan.* Retrieved from https://www.businessinsider.com/this-whole-line-of-infidel-gear-cant-be-helping-international-relations-in-afghanistan-2012-3
Lamothe, R. (1998). Sacred Objects as Vital Objects: Transitional Objects Reconsidered. *Journal of Psychology and Theology, 26*(2), 159–167.
Lincoln, B. (2003). *Holy Terrors: Thinking About Religion After September 11.* University of Chicago Press.
Lindsay, D. M. (2007). Evangelical Elites in the U.S. Military. *Journal of Political and Military Sociology, 35*(2), 161–176.
Lippy, C. H. (1994). *Being Religious, American Style: A History of Popular Religiosity in the United States.* Greenwood Press.
Loveland, A. C. (1996). *American Evangelicals and the US Military, 1942–1993.* Louisiana State University Press.
Maldonado-Estrada, A. (2020). *Lifeblood of the Parish: Men and Catholic Devotion in Williamsburg, Brooklyn.* New York University Press.

Myers, M. (2019, March 19). *A Muslim Soldier Says Her Command Sergeant Major Forced Her to Remove Her Hijab*. Retrieved from https://www.armytimes.com/news/your-army/2019/03/12/a-muslim-soldier-says-her-command-sergeant-major-forced-her-to-remove-her-hijab/
OCF Communications. (2019). OCF Leaders Recount Importance of Spiritual Commissionings. *COMMAND, Fall*, 10–11.
Orsi, R. A. (2010). *The Madonna of 115th Street: Faith and Community in Italian Harlem, 1880–1950*. Yale University Press.
Pargament, K. I. (1997). *The Psychology of Religion and Coping: Theory, Research, Practice*. Guilford Press.
Rahimi, S., & Rubin, A. (2012, February 21). *Koran Burning in NATO Error Incites Afghans*. Retrieved from https://www.nytimes.com/2012/02/22/world/asia/nato-commander-apologizes-for-koran-disposal-in-afghanistan.html
Sandhoff, M. (2017). *Service in a Time of Suspicion: Experiences of Muslims Serving in the U.S. Military Post-9/11*. University of Iowa Press.
Settles, I. H. (2004). When Multiple Identities Interfere: The Role of Identity Centrality. *Personality and Social Psychology Bulletin, 30*(4), 487–500.
Sharlet, J. (2009, May). Jesus Killed Mohammed: The Crusade for a Christian Military. *Harper's Magazine*.
Smith, C. (2003). *Moral, Believing Animals*. Oxford University Press.
Smith, Z. B. (2019). *Age of Fear: Othering and American Identity during World War I*. Johns Hopkins University Press.
Steuter, E., & Wills, D. (2008). *At War with Metaphor: Media, Propaganda, and Racism in the War on Terror*. Lexington Books.
Swidler, A. (1986, April). Culture in Action: Symbols and Strategies. *American Sociological Review, 51*(2), 273–286.
Taylor, C. (1989). *Sources of the Self: The Making of the Modern Identity*. Harvard University Press.
Turner, V. (2008). *The Ritual Process*. Cornell University Press.
Walters, K. L. (2013). *Beyond the Battle: Religion and American Troops in World War II* (Unpublished doctoral dissertation). University of Kentucky.
Wood, D. B. (2016). *What Have We Done: The Moral Injury of Our Longest Wars*. Little, Brown and Company.
Zubrzycki, G. (2006). *The Crosses of Auschwitz: Nationalism and Religion in Post-Communist Poland*. Univesity of Chicago Press.

CHAPTER 5

Finding Resonance: Religion and Moral Injury

An impending cloud of potential moral hazard and trauma has loomed over the previous chapters. As we investigated the ways the military produces religious resources—including beliefs, narratives, communities, expectations, and moral frames—we have also seen how these resources remain ambiguous, left precariously at a tipping point between resources that benefit the counsel and well-being of service members and ones that endlessly maintain service member readiness for violence. The religious resources we have seen have largely been woefully inadequate to capture the reality of participation in violence in war. Moreover, these ambiguities likely intensify moral trauma when it happens. As we will see, there is variation in how service members rely on religious resources when confronting trauma. For some, previous religious narratives, military frameworks, and religious culture and communities can help them preempt or mitigate trauma. For others, those same resources exacerbate it.

Portions of this chapter were originally published in Suitt, Thomas H. "Finding Resonance Amid Trauma: Moral Injury and the Role of Religion Among Christian Post-9/11 U.S. Veterans." *Sociology of Religion*, Summer 2021, Volume 82, Issue 2, Pages 179–207, https://doi.org/10.1093/socrel/sraa044. Reprinted by permission of Oxford University Press on behalf of the Association for the Sociology of Religion.

T. H. Suitt, III, *Narratives of Trauma and Moral Agency among Christian Post-9/11 Veterans*,
https://doi.org/10.1007/978-3-031-31082-9_5

The Global War on Terror is the US's longest war and has resulted in the deployment of between 2.5 and 2.75 million troops to combat zones since September 11, 2001, attacks on the World Trade Center (Goepner, 2016; McCarthy, 2018). Our longest war has been the source of significant trauma among military personnel, and suicide rates among service members and veterans have trended upward since the mid-2000s. The rate of active-duty personnel suicides has also been called an "epidemic of soldier suicides" (McDermott, 2012). The DoD and others have maintained that, apart from 2012, the suicide rates when adjusted for age, sex, and population are almost the same between active-duty service members and those of the general population (Under Secretary of Defense for Personnel and Readiness, 2020; Pruitt et al., 2019). However, while rates of active component suicides initially decreased after the 2012 peak, they have trended on an upward slope since 2013 and have now surpassed that 2012 rate. The number of suicides and the rate worsened in recent years as 2018 and 2019 consecutively marked the worst years of active service member suicide since the previous peak year in 2012 with 2020 on track to be even worse (Orvis, 2020).

Furthermore, veterans aged 18 to 34—those veterans who served in post-9/11 conflict—have a suicide rate higher than any other age group at 45.9 suicides per 100,000 (Office of Mental Health and Suicide Prevention 2020). That is about 2.5 times the suicide rate of the adjusted general population (18 per 100,000) and over 1.5 times the rate of men alone in the same age group (27 per 100,000) (National Institute of Mental Health, 2019). Having passed the twentieth anniversary of the Global War on Terror, the toll military experience has taken on service members has continued to get worse, despite new programs and increasing research on lasting traumatic conditions like moral injury and PTSD.

The range of potential traumatic events service members experience in the military is vast and varied. Combat exposure and morally injurious events are common, and there are, of course, other ways service members experience trauma. As one veteran told me, "I'm not a combat veteran, but I didn't have to go to combat to go through something incredibly horrifying." The veteran in question experienced MST far from the theater of war and continues to deal with negative mental health symptoms since her attack. Others experience physical trauma during training or on base during a deployment. Others witness or hear a traumatic event, opening them up to trauma. The military experience is one that can expose service members to trauma by their simply being a part of the military. Indeed, the lives of these veterans were clearly affected by their time in the service. Thirty-one of the participants reported trauma of some kind, whether physical, mental, spiritual, or sexual, resulting in PTSD, moral injury, spiritual struggle, MST, physiological complications, or anatomical wounds.

The rate of exposure to traumatic events in the military is not well documented. However, a study on exposure to traumatic events among US allies in Afghanistan found that a little less than half of all deployed service members experienced at least one traumatic event, and just less than 13% experienced more than three (Wittchen et al., 2012). In a study of over 100,000 surveyed households around the world by the World Health Organization, psychiatrists determined that exposure to traumatic events had a strong association with suicidal behavior, with exposure to multiple events increasing this association (Stein et al., 2010).

Among the many potential sources of trauma, this chapter focuses on the morally traumatic events veterans experienced and the moral injury that resulted. While significant moral trauma affected 23 participants, moral quandaries were present for most participants, even if their responses were not all the same. My account of moral injury comes directly from the veterans' and service members' expressed narratives and their feelings of shame, guilt, betrayal, anxiety, anomie, withdrawal, suicidal ideation, and self-sabotaging or vicious behaviors common to those experiencing moral injury but presented as possibly distinct from PTSD. In unpacking these stories, we will see how they differ depending on the source of the injury. Eleven participants described moral stress from questions about God. Seven reported experiencing being betrayed by the organization they served, and ten described experiencing personal moral injury. Some veterans experienced moral stress from multiple sources.[1]

In this chapter, then, I will explore how veterans of post-9/11 wars and conflicts used religious resources to navigate potentially morally injurious events (PMIEs) and lasting moral trauma. I will begin with an explanation of moral injury, the dimensional problem stemming from morally traumatic events, and how it tests deeply held cultural beliefs and interrupts habits developed before and during military service. Moral injury results from the kind of moral trauma the service member experiences and the

[1] I should highlight that I am not a mental health professional and could not, for instance, diagnose someone as having or not having PTSD. I had to rely on veterans' self-reporting, which may or may not have been representative of everyone with PTSD, MST, physical wounds, and the like.

religious resources available for them while in the service. Service members must either establish coherence between values and experience or abandon them amid dissonance. This process results in confirmation, rejection, or adaptation of belief and practice. As we will see, the role of religion in moral injury comes down to resonant versus dissonant beliefs.

Moral Injury

Moral injury is a betrayal of "what's right" (Shay, 1994: 5). It is a "violation of core moral beliefs" (Brock & Lettini, 2013: xiv). Although service members indeed come home with other psychological and physical injuries, moral injury is a "trauma as real as a flesh wound" and one that is distinct from post-traumatic stress disorder, which is a physiological response to trauma as opposed to a wound of the soul (Wood, 2016: 8). As one sailor explained to me, "Anytime you are involved in the military, you are connected to something that is constantly doing both ill and good. It's just inevitable. There is enough moral stain in the mix that just by joining, you are going to come out stained." These stains can create a massive disconnect between who the service member believes herself to be and what she has seen and experienced, leading to intense feelings of anger, guilt, and shame. That disconnect can destroy a sense of meaning and often disrupts a service member's connection to religious faith as well.

Significant, even authoritative, relationships often support our sense of who we are in a moral order, and the violation of trust and legitimacy inherent in moral injury disrupts our sense of place in society. Shay initially envisioned the precipitating incident as a betrayal from a trusted figure, like a superior officer. However, this is too narrow. Litz et al. (2009: 700) also point to moral injury stemming from acts of perpetration, which "may entail participating in or witnessing inhumane or cruel actions, failing to prevent the immoral acts of others, as well as engaging in subtle acts or experiencing reactions that, upon reflection, transgress a moral code." Indeed, both formulations—moral injury as victim and perpetrator—describe the experiences of service members. A recent study, which included Litz, by Jordan et al. (2017), showed that both models, one of perpetration and one of betrayal, correlated with diagnoses of PTSD, suggesting that morally injurious events can involve both the action itself and how one perceives the action in the context of significant relationships and self-identities.

In understanding the relationship between religion and moral injury, we must also consider spiritual relationships. As we have seen, people join the military with expectations about their relationship with the divine, its presence in their lives and the world. Unfortunately, the realities of war can upend these expectations. Broadly, psychologists and military chaplains have described "spiritual injury" as the unease with one's beliefs, one's relationship with God, and difficulty in participating in religious communities due to cognitive stress (Lawson et al., 1998; Berg, 2011), while others have pointed to spiritual/religious/divine struggle (Pargament et al., 1998, b; Exline et al., 2014). Although scholars often treat it as distinct from moral injury, divine struggle can hinge upon a feeling of divine betrayal. Trauma disrupts the individual's relationship with God, precipitating anger, a loss of faith, and ending participation in faith communities. Like moral injury, it also highly correlates with depression and suicidality (Exline et al., 2000). It is this aspect of spiritual injury, divine betrayal and a breaking down of faith-based relationships, that characterizes my understanding of divine moral injury. That is, I argue that events that destroy one's relationship with the divine are morally injurious.

We can understand moral injury, then, as involving three kinds of breakdowns in significant relationships. In each case, the betrayal is agential. Pete Kilner (2017), a veteran and former ethics professor at West Point, proposed this useful understanding. Personal moral injury, summed up by a service member thinking, "I did something terrible. I'm a bad person," may lead to a breakdown in one's relationship with one's moral community, fearing judgment or feeling unworthy. This captures Litz and associates' (2009) understanding of moral injury as perpetration or bearing witness to moral trauma but choosing to or being unable to prevent it. It is a feeling of betraying oneself. Second, there is organizational moral injury, summed up by a service member thinking, "I was screwed by 'higher-ups.' I trusted them literally with my life but was used and abused" (Kilner, 2017). Perhaps they blame a superior officer for an unjust command leading to a friend's death, a weapon failure, or persistent abuse. This leads to a breakdown in one's trust in perceived moral authority figures and captures Shay's (1994) understanding of moral injury as betrayal. Finally, there is what Kilner refers to as "divine moral injury," which can be summed up by a service member thinking, "No real God would allow this situation to take place. This is irrational, horrifying, unfair, more than I can handle" (Kilner, 2017). This form marks a breakdown in one's relationship with God. This final category sufficiently captures the divine betrayal that prevents participation in religion or religious communities captured by scholarship on divine struggle.

In personal moral injury, the self is the moral agent perpetrating or bearing witness to a betrayal of what is right. In organizational moral injury, specific superior officers or the military organization are the moral agents perpetrating the immoral act. Finally, divine moral injury makes God the moral agent perpetrating or failing to prevent a betrayal of one's moral expectations. In the spirit of Luhrmann's (2012: 301) explanation of Evangelicals' personal relationship with God as "real and integral to one's experiences of self," this move to include a divine relationship alongside personal, interpersonal, and organizational ones is an effort to take divine relationships seriously as an important significant social relationship no less real than the other relationships one experiences. While a perceived betrayal by God would clearly disrupt one's faith, moral injuries of the personal or organizational kind can disrupt one's faith as well. This three-tiered schema of understanding moral injury (personal, organizational, or divine) allows us to see that we must understand moral injury in terms of moral expectations and disruptions of these significant relationships.

There is a growing body of literature on the relationships between moral injury and religion, but much of the scholarship attends to moral injury in therapeutic terms—causes, consequences, and treatments (Schorr et al., 2018; Currier et al., 2015; Litz et al., 2009; Nash & Litz, 2013). Where scholars consider religion, neither its definition nor its social dimensions are specified. A recently published literature review by Suzette Brémault-Phillips et al. (2019), in addition to other peer-reviewed studies, show a close relationship between moral injury and religiosity (or spirituality), but the mechanisms and effects are less clear. Different studies emphasize different pieces of religiosity, focusing upon practice in some cases and individual beliefs in others while simultaneously focusing on individual experience of moral injury rather than the essential relationships and social contexts that inform individual moral beliefs before, during, and after the military experience.[2]

Current research on moral injury and religion presents an inconsistent image of religion's role in the lives of service members and veterans'

[2] That psychiatrists and the military treat moral injury solely in an individualistic fashion is a problem of the study of moral injury in general. The social mechanisms that inform competing moral codes are often completely ignored. See Molendijk et al. (2018) who raises this very issue.

experience of moral injury. It focuses on different aspects of religion at different times in the average life cycle of a military service member. Moreover, scholarship focuses primarily on the potential therapeutic benefits of specific aspects of religious belief or practice for coping. There is little attention either to the breadth of religious belief and practice—before, during, and after service—or to the relationship between particular religious moral narratives and the moral disruptions experienced by service members. Despite this apparent connection between moral injury and religion, we have relatively little research to guide our understanding of *how* they are related. Are highly religious service members more or less susceptible? What mechanisms, if any, absolve or justify service members' experiences to avoid moral injury? Are there differences between the religious traditions or religious practices of those who avoid moral injury and those who manifest it? Does moral injury always lead to a loss of faith or disaffiliation from religious communities?

This chapter, then, responds to the proposal from Brémault-Phillips et al. (2019) for more research on the specific mechanisms at work in religion's interaction with moral injury and what accounts for differences between those with or without moral injury, revealing that the interaction among previous religious narratives, military religious culture, and traumatic events can either help to avoid or anticipate moral injury or exacerbate it.

Moral Belief and Expectations as Cultural Products

Culture influences our actions by producing moral scripts that affect us consciously and unconsciously throughout our lives. Over time, cultural influences and scripts form the basis for our *habitus*, replete with cognitive and bodily dispositions that unconsciously guide behavior, including moral behavior and ethical dispositions (Sayer, 2005; Ignatow, 2009). Experience produces habits, "energetic and dominating ways of acting" that propel our usually uncritical actions (Dewey, 1922: 25). Referred to as Type I cognition (Lizardo et al., 2016; Luft, 2020), these habits motivate action in patterned ways based on social situations, experience, and expectations (Dewey, 1922). Naturally a part of non-discursive practical cognition—itself part of our personal culture (Lizardo, 2017)—the morality resting in *habitus* is more akin to the reactive attitudes (Strawson, 1974), which arguably expose how morality is socially constructed and internalized (Lukes, 2010). An action is right or wrong insofar as a situation produces an emotion, confirming habits and dispositions or interrupting and disquieting them. The reactive attitudes are how we know we have a moral compass. We feel bad when we do something that feels morally wrong.

Culture also produces more explicit scripts for action through resources that organize experience and regulate conduct, often motivating kinds of moral behavior (Swidler, 1986). This declarative form of personal culture (Lizardo, 2017) affects our conscious thinking, or "discursive consciousness" (Vaisey, 2009: 1687), that allows people to reason through and make explicit decisions about what parts of culture they will use to guide action in specific situations. Called Type II cognition (Lizardo et al., 2016; Luft, 2020), relying on explicit cultural toolkits for action allows persons to break from habit consciously. Although Vaisey's (2009) treatment of Type II cognition in his dual-process model is preeminently one of post-hoc justifications, discursive consciousness motivates action amid "unsettled lives" (Swidler, 1986: 278) or "disturbed habits" (Dewey, 1922: 76). In this way, culture creates both explicit and deeply implicit moral strategies for action, and individuals navigate this dual process of unconscious disposition and conscious deliberation to act morally—or not—as society and experience dictate. These strategies for moral action make up what theologian Zachary Moon (2019: 3) calls a "moral orienting system."

However, people are always many things at once, and there is no monolithic culture guiding all actions. Far from it, there are significant, often competing social spheres that influence action and produce multiple moralities. To speak of Lukes' (2010) caution, this is not to endorse moral relativism. Indeed, different cultures overlap, sharing morals in places and competing in others (Hitlin & Vaisey, 2013). Individuals, then, navigate different public cultural spheres as one selecting pieces from a larger personal repertoire, some cultures mastered and effortless and others half-learned and easy to forego (Swidler, 2001). As one takes on new moods, justifications, and strategies, so too do they set up social boundaries (Lamont & Molnár, 2002), prioritize moral views based on social context (Sayer, 2005), or cross boundaries as situations dictate (Luft, 2015).

As explicit and implicit public culture (Griswold, 2004) come to shape one's normative beliefs and practices and embodied and cognitive dispositions, so too will they influence beliefs and practices that maintain a community or individual narrative sense of self (C. Taylor, 1989). Often unconsciously held, experience can reinforce belief. However, experienced transgressions against these beliefs and practices can cause moral dissonance (Guhin, 2016). When habituated dispositions are "ill-adjusted" to novel situations, a *hysteresis* effect occurs (Bourdieu, 1990), and habit "swells as resentment and as an avenging force" (Dewey, 1922: 76). Precipitating emotion spurs reflection while disturbed habits attempt to correct themselves, heightening their "salience," or a "profound emotional connection to a particular issue that makes the issue worth more of an individual's or community's time, energy, and attention" (Guhin, 2016: 152). Type I cognition gives way to Type II cognition; that is, discursive consciousness takes hold. These "unsettled" times compel persons to seek new forms of action (or belief) from their cultural repertoires, which may later become habituated (Swidler, 1986). This reflection then promotes reinterpretation, motivation, and the construction of new aims that guide behavior to return to a reliance on habit (Dewey, 1922; Winchester & Green, 2019).

The result of working out a disturbed habit is called resonance (McDonnell, 2014). Beyond mere congruence between cultural objects—like moral beliefs and expectations—and experience, resonance is marked by active deliberation (McDonnell et al., 2017). One can already have the necessary resonant belief within their cultural repertoire, or they find and use a new one, assigning meaning to experience retroactively. Dissonance stems from an inability to reconcile experience with a belief or expectation with moral salience (Guhin, 2016). In the absence of a personally held declarative cultural object to reconcile that dissonance, individuals seek resonance by searching for new cultural objects (McDonnell et al., 2017). The new resonant end then becomes internalized and habituated, becoming the new means by which actions are taken (Dewey, 1922). Post-hoc justifications lead to future motivations (Winchester & Green, 2019).

While dissonance and resonance describe a process of deliberation over one's *personal* culture, the process of establishing habits of belief and action or of finding resonance post-disruption is one of interaction between personal and public culture. Both religion (Bader & Finke, 2010) and the military (Tiryakian, 2010) are sites that produce implicit (bodily/habitual) and explicit (discursive/organizational) public culture. Religion produces culture, for example, in theological belief (explicit) and embodied practice (implicit), while the military produces its culture, for example, in ethics training (explicit) and reflexive-fire shooting (implicit). Both produce unique moral scripts that can overlap or compete, contributing to resonance or dissonance in the novel experience of trauma. Moreover, there are plural and often competing religious cultures, and the military's own institutional religious culture is among them. Service members and military clergy bring multiple religious cultures with them, while institutional military religious culture attempts to ensure combatants achieve mission success (Waggoner, 2014). In the working out of moral trauma, Christian service members have access to these cultural toolkits—brought to or found in the military. In the face of a PMIE, they seek new cultural frameworks for establishing coherence amid felt dissonance. Absent that, dissonance can lead to the abandonment of beliefs and frames that failed to achieve resonance.

Specifically, I will show how military moral trauma affects Christian identity and moral frameworks and varies depending on timing and access to differing religious resources. What sort of meaning-making toolkit or habits did service members have, and how was that supported and reinforced by religious guides and communities? Did it matter whether service members' various cultural toolkits had competing or congruent moral beliefs? Analyzing these factors across experiences of trauma and access to religious resources, I will discuss the different ways Christian faith played a role in the traumatic experiences of post-9/11 veterans, thus elucidating the social process by which people seek resonance amid trauma.

Resonant Beliefs amid Military Service

Despite experiencing PMIEs, about a third of the veterans I interviewed appeared to avoid or preemptively manage manifestations of personal moral injury (see Table 5.1). That the killings were perfectly justified because the targets were evil and deserved to be eliminated was the most common justification among them. For them, just killings were distinct from murder.[3] Moreover, when non-combatants were harmed or killed, it was perceived to be the fault of the enemy combatants putting others in harm's way or manipulating them to take part in military actions. As Army Intelligence Officer Scott Michaels recalled from his ethics education at West Point:

> We all have this bubble around us, and once another person endangers another, they then lose that protective bubble that they have. They no longer have the right to have that protection around them. And so, that's

[3] Recall reference to Grossman (1996: Section IV, 1) in Chap. 3 for a Biblical justification for killing. This formulation—and Grossman's book in general—was cited by both veterans and chaplains as a critical source for such a justification.

Table 5.1 Dissonance, strategies of resonance, and relational sources of moral injury

Categories of informants	*Number of informants*
Reported trauma[a]	
MST	5
Moral injury	23
Physical trauma	15
PTSD	25
No significant moral dissonance	
No PMIE	4
Continuity with existing frame	16
Compartmentalization	4
Significant moral dissonance resulting in:	
Adaptation of existing frame	7
Post-service adaptation	7
Ongoing struggle	9
Sources of moral injury	
Divine alone	7
Personal alone	7
Organizational alone	4
Organizational and divine	2
Personal and divine	2
Personal and organizational	1

[a]Forms of reported trauma are not mutually exclusive; not all informants reported trauma

> how we justify using lethal force is when somebody breaks this contract we have with society, and they decide to impose lethal force on somebody. That's where society can then say, 'This person does not deserve to have their right not to be stopped from doing that.' Obviously, the goal's not to put lethal force on them. The goal's to stop them from doing that, and sometimes that results in lethal force.

Michaels then cited the Good Samaritan parable to offer a religious backing for this distinction. He posited, "What would that Good Samaritan have done had he encountered the man while he's being robbed and while he's being beaten up? Should the Good Samaritan have tried to stop that incident? And so, that anecdote kind of reconciles for me the need to and the justification of using force to stop something bad from happening, if needed." The enemy combatants in war had lost protections to life; therefore, they were justified targets of lethal force.

This reasoning mixed a learned secularized just war theory approach, his Joint Chiefs of Staff (JCS) basic standing rules of engagement for self-defense training, and a novel interpretation of a biblical parable to justify the use of force. As an officer, Michaels underwent rigorous ethics training, including an emphasis on just war theory. Simultaneously, he brought certain religious beliefs and interpretive strategies from his Presbyterian community at home. Upon facing the novel problematic of participation in violence, he paired personal cultural strategies learned in the military with religious resources brought from home to establish resonance, thus preventing moral injury. This pairing between military ethics training and religious narratives was typical of veterans, particularly officers, who were apparently able to preempt moral stress wounds with justifications for their participation. With ample moral justification from both the military and their religious resources, an existing moral *habitus* found resonance within the military status quo. They articulated what was likely an unconsciously held justification for action in terms of a newly salient issue (Guhin, 2016). They could readily maintain their moral narratives using military and religious tools to construct a life narrative reflective of experience.

About half of the veterans who explicitly stated killing was justified pointed directly to biblical texts to rationalize their participation in violence and the use of force, as Army Sgt. Joseph Daniel reflected, "I didn't do anything I'm ashamed of. God had his warriors too. I tried to make sure my actions lined up with my values as a person, first inclination being to protect others." Similarly, Army military police officer (MP) Thomas Meyer explained:

> I've been in those situations, and it is hard. I always come back to Romans. I believe it's Chapter 13 when it talks about doing what the government has you do because God put the government in existence for a reason. … You've got to do what's right for your government. They were going to send you there. You're doing what your leadership says, not just going out and murdering people. Yes, it's something that's very hard to live with because you don't know if you've done it or not, but you know you've had to pull and squeeze that trigger off.

In these cases, biblical texts and religious teaching worked together to justify participation in violence, preemptively helping the veteran avoid potential moral stress injury or helping them to establish resonance in hindsight.

Additionally, their religious cultural resources could preemptively provide them with paths to forgiveness. Navy LCDR Ian Davison reflected on his use of religious resources when he found himself "stained." As he put it, "[T]here is enough guilt floating around that some of this is going to stick. Having the religious beliefs that I have, I know what to do when that sticks, and I anticipate it sticking. I don't need to wallow in it when it does." He relied upon religious texts to help him "meditate" and maintain his composure when he felt angry or stained. This reliance on religious practice, private or communal, was common to veterans and service members whose religious moral narratives justified participation in violence. As a result, they often reported feeling that no moral dissonance occurred or, at least, that the violence was justified. With non-competing cultural repertoires of religious and military tools at their disposal, they expressed no feeling of moral stress. These toolkits allowed them to maintain or confirm coherence in their expected moral narratives, and their habits remained undisturbed (Dewey, 1922).

The religious resources of the military itself played only a minor role for the veterans who came with built-in religious justifications. Apart from participating in some religious services when available, none of the service members who brought built-in mechanisms for justification or forgiveness to the military ended up seeking counsel from military chaplains about their beliefs. They continued private religious practices while performing their duties, but their resonant beliefs did not require explicit discursive working out for their maintenance. The religious cultural objects of embodied practice and private prayer are enough because they privately articulate declarative cultural beliefs that existed only unconsciously, giving existing tools resonance. That is, certain reflective practices are an articulation of internalized salient schemas (McDonnell, 2014). Furthermore, since their religious frameworks aligned with military service, culture, and values, each reinforcing rather than clashing with the other, there was no apparent need for moral guidance. As a result, they did not report an experience of moral trauma, even if PTSD or physical trauma were still possible.

Fighting for Resonance amid Trauma

Reestablishing Moral Coherence in One's Self-Narrative

Most veterans reported that making decisions about the use of force aligned with the beliefs they brought to the military, but 11 of them initially experienced dissonance. In the face of this disruption in the moral narrative they brought from home, these veterans sought to establish resonance either by adjusting their religious beliefs or learning to compartmentalize, that is, relegating religio-ethical values to an outside social sphere that would allow their military experiences to remain largely unquestioned from a moral standpoint.

The seven who adjusted their beliefs tended to find themselves questioning their morality, coming to the point of a moral stress injury. Special Forces SFC José Martinez remembered asking himself, "'My gosh, am I a sociopath? Do I enjoy killing human beings?' Like, 'What the hell?' I was taught not to do that. You're not supposed to do that. It's one of the Ten Commandments!" He reflected on how some formative meetings with military chaplains, coupled with closer readings of the Bible, allowed him to mitigate these questions that had appeared to misalign with his Catholic upbringing. In one encounter, he remembered the chaplain saying, "'You have a job to do. And the good Lord is pleased you're here to do it.' And he gave me the guidance." The chaplain reminded him of good work he was doing, building schools and protecting civilians; he was right where he needed to be. The chaplain also explained to him, "Look, it's going to be a journey. You're going to figure it out. But don't ever forsake God." Martinez said this and similar interactions, coupled with Bible readings, helped him to avoid worrying that he was a fallen person, that he was evil himself. He would also pair these moments with daily meditation. In finding a faith-based justification for his participation in violence from a figure with religious authority, Martinez and others like him adjusted their religious moral narratives to fit the military experience, thus establishing resonance (i.e., "I am still a good person doing what God intended of me"). This simultaneously allowed him to continue killing, or what Luft (2015: 162) referred to as "combat socialization."

Examples like these illustrate how the military organization supplies service members with religious military cultural frameworks that align with strategic aims of the military (Waggoner, 2014). When military personnel found their homegrown religious repertoire could not establish coherence in the face of trauma, new military-based religious cultural objects replaced the failed ones. In this way, new resonant frameworks reinforced the status quo of military life through discursive justifications for action promoted through official authorities. At the juncture of competing moral beliefs (i.e., killing is wrong vs. killing is justified), Martinez abandoned the dissonant belief for a resonant one that allowed him to reestablish narrative coherence. When killing disturbed his habits of belief and expectation of himself, his reactive attitude of blameworthiness (Lukes, 2010) triggered a "cognitive manual adjustment" of his habits (Luft, 2020: 3). The issue of killing gained salience amid the dissonance (Guhin, 2016), and he sought a resonant belief to solve the problem however he could. The result of the deliberation was a post-hoc justification for action (Vaisey, 2009), but it was also a reflexive reconfiguration of means for action (Dewey, 1922) by drawing on a newly found resonant religious resource.

Other veterans did not bring many or any religious resources with them to the military. Instead, they found religion after an experience of dissonance while still in the military. The novel problems they experienced during their careers motivated a similar strategy of active moral discourse. For these service members, the new religious toolkits that encompassed their traumas represented a significant transformation rather than an accommodation with past beliefs. These veterans and service members would often refer to moments of being "saved" when they adopted a new set of religious resources. The new encompassing toolkits had resonance and came with attendant "heightened emotions" (McDonnell, 2014: 262). For example, Special Forces MSG Mike Thompson reflected on his experiences using his weapon:

> I knew I was not evil or at least evil enough to kill somebody. And I knew that they were all bad guys. There was no doubt in mind that they were the enemy and that they were being controlled by the enemy, and they had to go. So, it was just strictly, 'Hey, we're here to do a job. We're here to kill these guys.' And the quicker and the more we kill them, the less innocent blood is going to be shed. [And] after being saved and eyes being opened, I do look back on it. There's no conviction [sense of spiritual guilt] there whatsoever. Whatsoever. And, therefore, if I'm not being convicted by it, then I know that I was where God put me to be.

In addition to the different ways military training can alter the moral trajectory of a life, so too did interaction with the military's religious moral frames. Structured to preempt moral stress, Thompson did not feel guilt or existential dread over the need to eliminate an enemy. He found resonance with new religious resources, which provided the framework and tools necessary to navigate such potential moral injuries and reorient future habits.

This process of belief maintenance shows the work of military culture and biopolitics (MacLeish, 2019) in action. Chaplains and the religious beliefs, justifications, and narratives they supply service members actively make participation in violence easier, reframing service members' work as "good." This is part of a larger socialization process that uses "psychological mechanisms that enable people to view, as a form of authentic professional activity, work that is actually or potentially genocidal" (Lifton & Markusen, 1990: 98).[4] This process of professional socialization, or combat socialization (Luft, 2015), situates the warrior identity—along with its pathways to violence and machismo—as a professional one replete with its own unique moral frameworks. Again, these frameworks are rooted in a military culture that maintains an ideology and narrative of "the necessity of war as sacrifice" (Denton-Borhaug, 2011: 93).

Finding Coherence in the Face of Evil

Among all the questions of faith and morality that military service members raised, the question of theodicy was by far the most common. When confronted with the existence of evil, 20 service members began to question their relationship to any divine power. Whatever moral order they had previously assumed could not account for what they saw. "Why did my best friend die?" or "How could God let women and children die in war?" The 11 service members who did not already have a sufficient built-in answer for theodicy typically spoke with either a confidante or a military chaplain to find an answer. The five who found an acceptable answer felt comfort in determining that God had nothing to do with the evil taking place, or that He was right there suffering alongside military service members. The first justification constitutes what sociologist Peter Berger understands as a shift from a question of theodicy to one of "anthropodicy," or the argument that good and evil are matters of human character

[4] Lifton (1986) and Lifton and Markusen (1990) focus on professional socialization moral numbing and non-feeling that allowed Nazi doctors to participate in the mass killings of Jewish, Romani, disabled, and other minority groups as well as the normalization of nuclear armament and the creation of nuclear-weapons professionals. I do not wish to claim that modern service members are akin to Nazis, which has potentially damaging value judgements, but the psychological socialization process is clearly similar. As Lifton (1986: 503) explains, "We are not all Nazis. … But we learn from the Nazis not only the crucial distinction between impulse and act, but the critical importance of larger ideological currents in connecting the two."

and action; the second is at the heart of a frequent Christian answer to theodicy, that Christ's suffering is simultaneously God's suffering and "genuine human suffering" (Berger, 1967: 77–8). God suffers as humankind suffers. National Guard Staff Sgt. Dave Cutter reflected:

> My understanding of the things that I experienced when I was in Iraq, about how when I was there, I really did not think that God was anywhere around, or really cared about what was going on, because if he did, he would have done something. That was my frame of reference. [But], now, really having a firm understanding of where sin comes from, and the trauma that results from it, and how God can still be in the midst of that, and he didn't cause it. Knowing all that now helps me understand more of what was going on at the time.

The religious counseling he received regarding his genuine questions of theodicy allowed him to reframe his experiences and mitigate the divine moral injury he experienced.

Finding new sources of resonance hinged on relationships, both human and divine. The service members who found ministers useful in answering these sorts of questions would often say, "they just comforted me" or "I knew I could go to them, and they wouldn't judge me." An emphasis on solidarity and on placing God in the trauma experience resonated the most with these service members. The ability to mitigate moral injury was, in part, about establishing or (re)ordering resonant theological beliefs, but with the divine relationship at risk, a human relationship with a moral and religious guide provided the solidarity necessary to reframe the service member's moral narrative to one in keeping with essential beliefs about themselves and their role in the military. Much like Martinez questioning his involvement in killing, service members with the question of theodicy were able to target and replace a disturbed habit of moral belief and expectation by reflexively absorbing a new resonant belief, if not an entire toolkit, thus altering future action. The ability to do so was dependent upon a successful social discourse.

Compartmentalization

Four of the interviewees appeared to avoid moral injury by also avoiding moral work. They claimed not to have had moral questions about their participation in the war, and they denied that their faith played a role in how they understood making decisions about the use of force.[5] Rather than relying on faith for answers or support, others replied to my questions about moral issues in war with a quick "no." As Army cavalry soldier, Frank Rivers, suggested, "When it's time to be strong and be a military guy, it's time to be a military guy. When it's time to talk and ask questions, then religion can come into that part." He would actively separate combat experiences from questions of morality even when pressed. Similarly, one career military man, CSM Sam Griffin, explained his thought process when asked if questions of morality came up for him while making decisions about the use of force. He explained, "We talked about how to fight and win and to execute the orders that were given to us by our superiors. I don't know anybody in the military that I've ever even talked to ever in my whole life that would talk about something like that. It sounds like something my Democratic mother would talk about." While blunt about the moral question, Griffin was not without religious faith or practice. He talked about daily self-reflection and prayer that helped him throughout his career, even mentioning that he felt a need to seek forgiveness. However, these acts had little to do with his experiences in the theater of war; instead, he reflected, "Well, I did some bad stuff. You name it—lie, cheat, steal, sin. So, I needed to get my stuff together. I had made a few mistakes in my life, and those are ones that I needed forgiveness for." He, and others like him, were able to section off questions about the use of force from whatever moral frameworks operated in the rest of life.

This sectioning off, which I call compartmentalization, asserts that there are two separate moral spheres at work in their lives, military action and civilian religion. The compartmentalization effect here described can be explained as "doubling," the psychological effect of military socialization Lifton (1986: 418) and Lifton and Markusen (1990) investigate. "Doubling" is the "division of the self into two functioning wholes, so that a part-self acts as an entire self." We can understand this process as being a product of the military socialization process wherein service members develop a warrior *habitus*. When I asked Rivers, for example, if he compartmentalized religion from his military experience, he replied, "they probably lean more to being separate. … You talk to God in your own way." Admitting that he has not done much reflection on the moral

[5] One can reasonably speculate the pattern of compartmentalization is far more common in the military, but those who did not rely on religion for moral work were probably unlikely to speak with me.

dimensions of his combat experience, he, like Griffin, emphasized social morality instead. The apparent avoidance of moral discourse does not necessarily reveal that compartmentalization is at work here, although suppression of moral reflection is doubtless a part of military culture (Wood, 2016). The military cultural frame of compartmentalization, stemming from high operational tempo and training techniques like reflexive-fire training, contributes to the avoidance of explicit moral discourse. Even though the post-hoc nature of interviews about morality occasioned moral reflection (Vaisey, 2009), internalized cognitive dispositions likely obtained within military culture appear to have contributed to a burying (and even pushback in Griffin's case) of moral work. In fact, over 80% of all interviewees reported feeling the military had changed the way they "walked and talked." As Rivers put it, "To this day, I'm still a soldier the way I talk, walk, everything." His military *habitus* blocked moral deliberation and allowed him to participate in violence. Illustrative of combat socialization (Luft, 2015), it was further enhanced by an implicit culture that prevents reflection. Even under duress, a military *habitus* designed to avoid reflection prevented the move from Type I to Type II cognition.

Recall that a person can have a dual or split-*habitus* (Bourdieu, 1990; Vest, 2013). Perhaps a civilian draws on multiple *habitus* depending on different social spheres in which they find themselves in everyday life. In the military context, however, this multiple *habitus* plays out as a "doubling" of the self (Lifton, 1986). Moral concerns for everyday life are different from those in war, so a "part-self" must act for a whole person. That part-self has been socialized to feel that their professional identity is both "good" and necessary, so certain cultural tools must be habituated by needs. Among those is a "radically diminished feeling, upon one's not experiencing psychologically what one was doing." This process of "psychic numbing" explains the biopolitical process that allows service members to fight and remain in the fight for years (Lifton, 1986: 442; MacLeish, 2019). Military culture is highly efficient at helping service members avoid moral anguish—strong people do not feel emotion after all—and when service members do feel moral emotion and have reactive attitudes, the military supplies them with a meaning-making toolkit to reframe experience positively after the moment of incoherence in their ongoing moral narratives.

By comparison to those who actively participate in intentional moral deliberation and discourse above, those that compartmentalized did not work out a problem by finding a new resonant belief or toolkit. They absorbed a military cultural framework that discourages moral reflection and instills obedience and hegemonic masculine culture. They used doubling to create a "separate reality" that allowed them to disassociate from the violent reality of the military experience. CSM Griffin's scoffing at moral consideration shows this doubling process played out. "We talked about how to fight and win," he said; moral considerations in war are for liberal civilians. Those that compartmentalize stand in contrast to those who maintain or find modes of consistent moral reflection. The ingrained military *habitus*, rooted in obedience and efficiency, prevents a cognitive alarm that moral work is required. It is likely not an explicit choice of compartmentalization so much as it is a cognitive disposition toward it. In this way, the military's public cultural resources inhibit articulating one's *habitus* (military or religious). The result is the postponement of feeling the disruption in one's beliefs and expectations in favor of a dominant military identity, which may delay the onset of moral injury.

Persistent Moral Dissonance

Nine veterans experienced acute moral injury and had lasting effects from those soul wounds. Given that participants knew I would be asking them about the role of faith in their lives, it is not surprising that divine moral injury was the most common form of lasting moral injury I came across in my sample. However, Christian faith was also implicated in the journeys of a few of the participants in the study who lost their faith and abandoned most of their religious connections as a result of other forms of moral injury.

Personal moral injury, for example, usually arose from a service member having to make decisions about the use of force. Bill Childs, a Southern Baptist 27-year Navy cook, found himself having to make that decision. As he told his story, he stopped short and said, "Things changed for me during my first combat deployment. Taking a life changes a man, and I'll leave it at that." His once consistent involvement in the Baptist church changed after military service. While he did seek a military chaplain who brought him some comfort, he still has questions of faith "quite often" today. Military religion never replaced or offered viable alternate beliefs to his Southern Baptist religious toolkit, which marked him as an immoral person for his actions. In reflection on his sense of relationship to God, he says, "It's never gone completely away, but for different reasons, I have chosen not to open that door. I've never turned my back. I guess I'm just on a lengthy vacation." The barrier to gaining renewed access to religious resources is a fear of judgment or unworthiness stemming from dissonant beliefs about a salient moral issue.

Organizational moral injury has long-lasting consequences as well. One participant became a convinced atheist after his previous faith came up short when addressing moral trauma. Joe Guthrie, an Air Force MP, revealed that his NCO spread lies about him that affected his career negatively, spurring serious reflection on Guthrie's own beliefs. The NCO "lied about me," he said. "And he clearly lied about me. And it was just a really clear, bold lie." He said his experience showed him "the world isn't so binary. ... it really called into question everything I had been taught as a Christian." This betrayal made him question his cultural repertoire of religiously motivated moral beliefs, making him doubt his faith entirely. In navigating the organizational moral injury, he found it easier to abandon the dissonant religious cultural frameworks entirely, leaving him to sort out his betrayal in other ways.

While personal moral quandaries and organizational moral challenges precipitated injury for some, two-thirds of service members with lasting manifestations of moral injury felt betrayed directly by God. Their questions about why God would allow evil to exist or why God would allow a friend to die were left unanswered or, if answered, unsatisfactorily. In critical moments of dissonance surrounding morally salient issues (e.g., protection to life of a friend), incoherence in the moral expectations and narratives of service members motivated them to challenge their relationship with God. Failing to find resonant beliefs to reestablish coherence led to a rupture in their sense of divine relationship. Neither the moral expectations in their personal cultural repertoires nor those provided by military religious sources could remedy that moral rupture, leading to an abandonment of religious frameworks of moral resolution in their entirety. Despite the dissonance initiating conscious deliberation, such an appraisal led to the abandonment of the entire meaning-making system. Without a new resonant framework, dissonance and, therefore, moral injury have remained.

As Army Sgt. Damien McDaniel put it, "I had put so much faith into this and so much trust, and that trust I felt was betrayed." Despite daily prayers, prayers before missions, and being a devout Catholic upon joining the military, he felt God had not held up His end. McDaniel reflected on one day that was particularly devastating for him. "A couple guys got hurt, and essentially I prayed, and I asked God for help, and at the end of that, I felt that no one was coming, and it was up to us, and that was a very alone, isolating feeling for sure, and I don't know if that went away after that." He remembered seeking out the chaplain; his faith was a large part of his life to this point, after all. Unfortunately, the chaplain was unable to answer his questions. Instead, McDaniel remembers the chaplain said "to just stay strong and that my faith will return. I just need to remember that God's grace is there even in wartime and that I was going to get past it, and unfortunately, I feel like I never did." Calling it a "defining moment," he remembered that as the interaction where he lost his faith. An improvised explosive device (IED) blast later left him wounded, and he retired from the military and has remained an atheist to this day.

Many veterans I spoke with had stories like McDaniel's. Marine Staff Sergeant Edgar Jansen also confronted the question of evil while in Afghanistan. Part of his team's job was to mine roll the pathways to and from base, using a large trawling device attached to the front of a tank to detonate pressure sensitive explosives before they injured someone. Unfortunately, his best friend happened to step on an IED just outside the rolled pathway, tragically killing his friend instantly. Jansen explained, "God and I had a disagreement while I was in Afghanistan, and that was taking my friend away." Much like McDaniel, he decided to seek out a chaplain immediately. He said the chaplain tried to explain his friend's death as serving some higher purpose beyond our understanding. Jansen recalled, "he started saying, 'God, this,' 'God, that,' I think I was still pissed off. Well, I know I was still pissed off. And I felt cheated." He stopped relying on either his Episcopalian upbringing or anything a chaplain had to say. He could not understand how God would allow his best friend to die, and the chaplain's response had not helped. In Jansen's words, "I wanted to hear a reasonable person give me reasonable advice. Instead of, I guess, in my mentality at that point, instead of chalking it up to some Higher Power, who takes friends away."

While Jansen has had a difficult time managing his divine moral injury along with PTSD, he said talking through it has been his best source of therapy, that and a supportive family. His account highlights the importance of significant relationships while searching for resonance (between God and Jansen, the chaplain and Jansen, and his family and Jansen). Including the breakdown of the divine relationship as a sociologically relevant one allows us to take seriously how Jansen's moral narrative was upended. Like narrative breaks that say "I am immoral" or "the military is immoral," a breakdown in this significant relationship shatters the expectation that God is moral. In attempting to correct this dissonance, Jansen attempted to participate in moral discourse but found only trite answers for a complex morally salient issue. Even if dissonance triggers discursive consciousness (Vaisey, 2009), habits are difficult to change—what Dewey (1922: 129) calls a "defense reaction." In the absence of resonance with religious resources, Jansen instead turned to other cultural communities (i.e., his family). These relationships allow him to confirm the veracity of his moral goodness and that he is not alone.

This was a common pattern among those who experienced divine moral injury. Whether it was losing friends or witnessing the horrors of war, coming face to face with atrocities shook the religious frameworks of many veterans with whom I spoke. Still, about a third of those who felt betrayed by God chose to wrestle with these questions alone. The reason they did not seek a chaplain did not have a consistent answer. They generally had good impressions of chaplains, yet other aspects of military culture promote machismo, stoicism, mental fortitude, and avoidance of moral reflection (Hockey, 2003; Wood, 2016). Like those who compartmentalized but maintained faith, those who avoided moral conversation likely did so because of the internalization of military cultural norms. If the thought of active moral deliberation arose at all, a socially ingrained military *habitus* would quell it. An unconsciously held habit prevented a reflexive attitude even when disturbed. These military cultural norms are so salient, I argue, that they present a predictable *habitus* that prevents reflection but exacerbates moral injury.

Beyond habituated compartmentalization, some service members avoided relational moral deliberation because they thought dwelling on emotional turmoil would make them appear weak. They embodied the debilitating machismo that is inherent in military culture. SFC Martinez revealed to me he had a subordinate who witnessed two of his team members die when a helicopter crane cable lifting an injured Green Beret to safety frayed and snapped ten feet from the bird. Back at base, the young man approached Martinez to say, "I just don't know what to do. I mean, I feel like I'm still in the helicopter. I still see him falling." Martinez, who has since apologized to that team member, responded to him at the time by commanding "him to quit being a fucking pussy and shut the fuck up. And suck it up and get back in the fight. We got a fucking job to do. And if he keeps doing this shit, we're going to fucking send him out. So, that's how we handled shit with questions on morality, and death, and stuff." While chaplains were not always available on more isolated bases, even when they were, service members might not seek them out for fear of looking less masculine in the eyes of their team members.

The lingering effects of moral injury, then, tended to be a loss of a connection to a higher power and religious community, apparently as a failure of service members to find resonance. The failure could stem from dissonance between religious resources brought to the military and disruptive military experience, an inability to find resonance among old religious frameworks or new military religious ones. Or active moral work was avoided altogether due to internalized habits of compartmentalization, itself a product of military moral culture. In the total abandonment of their religious repertoire, civilian or military, veterans reported seeking out other meaning-making resources with varying success.

Conclusions

Service members and veterans work with multiple cultural toolkits. Some tools are brought from home and some are supplied by the military. Traumatic experience is nearly inevitable in their wartime service, and those toolkits provide varying assistance as they seek resonance amid moral trauma. Often, the religiously steeped personal culture these toolkits produced provided them with explicit and implicit values and moral expectations that shaped their beliefs about themselves as good persons. These expectations and beliefs extended from often uncritically held habits established throughout their lives by the public cultures with which they interacted (Dewey, 1922; Lizardo, 2017). Military culture and experience support and confirm these values and beliefs, allowing service members to maintain significant relationships and moral narratives that reinforce who they are within the moral order of faith communities, the military, and other social spheres. However, when potential moral trauma presented a novel problem that upended the coherence of their expected moral narrative, thus forcing reflection (Dewey, 1922), service members who reestablished resonance responded in varied ways, using established beliefs from their cultural repertoires, finding new resonant beliefs, or avoiding moral deliberation altogether. Service members who failed to reestablish coherence in their moral narratives continued to feel dissonance with attendant feelings of guilt, shame, anger, and a loss of meaning—a moral injury.

The clear horror of moral trauma stemming from the breakdown of significant relationships (self, organization, or God) activates the salience of moral issues like killing, human dignity, or the right to life in some (Guhin, 2016). This breakdown often triggered Type II cognition through discursive consciousness either immediately or, as we will see, *years* after the PMIE. A traumatic disruption in one's moral expectations does not necessarily initiate immediate reflection if ever. When moral reflection followed, it emphasized reestablishing coherence in the expected moral narrative of the service member by relying on old beliefs (often previously unarticulated) or newfound ones that resonated with the narrative they hoped to reconstruct. New beliefs then became habituated, easy to draw upon in giving a later account (Dewey, 1922; Winchester & Green, 2019).

By contrast, a proportion of those who appeared to avoid moral injury were those who avoided moral deliberation and discourse altogether. I argue that this is a result of the military culture that inhibits emotion and reflection in favor of stoicism and high operational tempo. That is, military culture is one that inhibits the process of disruption that would trigger deliberation. As military training alters the *habitus* of its service members (Ben-Ari, 1989), they often develop habits and hold beliefs that prevent conscious awareness of a PMIE (Dewey, 1922). In fact, three of the participants admitted that the interview was the first time they had ever reflected morally on their careers, suggesting that the discursive practice of the interview itself activated the salience of moral issues. The post-hoc account triggered reflection on moral quandaries and drew attention to justifications for action that could become motivations in the future. However, as I have shown, while many acted solely out of a military *habitus*, almost two-thirds of those who experienced moral injury reported relying on moral discourse to navigate it with varying degrees of success.

The process of belief maintenance illustrates the process of biopolitics (MacLeish, 2019) that systematically and efficiently socializes service members for brutalization. Military culture and military religious resources indeed supply justifications and narratives that contribute to moral coherence even after dissonance activates Type II cognition. However, military culture also socializes service members to a professional identity (Lifton & Markusen, 1990) and combat (Luft, 2015) that frames the warrior identity as both good and necessary. Part of the process is doubling and gradual psychic numbing that makes participation in violence possible and makes killing not only easier but desirable (Lifton, 1986; Lifton & Markusen, 1990). This process of derealization positions service members in an alternate reality of sorts where killing does not stir the reactive attitudes (Strawson, 1974)—the very moral emotions that make us moral beings—and the hindrance of empathy vanishes. Recall MSG Thompson's framing: "The quicker and the more we kill them, the less innocent blood is going to be shed." The cultural frames he received from training, religious counsel, ethics education, and the inculcation of the warrior identity culminated in framing killing as an essential and beneficent end. These cultural frames are endlessly habituated in service members and are, in many ways, the pathways that makes participation in the military possible.

Indeed, while McDonnell et al. (2017) push back against formulations of resonance that rely on old habituated cultural frames having mere congruence with experience, I believe this is too limiting. It is clear in these stories that PMIEs present novel problems individuals must work through using cultural frameworks to reestablish their moral expectations and narratives. Contrary to McDonnell, old beliefs do appear to create feelings of resonance, and it is because they are deployed in a new way. That is, the novelty of the traumatic problem means the service member is using a belief in a way they would never have previously, allowing them to articulate a previously uncritically held tool from their repertoire. At the absence or failure of a cultural frame from one's repertoire, new ones found during or after military experience find resonance if they can reestablish coherence.

The long-term success of this resonant framework depends on both the source of the disruption and the goal of the new narrative. Typically, the interrupted habit was a part of their personal religious declarative culture (to use Lizardo's, 2017 schema), but military situations and nondeclarative military cultures initiated dissonance, causing guilt, shame, and anger—a moral injury. In every case, the breakdown in a significant relationship (self, superior officer, organization, or God) perpetuated the trauma. Establishing resonance required sorting through cultural toolkits, some already established, some previously unarticulated, and some newfound. The source of those cultural tools, in turn, shaped the moral narrative that emerged and usually involved the suppression of empathy (Lifton & Markusen, 1990). For military religious resources and frames, for example, it is clear that the goal is a strategic reinforcement of the status quo of military culture and troop readiness (Waggoner, 2014), which continues to raise significant ethical questions.

Bibliography

Bader, C. D., & Finke, R. (2010). What Does God Require? Understanding Religious Context and Morality. In S. Hitlin & S. Vaisey (Eds.), *Handbook of the Sociology of Morality* (pp. 228–242). Springer.

Ben-Ari, E. (1989). Masks and Soldiering: The Israeli Army and the Palestinian Uprising. *Cultural Anthropology*, *4*(4), 372–389.

Berg, G. (2011). The Relationship between Spiritual Distress, PTSD and Depression in Vietnam Combat Veterans. *Journal of Pastoral Care & Counseling: Advancing Theory and Professional Practice through Scholarly and Reflective Publications, 65*(1), 1–11.

Berger, P. L. (1967). *The Sacred Canopy: Elements of Sociological Theory of Religion.* Doubleday.

Bourdieu, P. (1990). *The Logic of Practice* (R. Nice, Trans.). Stanford University Press.

Brémault-Phillips, S., Pike, A., Scarcella, F., & Cherwick, T. (2019). Spirituality and Moral Injury Among Military Personnel: A Mini-Review. *Frontiers in Psychiatry, 10*, 276.

Brock, R. N., & Lettini, G. (2013). *Soul Repair: Recovering from Moral Injury after War.* Beacon Press.

Currier, J. M., Holland, J. M., & Malott, J. (2015). Moral Injury, Meaning Making, and Mental Health in Returning Veterans. *Journal of Clinical Psychology, 71*(3), 229–240.

Denton-Borhaug, K. (2011). *U.S. War-Culture, Sacrifice and Salvation.* Routledge.

Dewey, J. (1922). *Human Nature and Conduct: An Introduction to Social Psychology.* Henry Holt & Company.

Exline, J. J., Yali, A. M., & Sanderson, W. C. (2000). Guilt, Discord, and Alienation: The Role of Religious Strain in Depression and Suicidality. *Journal of Clinical Psychology, 56*(12), 1481–1496.

Exline, J. J., Grubbs, J. B., & Homolka, S. J. (2014). Seeing God as Cruel or Distant: Links with Divine Struggles Involving Anger, Doubt, and Fear of God's Disapproval. *The International Journal for the Psychology of Religion, 25*, 29–41.

Goepner, E. W. (2016). Measuring the Effectiveness of America's War on Terror. *Parameters, 46*(1), 107–120.

Griswold, W. (2004). *Cultures and Societies in a Changing World.* Pine Forge Press.

Grossman, D. (1996). *On Killing: The Psychological Cost of Learning to Kill in War and Society.* Little, Brown.

Guhin, J. (2016). Why Worry about Evolution? Boundaries, Practices, and Moral Salience in Sunni and Evangelical High Schools. *Sociological Theory, 34*(2), 151–174.

Hitlin, S., & Vaisey, S. (2013). The New Sociology of Morality. *Annual Review of Sociology, 39*(1), 51–68.

Hockey, J. (2003). Military Masculinities: Identity and the State. In P. R. Higate (Ed.), *The Criminology of War* (pp. 15–25). Praeger.

Ignatow, G. (2009). Why the Sociology of Morality Needs Bourdieu's Habitus. *Sociological Inquiry, 79*(1), 98–114.

Jordan, A. H., Eisen, E., Bolton, E., Nash, W. P., & Litz, B. T. (2017). Distinguishing War-Related PTSD Resulting from Perpetration- and Betrayal-Based Morally Injurious Events. *Psychological Trauma: Theory, Research, Practice, and Policy, 9*(6), 627–634.

Kilner, P. (2017, March 28). *Moral Injury--Personal, Organizational, and Divine Betrayals.* Retrieved from http://soldier-ethicist.blogspot.com/2017/03/a-third-form-of-moral-injury.html

Lamont, M., & Molnár, V. (2002). The Study of Boundaries in the Social Sciences. *Annual Review of Sociology, 28*, 167–195.

Lawson, R., Drebing, C., Berg, G., Vincellette, A., & Penk, W. (1998). The Long Term Impact of Child Abuse on Religious Behavior and Spirituality in Men. *Child Abuse & Neglect, 22*(5), 369–380.

Lifton, R. J. (1986). *The Nazi Doctors: Medical Killing and the Psychology of Genocide.* Basic Books.

Lifton, R. J., & Markusen, E. (1990). *Genocidal Mentality: Nazi Holocaust and Nuclear Threat.* Basic Books.

Litz, B. T., Stein, N., Delaney, E., Lebowitz, L., Nash, W. P., Silva, C., & Maguen, S. (2009). Moral Injury and Moral Repair in War Veterans: A Preliminary Model and Intervention Strategy. *Clinical Psychology Review, 29*(8), 695–706.

Lizardo, O. (2017). Improving Cultural Analysis: Considering Personal Culture in Its Declarative and Nondeclarative Modes. *American Sociological Review, 82*(1), 88–115.

Lizardo, O., Mowry, R., Sepulvado, B., Stoltz, D. S., Taylor, M. A., Ness, J. V., & Wood, M. (2016). What Are Dual Process Models? Implications for Cultural Analysis in Sociology. *Sociological Theory, 34*(4), 287–310.

Luft, A. (2015). Toward a Dynamic Theory of Action at the Micro Level of Genocide: Killing, Desistance, and Saving in 1994 Rwanda. *Sociological Theory, 33*(2), 148–172.

Luft, A. (2020). Theorizing Moral Cognition: Culture in Action, Situations, and Relationships. *Socius: Sociological Research for a Dynamic World, 6*, 1–15.

Luhrmann, T. M. (2012). *When God Talks Back: Understanding the American Evangelical Relationship with God.* Alfred A. Knopf.

Lukes, S. (2010). The Social Construction of Morality? In S. Hitlin & S. Vaisey (Eds.), *Handbook of the Sociology of Morality* (pp. 531–541). Springer.

MacLeish, K. (2019). Imagining Military Suicide. In C. Lutz & A. Mazzarino (Eds.), *War and Health: The Medical Consequences of the Wars in Iraq and Afghanistan* (pp. 190–208). New York University Press.

McCarthy, N. (2018, March 21). 2.77 Million Service Members Have Deployed Since 9/11." *Statista.* Retrieved from www.statista.com/chart/13292/277-million-service-members-have-deployed-since-9-11.

McDermott, J. (2012, August 1). Soldier Suicides, An Epidemic We Must Defeat. *TIME.* Retrieved from https://nation.time.com/2012/08/01/soldier-suicides-an-epidemic-we-must-defeat/

McDonnell, T. E. (2014). Drawing out Culture: Productive Methods to Measure Cognition and Resonance. *Theory and Society, 43*(3/4), 247–274.

McDonnell, T. E., Bail, C. A., & Tavory, I. (2017). A Theory of Resonance. *Sociological Theory, 35*(1), 1–14.

Molendijk, T., Kramer, E., & Verweij, D. (2018). Moral Aspects of "Moral Injury": Analyzing Conceptualizations on the Role of Morality in Military Trauma. *Journal of Military Ethics, 17*(1), 36–53.

Moon, Z. (2019). *Warriors between Worlds: Moral Injury and Identities in Crisis.* Lexington Books.

Nash, W. P., & Litz, B. T. (2013). Moral Injury: A Mechanism for War-Related Psychological Trauma in Military Family Members. *Clinical Child and Family Psychology Review, 16*(4), 365–375.

National Institute of Mental Health. (2019). *Suicide* (Report). Retrieved from www.nimh.nih.gov/health/statistics/suicide.shtml.

Office of Mental Health and Suicide Prevention. (2020). *2020 National Veteran Suicide Prevention Annual Report* (Report). US Department of Veterans Affairs, Retrieved from https://www.mentalhealth.va.gov/docs/data-sheets/2020/2020-National-Veteran-Suicide-Prevention-Annual-Report-11-2020-508.pdf

Orvis, K. A. (2020). Department of Defense (DoD) Quarterly Suicide Report (QSR) 3rd Quarter, CY 2020. Department of Defense Suicide Prevention Office, Retrieved https://www.dspo.mil/Portals/113/TAB%20A_20201112_OFR_Rpt_Q3%20CY%202020%20QSR_final_1.pdf.

Pargament, K. I., Smith, B. W., Koenig, H. G., & Perez, L. (1998). Patterns of Positive and Negative Religious Coping with Major Life Stressors. *Journal for the Scientific Study of Religion, 37*(4), 710–724.

Pargament, K. I., Zinnbauer, B. J., Scott, A. B., Butter, E. M., Zerowin, J., & Stanik, P. (1998). Red Flags and Religious Coping: Identifying Some Religious Warning Signs among People in Crisis. *Journal of Clinical Psychology, 54*(1), 77–89.

Pruitt, L. D., Smolenski, D. J., Bush, N. E., Tucker, J., Issa, F., Hoyt, T. V., & Reger, M. A. (2019). Suicide in the Military: Understanding Rates and Risk Factors Across the United States' Armed Forces. *Military Medicine, 184*(Supplement_1), 432–437.

Sayer, A. (2005). *The Moral Significance of Class.* Cambridge University Press.

Schorr, Y., Stein, N. R., Maguen, S., Barnes, J. B., Bosch, J., & Litz, B. T. (2018). Sources of Moral Injury among War Veterans: A Qualitative Evaluation. *Journal of Clinical Psychology, 74*, 2203–2218.

Shay, J. (1994). *Achilles in Vietnam Combat Trauma and the Undoing of Character.* New York, NY: Scribner.

Stein, D. J., Chiu, W. T., Hwang, I., Kessler, R. C., Sampson, N., Alonso, J., Borges, G., Bromet, E., Bruffaerts, R., de Girolamo, G., Florescu, S., Gureje, O., He, Y., Kovess-Masfety, V., Levinson, D., Matschinger, H., Mneimneh, Z., Nakamura, Y., Ormel, J., Posada-Villa, J., Sagar, R., Scott, K. M., Tomov, T., Viana, M. C., Williams, D. R., & Nock, M. K. (2010). Cross-National Analysis of the Associations between Traumatic Events and Suicidal Behavior: Findings from the WHO World Mental Health Surveys. *PLoS One, 5*(5), e10574.

Strawson, P. F. (1974). *Freedom and Resentment and Other Essays.* Methuen.

Swidler, A. (1986, April). Culture in Action: Symbols and Strategies. *American Sociological Review, 51*(2), 273–286.

Swidler, A. (2001). *Talk of Love: How Culture Matters.* University of Chicago Press.

Taylor, C. (1989). *Sources of the Self: The Making of the Modern Identity.* Harvard University Press.

Tiryakian, E. A. (2010). The (Im)morality of War: Some Sociological Considerations. In S. Hitlin & S. Vaisey (Eds.), *Handbook of the Sociology of Morality* (pp. 67–88). Springer.

Under Secretary of Defense for Personnel and Readiness. (2020, August 20). *Annual Suicide Report - CY 2019* (Rep. No. 4-CFF293C). Department of Defense. Retrieved from https://www.dspo.mil/Portals/113/Documents/CY2019%20Suicide%20Report/DoD%20Calendar%20Year%20CY%202019%20Annual%20Suicide%20Report.pdf?ver=YOA4IZVcVA9mzwtsfdO5Ew%3d%3d

Vaisey, S. (2009). Motivation and Justification: a Dual-Process Model of Culture in Action. *American Journal of Sociology, 114*(6), 1675–1715.

Vest, B. M. (2013). Citizen, Soldier, or Citizen-Soldier? Negotiating Identity in the US National Guard. *Armed Forces and Society, 39*(4), 602–627.

Waggoner, E. (2014, September). Taking Religion Seriously in the U.S. Military: The Chaplaincy as a National Strategic Asset. *Journal of the American Academy of Religion, 82*(3), 702–735.

Winchester, D., & Green, K. D. (2019). Talking Your Self into It: How and When Accounts Shape Motivation for Action. *Sociological Theory, 37*(3), 257–281.

Wittchen, H., Schönfeld, S., Kirschbaum, C., Thurau, C., Trautmann, S., Steudte, S., Klotsche, J., Höfler, M., Hauffa, R., & Zimmermann, P. (2012). Traumatic Experiences and Posttraumatic Stress Disorder in Soldiers Following Deployment Abroad. *Deutsches Aerzteblatt International, 109*(35–36), 559–568.

Wood, D. B. (2016). *What Have We Done: The Moral Injury of Our Longest Wars.* Little, Brown and Company.

CHAPTER 6

Religion, Trauma, and PTSD

Army Special Forces Chief Warrant Officer 2 Greg Bush served for thirteen years before his forced retirement in 2012. Constant achievement and a pursuit of higher leadership positions characterized his journey through the military. He enlisted as an E-1 private and worked his way up in rank until he could apply to become an officer, eventually becoming an E-7, Sergeant First Class. He deployed with peacekeeping forces in Kosovo, attended Airborne School to become a paratrooper, and did three tours in Iraq, where he dismantled opposition networks and fought militias. By the end of his time in Iraq, he recalled, "I kind of had a reputation as being pretty. … I was very good at my job, which was pretty much killing terrorists, so I got a name for myself as being kind of ruthless and methodical. And it seemed like I was the only one that could get it done." He became "a lot harder and callous and jaded," and, upon returning from his last deployment in Iraq, he was screened for and diagnosed with PTSD.

While PTSD marks the end of a career for many service members, Bush's diagnosis did not. They prescribed medicine for anxiety and sleep deprivation with hopes that doctors would follow up with him in his next Special Forces Group. They never did. Bush did not want to risk his career, nor did he want to relive his trauma by talking about it. He wanted to "put the mission first." Talking about his trauma would not help him perform his job, which he was proud to say he performed well. Bush was accepted

T. H. Suitt, III, *Narratives of Trauma and Moral Agency among Christian Post-9/11 Veterans*,
https://doi.org/10.1007/978-3-031-31082-9_6

to the Warrant Officer Candidate School, and, after a brief break from combat, he deployed to Afghanistan. Despite the PTSD diagnosis and increasing troubles with complications from a herniated disc, he continued to see combat with near nightly missions. His medication, which included opiates and other pain killers, increased, but the Army kept deploying him. He deployed to Afghanistan three times.

One night, on his last deployment, he was "clearing a house and came face-to-face with an anti-personnel mine." As the mine exploded, his "life flashed before [his] eyes," but he was able to get himself and his men to safety. Upon returning to base hours later, however, they found nothing wrong with him because he "wasn't bleeding." He continued to serve out the rest of his tour with more combat missions over the course of months. It was not until he was sent back home that everything caught up with him. "Once I got back from my last tour, I went to see someone, and my entire military career ended," Bush said. "It was severe. My doctor actually said … it was the most severe case [of combat-related PTSD] that he had to deal with so far in the military." In addition to PTSD, he was also diagnosed with a TBI. The mortar that had exploded by his head caused damage left untreated for months, not including addiction to the pain medications he was already taking for his back. With the doubling down on his diagnosis of PTSD along with the TBI, the military could not continue to deploy Bush. "I wasn't able to do my job anymore, and so my clearance was removed. Pretty much when I couldn't deploy for them anymore, they kind of just said, 'Thanks for your service, and it's time for you to retire.'" He returned to the civilian sector broken and not sure what to do next.

Despite a bad interaction with a chaplain in the military who made him feel "judged," he credits his faith with helping him navigate his PTSD. It has allowed him to make meaning of some of his experiences and allowed him to avoid feelings of despair. It was, however, not a cure-all. "I'm still dealing with PTSD, and I have regrets and shame for some of the things that I've done, but I know that God loves me and is proud of me. So, without that faith, then a lot of those other things would probably overcome my thoughts," he said. His faith has allowed him to find some comfort in his life even though it could not completely resolve his PTSD.

The dynamic between his PTSD and his faith remains a complicated one. Although he has a good relationship with God on his own, his symptoms prevent him from participating in a religious community. "I had a hard time at church, and I still have a hard time at church, mostly the crowd. I have a really hard time with babies crying and little kids running around. That's going back to when I had collateral damage, and I killed women and children. That goes back to that," he paused. "So, I have a difficult time at church now." CWO-2 Bush has come to terms with his soul wounds using his religious resources to make sense of his role in the military; however, his religious resources cannot prevent his PTSD symptoms that manifest as nightmares, flashbacks, night sweats, and flight responses. His constant exposure to combat, the sights and sounds of death, and the real fear that people were trying to kill him have left their mark over the last seven years. "I have a lot of issues like racially profiling and just [being] untrusting of my fellow man in general." However, his faith has "sustained [him] and kept [him.]" He now tries to rely on his faith to work on himself. "I think [my faith has] helped me with my PTSD, it's helped me try to get back to the person I was before I joined."

Bush also had moral injury and a TBI, yet his experience with PTSD and his use of religious resources to cope was like that of other veterans with whom I spoke, even when the range of traumatic events and subsequent conditions varied. Extending from our previous discussion on moral injury, this chapter will explore the role of religion in navigating experiences of trauma and the development of PTSD. When religious resources could preempt or make meaning of traumatic experiences void of a perceived moral dimension, they tended to allow service members to cope with trauma and maintain a positive affect. In the apparent absence of moral trauma, religion played a more uniformly positive role among participants. This, however, did not mean that religious resources could not be destructive.

Traumatic Experience and PTSD

Although strongly associated with moral injury (Koenig et al., 2019), PTSD is a separate psychological condition that has more to do with mental and physiological responses to trauma than to wounds of the soul. For instance, a person who has PTSD likely perpetrated, witnessed, or experienced a horror of war, like Bush did, causing an overwhelming sense of fear that "triggers an alarm system set deep in the amygdala." The individual is then incapable of turning off the biological fight or flight response to danger.

When false alarms, like loud noises—even the sounds of children—trigger that reaction, there is "perceived threat and automatic response," which we can understand as "fear-circuity dysregulation" (Wood, 2016: 15–16). PTSD is a "technical name for a complex of symptoms that arise in the wake of trauma" (Finley, 2012: 5). A psychological response, it requires a "minimum number of symptoms in each of three categories: reexperiencing (e.g., recurring nightmares about the traumatic event); avoidance (e.g., avoiding conversations about the traumatic event); and arousal (e.g., difficulty sleeping)" (Bagalman, 2011: 3). Note that CWO-2 Bush had all three. The symptoms must last for more than one month and must result in distress and impairment in social functioning. The symptoms tend to only be diagnosable as PTSD six months after a traumatic event, although some symptoms occur immediately. Each year, between about 11% and 20% of veterans are diagnosed with PTSD with 27% of all Global War on Terror veterans who seek VA health care services having a PTSD diagnosis ("How Common Is PTSD in Veterans?," 2018).

While this project emphasized moral questions and how religious resources interacted with the moral quandaries service members faced, PTSD did come up. I found that twenty-five of the 47 veterans revealed a PTSD diagnosis, a rate of over 50%, which is significantly more than the rates mentioned above. Beyond that, a few revealed they have actively tried to avoid receiving a diagnosis for various reasons, with some still avoiding treatment and others only recently seeking it. The DSM-5 (2013) lists an array of traumatic experiences that could be sources of the condition, and the participants of this study revealed experiences where they were exposed to the sorts of traumatic events that could cause PTSD. According to the DSM-5, a major source of PTSD is exposure to death, with combat experience—and combat trauma by extension—having significant correlation with the onset of the condition (Fontana & Rosenheck, 1999). Nevertheless, there are indeed many sources of PTSD. Service members need not have a combat role to experience trauma, but killing in war is "a better predictor of chronic PTSD symptoms than other indices of combat" (Litz et al., 2009: 697).

Combat Trauma

Among my sample, fifteen reported having experienced frequent combat. They were all men in the Army, Army National Guard, Army Special Forces, or the Marines. They tended to say that they had chosen to be in combat roles. MSG Mike Thompson, for example, said, "I was setting myself up always for the ground soldier, to do the hardest, to live off the land, to walk on the land, to be the closest into battle, face to face sometimes with the enemy." They had no misconceptions about their job. As one soldier put it, "you know infantry, you're the ones inflicting the wounds. Your job is to inflict the wounds." Even if they started in support roles, they would eventually seek out the more involved combat role. SFC Martinez, for example, revealed that he was initially an "air defense guy," but he admired the Green Berets and wanted to join them. "They were always doing more than we were," he said. "They seemed to have a larger impact. They were more engaged with the local communities. They didn't have to wear all the crap we did. They seemed a lot more comfortable, a lot more mature. You know, less bull crap, and I was like, 'You know, I want to try that.'" Some referred to themselves as "bottom of the totem pole" or "nothing but a simple grunt," but they were the exception. Most of the participants with explicit combat roles were proud of their work, particularly the Green Berets who viewed themselves as "professional" and having "big-boy rules." In every case, they understood their job was to be the "tip of the spear."

Some responded to this with hesitancy, despite choosing their position; "I'm not a killer. I love the challenges of combat, but I don't get any enjoyment out of shooting at anybody or shooting anybody. It's not. … That's just not my personality." Others, however, felt they were doing good work and found enjoyment in fighting against the enemy: "Some guys feel bad about it. I don't. And I can say this with the utmost certainty, those are still some of the most joyous moments of my life was doing my job." Regardless of their feelings about killing, however, PTSD was still common. Twelve of the 15 revealed a PTSD diagnosis to me, and others were likely left unreported.

Of course, one did not have to be in a combat position to see combat. An additional 15 of my participants characterized their careers as having "infrequent combat experience." There was more variation in their branches of service with a few participants from the Navy and Air Force, though the majority remained Army, Army National Guard, or Marines. These participants could be in combat roles but did not come across enemy combatants frequently. SSgt Trey Underwood, for example, had a communications MOS for most of his career and reported infrequent combat experience. However, a change of roles to Convoy Operations Leader exposed him to a significant amount of combat, and he experienced trauma during that relatively short window of his career. Others were in support roles but experienced something like mortar fire or a short engagement with the enemy. Air Force civil engineer Hailey Freeman remembered, "[W]e were going to inspect a school and we were halfway between the school and the trucks and they started shooting RPGs at us." Eight of those 15 with infrequent combat experience were diagnosed with PTSD, and again some were likely unreported. Here, however, the source of the PTSD was less likely to have been their own actions.

Exposure to Death

While killing is cited as the best indicator of who develops PTSD in combat (Litz et al., 2009), there are other traumatic experiences in the theater of war that could also cause PTSD. Exposure to death off the battlefield was one such experience. For example, Special Forces Captain Marcus Russo witnessed "a pickup truck of fifty headless bodies being brought to [him] and somebody saying, 'What do I do with these things?'" Similarly, a cryptologist technician in the Navy, Justin Page, recalled being stationed in Burma while doing intelligence work to protect the Burmese president. He said, "While sitting off the coast, I was standing outside and just happened to see a body floating by. And they basically didn't even care … that one of their citizens had been floating by. And it felt like they basically just put him back in the water kind of thing. And that one instance has stuck with me because it kind of shows some people just don't have a respect for life." By contrast to Russo who saw frequent combat and engaged with the enemy on a regular basis, Page never saw combat. Page did not report a PTSD diagnosis, but experiencing death left an indelible scar on his life. As Litz et al. (2009: 696) relate, "Research has shown that for those who are unaccustomed or unprepared, exposure to human remains is one of the most consistent predictors of long-term distress," yet even for service members who are aware of the possibility of witnessing death, who are trained to be prepared for it, the sight of death is distressing all the same.

Physical Trauma and Threats to Life

The DSM-5 also posits that being threatened with death can lead to PTSD. This was certainly true of those in combat positions, like MP Thomas Meyer, who reported feeling "jumpy" and said, "You watch your back. You're trying to make sure nothing happens." The constant feeling of threat in a war zone can lead to a fear and startle response that is common to PTSD. Threats to life, however, do not always occur in the theater of war. Taylor Vaught, for example, was threatened by a superior officer who then hit her in the head with a tank wrench. Similarly, George McClintock, a light wheel mechanic in the Army National Guard, developed PTSD after his experiences with an NCO. McClintock entered the military with Wiccan beliefs and practiced his faith openly. After being accused of "sorcery" by his commanding officer, he received a death threat and feared for his life. One day, while going through Baghdad in a convoy, he let "this little blue Datsun pickup truck full of little kids in the back cut through …, and [his] NCO started freaking out and he started threatening to kill [him] if I didn't run over the truck." After refusing to stop the Datsun, McClintock's commanding officer "put his M16 right up in the corner of [his] Kevlar and into [his] temple and threatened to kill [him] if [he] didn't run over the truck." McClintock refused, and the NCO "threw [him] up against the truck, punched [him] in the stomach a couple times, and said, 'If you ever disobey my direct order again, I will fucking kill you.'" McClintock was soon honorably discharged from duty. The constant threat to his life resulted in PTSD.

Actual or threatened serious injury can also contribute to PTSD according to the DSM-5. Fifteen of the participants experienced some form of physical injury during their time in the military, from a broken pinky to losing limbs, with 13 of these also developing PTSD for various reasons. MSG Mike Thompson, for example, developed PTSD after being medically discharged from the military. He stepped on an IED while in Afghanistan back in 2010 and lost both of his legs, most of his dominant arm, and injured his groin and stomach as well. "I was pretty bad off," he said. "The moment I stepped on that IED, I was dead. And I was dead because I know what I was looking at. And what I was looking at was completely darkness. It was just absolute complete darkness. And I felt as though I was floating in the air. I knew I stepped on an IED, and I knew it sent me up in the air. But I just felt like I was suspended there. And at that moment in time, it's pure darkness." In what he calls an unlikely miracle, he was airlifted out on a JTAC helicopter nearby. While trying to maintain consciousness, Thompson recalled, "I just knew that all I had to do was hold on until the helicopter got there, and then hold on until they loaded me, and then hold on until we landed in Kandahar, and then hold on until they speak to that surgeon. And when I spoke to that surgeon, I was just so tired. And I was just … I just had to give up. I wanted to give up so bad. It was exhausting, the most exhausted that you could feel ever." He made it to the surgeon but wound up in a coma. He recovered but had to deal with his new reality. He was awarded the Purple Heart and a Bronze Star, but his injuries and the onset of PTSD forced him to retire medically.

Military Sexual Trauma

The DSM-5 also explains that actual or threatened sexual violence can cause PTSD. Four of the women I interviewed revealed that they had been the victims of sexual assault or rape with one additional service member having to navigate constant sexual threats. Each of them developed PTSD because of their sexual trauma or in addition to other traumas.

One of the kinds of traumatic events that can precipitate PTSD is the threat of or actual sexual violence. The repeated threat or experience of sexual violence, harassment, or assault within the military context has come to be known as MST, which affects over 23% of women in the military, though a significant portion likely goes unreported. These incidents include "rape, forcible sodomy, indecent assault, and any attempts of these violations [as well as] sexual coercion, unwanted sexual attention, or threatening attempts to initiate a sexual relationship" (Conard et al., 2014: 282). There is a significant link between MST (the traumatic event) and PTSD (the psychological and physiological response to the trauma). Murdoch et al. (2004) revealed that 71% of women veterans seeking treatment for PTSD had experienced MST. Moreover, Surìs et al. (2007) discovered that women veterans who had experienced MST were five times more likely to develop PTSD than their peers who had not experienced it. Despite this link to PTSD, MST does not always result in the mental disorder, but it can lead to other mental health disorders strongly associated with sexual trauma among women veterans like "major depressive disorder (MDD), anxiety, and substance abuse" (Kelly et al., 2011: 458).

MST is also, for various reasons, often separated from other forms of trauma like combat trauma, morally injurious events, and the like, even though it can, like other traumas, result in PTSD and moral injury, particularly because it is such an act of betrayal. In fact, the feeling of betrayal is part of what makes MST distinct from sexual trauma in the civilian sector. Health scientist Patricia Conard explains, "MST is unique in that it usually occurs in the workplace setting and often by someone known," and the victim likely must continue to work with their attacker, which leads to feelings of betrayal, shame, and hopelessness (Conard et al., 2014: 282). A service member usually cannot just leave the service whenever they choose. Flight manager Karen Black, for instance, noted that she could not simply "quit." She explained, "You can't just leave. You know, like, most people go, 'Why didn't you just leave?' How can I leave? I'm going to go to jail." Part of what makes MST so horrific is that it is accompanied by a very real feeling of being trapped with the attacker. Black shared the same space with her attacker.

Victims' attempts to speak out against their attackers, too, often fall on willingly deaf ears. Army mechanic Taylor Vaught, for example, was assaulted before her head injury from the tank wrench. "I was always kind of like one of the boys," she recalled, and this extended to having her guard down with men who were harassing other women. She was typically not the target of it. But one day, an NCO in her unit, who had a history of "sexually harassing people," "one day ... took it too far, and it turned into [trying] to sexually assault me, which turned into a physical altercation, which turned into the good ole' boy system versus me because I wasn't really a part of the unit." Despite feeling like an insider to her unit—being one of the guys—that all changed when she was the victim of sexual assault. Her attacker faced no repercussions for his attempted assault. She had invaded their "boys' club" and was largely ignored.

Likewise, Navy airman Ruth Hannon, who was repeatedly threatened by a Marine soon after 9/11, was unable to escape her abuser. She said, "He'd come up to me, he'd have knives in his hands pointing." She had a difficult time telling me her story. "I finally said something to my temporary chain of command, and they, for some reason, ... sent me to the chaplain's office to deal with this issue. And they also got him and put him in the chaplain's office in front of the chaplain, ... me, the chaplain, and this guy threatening me with a knife, to work it out." Being forced to face the man who threatened her in a closed room did not help the situation at all. "It didn't get worked out, and it made things a lot more stressful. I don't know, I don't know why but I didn't really say anything to anybody except that because then it was like, well, they didn't help me. What is anybody else going to do?" The trauma of the threats has remained with her to this day, and it is clear that the sense of hopelessness and inescapability that is a major part of MST deeply affected her.

Chaplain Experiences of Trauma

Potential trauma extended beyond service members in combat and operational support roles; chaplains could experience trauma too. As we have seen, traumatic events need not exist solely on the battlefield. One need not perpetrate violence or experience the horrors of war directly to experience trauma. Rather, a deeply held belief in one's failure to do more could constitute a personal betrayal of one's sense of right. A feeling of abandonment by God could precipitate divine moral injury. And the exhaustion of service and the military life develops can result in PTSD. Knowing this, it is important to consider those serving the military in roles set apart yet embodying the military *habitus* all the same. Military chaplains themselves experience trauma even if they never pick up a weapon.

Ch. (Maj.) John Williams experienced trauma during his 14-year career as an Army chaplain. Calling himself a "terrible chaplain," he implicated his entire career as the inciting traumatic experience. "I feel like I didn't do enough," he said. "I just didn't do enough. There was always more places to go. More people to visit, more people to pray with and I didn't do it all the time. Sometimes I was just tired lazy and because I had a lot of freedom to come and go as I pleased over there." He felt he had been dismissive of soldiers needing marriage advice or bad at listening for soldiers who came to him with questions about a recent killing of an enemy combatant. Service members told him he was a "good chaplain," but he said the remarks did not help. Calling war a "real slow-drip trauma," he explained, "you don't always get PTSD from big awful things." Rather he felt the "very simple stories" where he (not to mention the service members he served) was not doing anything sensational but felt he could have done more were the memories that haunted him and led to PTSD (and moral injury).

While the other chaplains I interviewed did not report any trauma, other research has pointed to this being an important and understudied area for investigation. There is some, albeit limited, research on military chaplain trauma and their susceptibility to PTSD despite their noncombatant role. Levy et al. (2011) and Besterman-Dahan (2012) studied the effect of deployment stress on military chaplains in the Air Force and Army National Guard, respectively. The studies reveal that in addition to other stressors that trigger the development of PTSD or even moral injury, much of the deployment stress has roots in vicarious experiences which create a burden on the caregiver, not unlike the experiences of military physicians (see Maguen et al., 2008). As Levy et al. (2011) show, among the possible issues, the most significant operational stressors for military chaplains that predicted PTSD were seeing wounded or disfigured service members, receiving hostile fire, and exposure to death. Vicarious exposure to trauma via counseling alone was not a significant indicator of PTSD, although it occurred in some cases. Interestingly, counseling others through trauma was linked with post-traumatic growth, or increased faith and perceptions of competence.

The Development of PTSD

These stories of trauma and their links to PTSD, even in these brief explications, do not cover the full spectrum of trauma among those I interviewed, let alone in all the experiences of US Armed Forces service members. These stories show how traumatic events happen outside the theater of war and happen even to those members who rarely if ever see an enemy combatant during their careers. Moreover, these stories highlight how individuals do not have to be the direct targets of the trauma but can witness the aftermath and still develop PTSD. To add one more layer, Andy Hannon explained, "I was a military firefighter, and I worked on military bases. So, just like a fire department in the city, you see suicides, you see shootings, car fires, house fires. So, you would see all those different things." Sometimes, the very nature of a job, even one that does not see combat, still results in a constant stream of potentially traumatic events; and these events eventually led to PTSD for Hannon as well. Both direct and indirect exposure to trauma—death, threats to life, actual or threatened harm, injury, and sexual assault—can all potentially result in PTSD. All these sources of trauma are common to the military experience, even if PTSD only officially affects a small portion of Global War on Terror veterans.

After one or more of these traumatic events takes place, PTSD may not necessarily occur. It is, instead, marked by the persistent re-experiencing of the trauma through unwanted memories, nightmares, flashbacks, or the like. As one veteran told me, "I no longer had dreams, but nightmares, staying awake to avoid crippling flashbacks, and the fear of being caught in similar situations again." This is then accompanied by avoidance behavior to prevent trauma-related stimuli. When the trauma stimuli cannot be avoided, it usually results in irritability, vicious or risky behaviors, hypervigilance, heightened startle response, difficulty breathing, or difficulty sleeping. PTSD results in unwanted thoughts and destructive behaviors that can make it difficult to function in life. Accompanying these behaviors are negative thoughts and feelings, including feelings of blame, that are compounded by recalling the trauma and lead to isolation and antisocial behaviors. When these symptoms last for more than one month and lead to the inability to function, then the individual will likely receive a PTSD diagnosis.

Notably, some veterans reported actively avoiding a PTSD diagnosis. Marine officer Owen Gray revealed that he wrestled with symptoms of PTSD and moral injury but avoided the diagnosis. "I guess, to some degree, it was a practical thing for me," he said. "No matter what, when you go and you spend a year in a combat zone or wherever, your mind works in a different way, and even if you're in a combat zone but you're not involved in combat, your mind still works in a different way. And so, anytime you come home, there is a level of adjustment. Again, even if you're not in combat—and I always tell people, people throw PTSD around like it's water." He felt that PTSD was over-diagnosed and that it was really a matter of "willpower and their own ability to overcome their own issue." For him, "there's always a little bit of anxiety there, and you live with that. But again, it's how you deal with it. If you allow it to be an excuse to go be an alcoholic or a drug addict or an abuser or whatever … I chose not to, and I probably saw more combat than most. But I know guys who went to combat, who didn't see a day of combat, who their whole life is screwed up because of PTSD." Only recently retired, Gray felt he had enough resilience and willpower to manage his "anxiety," and he avoided a diagnosis and focused on his civilian life. Like others, he stigmatized a PTSD diagnosis and avoided one lest it affect jobs or reserve status.

This stigmatization toward mental health is not surprising. Despite advocacy and scholarship that seek to promote positive attitudes toward help-seeking behaviors, "stigmatizing views about mental illness persist among the public, especially the desire for social avoidance and the assumption of dangerousness." This stigma can lead to "discriminatory actions by those in powerful positions." Veterans and service members can risk losing their jobs or even finding housing with a PTSD diagnosis (Mittal et al., 2013: 87). CWO-2 Greg Bush, for example, explained that despite avoiding retirement for years after his initial PTSD diagnosis, his eventual forced medical retirement left him feeling "jaded." He would have remained in the military longer if he could have, but when a doctor claimed his PTSD was the worst he'd seen, Bush was shown the door. He blamed the diagnosis above all else. The avoidance of help-seeking behaviors can also be a result of self-stigma, feeling that seeking treatment would be considered a weakness making the veteran appear weak to himself. As Mittal et al. (2013: 90) explain, this view of PTSD and other mental health issues "may relate to … military culture, which promotes invincibility among soldiers, and acknowledging mental illness is likely to be viewed as a sign of weakness and a potential threat to their careers. Once veterans move into a civilian life, they may perceive and internalize negative public views about PTSD and mental illness." Veterans like Gray admit to having symptoms of PTSD and moral injury, like anxiety or shame, but they refuse help and a diagnosis because of a negative stigma. As this phenomenon continues to be an issue, advocating for positive attitudes toward treatment remains an important concern, particularly as veteran suicides remain a nationwide issue.

PTSD and Religion

There is a large body of scholarship on the relationship between religion and PTSD, although most studies deal with the general population. Studies of the veteran population, like the scholarship on moral injury, show a mixed picture. Religious resources can both alleviate and worsen the symptoms of PTSD. In one of the most recent and significant studies on the connection between religion and PTSD, Koenig et al. (2018: 2336) found "a weak positive relationship between religious involvement and PTSD … indicating some level of mediation for anxiety/depression in the relationship between religiosity and PTSD symptoms." This suggests that particular religious frames and communities can be useful in the treatment of PTSD's symptoms of anxiety and depression. Other studies have shown that high religiosity and frequent faith practices help prevent or alleviate PTSD symptoms. Pietrzak and Cook (2013), for example, show that high religiosity has also been associated with more resiliency against distress and PTSD symptoms, particularly among veterans who engage in private religious practice at least once per week. Hourani et al. (2012) likewise found that the use of religious resources in making life decisions contributed to the amelioration of PTSD among veterans.

By contrast, other research indicates that religious beliefs could exacerbate symptoms. Cornish et al. (2017: 307) reveal that positive religious coping (that is, a strong relationship with a higher power and help-seeking attitudes) can worsen PTSD symptoms. "For individuals who seek comfort in their religion but do not find it … *greater distress* is not an unexpected result [emphasis in original]." This is not unlike Sgt. Damien McDaniel's experience of praying but never feeling God showed up on the battlefield. Seeking God amid the horrors of war precipitated his trauma and a sense of betrayal when God failed to show up to save him and his unit. Similarly, Park et al. (2017: 18), also found that "*positive* [religious/spiritual] *coping* may have not only been ineffective in alleviating symptoms of PTSD but may actually have strengthened the influence of high *combat exposure* [emphasis in original]." In cases of higher combat exposure, the use of religious resources to cope with PTSD symptoms worsened veterans' mental health issues. The explanation for these divergent results is not well-understood, mirroring gaps in scholarship on moral injury.

Religion did play a role in how the veterans with whom I spoke navigated PTSD, although this was not always easy to determine. Since a veteran can have both moral injury and PTSD, it was not always clear how the *source* of PTSD or moral injury affected the likelihood of a PTSD diagnosis or subsequent attempts to cope. As with moral injury, dissonance between religious beliefs and military experience likely played a role in the traumas that led to PTSD. In certain cases, however, it was clear that religious resources affected the *outcomes* that followed.

Mitigation of Symptoms via Coping

Contrary to literature that showed religious resources exacerbating the effects of PTSD, the veterans I spoke with tended to cope "better" by relying on religious resources. For example, Special Forces MSG Mike Thompson, who sustained catastrophic injuries from an IED, used positive religious coping to reframe his experience. As a medic in the Special Forces, he was aware of what his injuries meant for him. He knew that had he not remained awake and aided his fellow medic in saving his own life, he would not have survived. Upon reflection on his injuries and trauma, Thompson said, "it's the most wonderful battlefield story to salvation or to God's mercy that one can have." His faith narrative aided him through recovery.

He remembered coming out of his three-day coma and feeling elation over surviving, rather than sadness over the loss of his limbs, attributing his survival to God's mercy. "The Holy Spirit was all over me," he said. "And I wasn't even upset. I wasn't even crying. I wasn't even sad." He was so grateful to be alive and for being able to see his family again that the loss of his legs and arm was secondary. Still, he admitted that he did not easily return to civilian life. His trauma led to risky and destructive behaviors, yet his faith continued to be a positive factor in his ability to cope.

"Even when I'd be partying, even when I'd be smoking, and driving, and doing just stupid stuff with one good arm, … He would be calling to me," he reflected. Eventually, he found a church that he committed to, and his faith helped him to reframe his experiences completely. Now, he sees himself as someone who has grown in his faith to "where the Holy Spirit gives [him] the strength to fight those temptations, and those trials, and those tribulations that the devil put [him] through." Despite genuinely missing the military life and the camaraderie that came with it and the full functioning of his body, he would not change a thing. "I would rather be a guy with one good arm in a wheelchair, knowing that I'm going to the Kingdom of Heaven rather than to have it all and wallowing in darkness, fearing hell."

Similarly, Special Forces SFC Martinez also highlighted the role of religion in allowing him to cope with and mitigate his PTSD. Toward the end of his career, his combat trauma started to lead him to partake in risky and destructive behaviors. He did not know it at the time, but he had undiagnosed PTSD. "I was drinking. I was an alcoholic. I was abusing my medication. And I was an addict. I wasn't smoking crack or anything, but if you gave me pills, I was going to take them all." He was soon diagnosed with PTSD, which made him "immediately pissed off about it." Martinez, who had great success in managing PMIEs by speaking with chaplains, sought out one again. The second chaplain explained, "Look, you have a job to do. As a Special Forces Green Beret your job is getting through this. The Lord has placed something in front of you [that] you have to negotiate. It's an obstacle. It's not a disability." Martinez had also suffered a TBI, started developing Parkinson's, had balance issues, knee issues, and other problems stemming from his time in combat. "I had like 18 different things wrong."

However, the chaplain helped him reframe his trauma, "Look, they're not disabilities. They're just obstacles." By reframing his trauma as yet another obstacle in his career as a Green Beret and as one that God put in his path, the chaplain encouraged Martinez to approach his trauma like a warrior. "I was a Special Forces Green Beret. I was the tip of the spear! I was the best of the best. I was whatever in my mind. But even though I was a father, a husband, a brother, a friend, a son, an uncle. All that other shit really wasn't on my radar. That was my sole focus. But he reminded me of that, and it saved my life."

Martinez's successes in coping with his PTSD, like moral injury, stemmed from active deliberation with a spiritual guide at the moment of experiencing dissonance. For moral injury, it was over the salient issue of killing; for PTSD, it was coming to terms with his diagnosis and attendant vicious habits. By reframing the diagnoses and behaviors as "obstacles," Martinez drew on new, reframed resonant beliefs to reconfigure his means for action reflexively (Dewey, 1922). Importantly, this reframing did not cure Martinez of PTSD, which is a physiological response; however, it motivated him to commit to treatment. Like moral injury, the readjustment required a search for and discovery of a new resonant belief that coincided with his all-encompassing warrior identity. In this case, the new resonant belief made the symptoms and manifestations of it appear more manageable; he was a warrior after all.

However, as with moral injury, there is an ethical dimension to consider. Unlike MSG Thompson, whose injuries barred him from future service, Martinez's PTSD—not to mention moral injury and other complications—manifested during his career. He had been diagnosed with PTSD and a TBI by a healthcare professional and had multiple serious physical and psychological wounds. Yet he continued his career until he was forced into a two-month inpatient treatment facility to address his PTSD and chemical dependency. The chaplain's advice may have had a "positive" impact on Martinez's coping, but it also kept him in the fight. It re-aimed him right back toward the mission objectives that resulted in his traumas in the first place. Whether done consciously or not, that chaplain thoroughly supported the military mission over Martinez's well-being. Religious guides and frameworks may facilitate more "successful" coping that benefits the military and an institution; that does not mean they are beneficial for the individual service member.

Belief resonance plays as strong a role in the PTSD story as it did in the moral injury one. The difference is that PMIEs were reframed as "good," while the PTSD diagnosis and the trauma leading to it had to be framed as "obstacles to overcome." Both approaches lessened dissonance and allowed for coping and more positive outlooks and affect. Despite tremendous trauma, Thompson and Martinez have been able to work consistently and were among the most warm and amiable veterans with whom I spoke. Their respective religious resources played a significant role in allowing them to cope with and make positive meaning of traumatic experiences and the military experience overall. The military's hand in supplying Martinez with religious and motivational frames that kept him in the service when he needed help much sooner reveals a significant ethical dimension to these stories, however.

In coping with PTSD, internal meaning systems appear more significant than participation in religious communities. CWO-2 Bush, who opened this chapter, reflected on how his PTSD prevents him from participating in a religious community because the sounds of children bring flashbacks. He reflected, "I'm still dealing with PTSD and I have regrets and shame for some of the things that I've done, but I know that God loves me and is proud of me. So, without that faith, then a lot of those other things would probably overcome my thoughts." Religious resources have been helpful in improving his outlook and affect by reframing his experience in a more positive light. Shaw et al. (2005) posit that religious participation benefits those with PTSD, "perhaps because it may lead to increased social support," but the most important religious factors helping trauma survivors improve "are the more intrinsic aspects of religiosity and spirituality because of the sense of meaning, purpose, and coherence that these may provide for people" (Shaw et al., 2005: 7). This held true for Bush. Despite an inability to engage in organizational religious activity, high intrinsic religiosity helped them to cope better with PTSD.

Religion and Military Sexual Trauma

Although there is significant scholarship on religion and trauma, examining religious coping or religious intervention with MST is less common, so we must draw on the growing body of work on religious coping and sexual assault among the general population. Some research suggests that both organizational participation and intrinsic religious resources have a beneficial effect on those who experienced MST. Chang et al. (2001) explain that those who have frequent organizational religious activity have better mental health and are less likely to have depressive symptoms. Moreover, private religious activity and intrinsic religiosity were "found to be associated with better mental health and less depressive symptomology regardless of the experience of sexual assault in the military" (Chang et al. 2001: 91). Contrary to some studies that show religious practices can exacerbate PTSD symptoms or moral injury, even when using positive religious coping, the scholarship on religion and MST suggests a largely positive relationship. The reasons for this difference deserve further study. It could be that scholarship on MST and religious coping is too sparse to have uncovered instances of detrimental effects, or it may be that the type of betrayal at the heart of MST and the questions that trauma raises for victims are distinct from the sorts of trauma or morally injurious events that are worsened by religious belief.

Gender may also be a factor. The military is "actively involved both in production and in reproduction of the established gender order"—that is, a hegemonic masculine order that honors toughness in spite of suffering. The military presents a challenging space in which women must navigate a professional service identity and a female gender identity. As linguist Joanna Pawelczyk (2014: 90) explains, "[W]ith its prevailing hegemonic discourse of masculinity, the military context puts women in a position of structural ambiguity. ... Thus women ... face a basic dilemma, i.e., whether they can be a soldier and a woman at the same time and not be viewed as deviating from what it means to be either." To do this, women service members construct a professional military identity that emphasizes "professional involvement," displays of "expertise," showing they are both "tough and agentive," "distancing [themselves] from the category of women," and rejecting "mental disorder" as a threat to professionalism (102–106). Passively enduring suffering is a means of maintaining that professional military identity. Moreover, religious beliefs, such as traditionalist evangelical emphasis on patriarchal hierarchies that prescribe female "submission" in the household (Bartkowski & Read, 2003)—not to mention the pulpit—can support it. Even if the women participants of this study do not engage in a rhetoric of "submission," it can remain a part of their religious cultural toolkit, motivating a habit of submission and internalizing trauma.

However, all the women veterans who revealed their experience of MST to me shared the belief that their faith played a positive role in how they managed their trauma. Flight manager Karen Black said, "[T]he Lord just protected me in certain situations because it could have been a lot worse, a lot, lot worse. At least I wasn't the one that was killed. You know?" She felt like being able to survive assault and years of harassment had everything to do with God. God had nothing to do with the trauma she experienced, but everything to do with surviving.

Similarly, Taylor Vaught found comfort in her faith. She recalled, "I've had to spend time with Jesus just going over it and letting God heal the wounds ... especially around the military and around the hurt and feeling betrayed. And I've had to go back and be like, 'Okay, God, in these situations, where were You when this was being said to me, when this happened? Where were You?' And He shows me where He was. And because of that, I can have peace." In these cases, their faith allowed them to feel comforted by a God present with them in their suffering. The divine was not the source of the trauma or the feeling of betrayal, so their positive religious framing allowed them to manage their trauma.

The women veterans who experienced MST were divided, however, on the usefulness of military religious resources, namely military chaplains, to aid them. On the negative side, there was Karen Black who felt military chaplains ignored her. Worse, Hannon recalled being forced to confront her attacker in front of the chaplain, which exacerbated her feeling of helplessness and trauma. In both cases, the women subsequently avoided military chaplains.

Conversely, Vaught sought out a chaplain after her experience of attempted assault and had nothing but positive experiences. She reflected, "The chaplain was very objective. I understand why—because he was a chaplain. So, I would go to church a couple times, and he was the only one I'd talk to that knew what happened really that was on my side and fought for me." Marine Lance Corporal Joy Harper, who also survived MST, similarly had a good opinion of chaplains. When her unit refused to acknowledge her assault or the ways she was being harassed, the chaplain stuck up for her. She recalled him receiving flack for trying to help her. "Those chaplains, they do a lot, they're pretty strong to deal with us Marines' craziness," she said. The chaplain may not have supplied her with explicit religious frameworks to work out her trauma, but he supplied support and advocacy, which likely came with religious foundations all the same. Religion, after all, works out in explicit and implicit ways in the military. As we saw in Chap. 2, variation in experiences with chaplains was common, and that was true of traumatic experience as well.

Military Chaplain Trauma and Religion

Along with isolation and the eventual divorce from his wife that followed, Ch. Williams' trauma shook his faith also. He reflected, "I disassociated from like reality to handle all of it. I thought that the military would, if I did a good job as a chaplain, that I'd have an easy life and family and stuff would work out, and it didn't. I really questioned God." The trauma stemming from his exhaustion and a persistent feeling that he could be doing more, the experiences that he saw that caused him to stay up at night with fear, the experience of returning to civilian life which shattered his identity, the experience of his wife leaving him while he served, and the experience of God betraying him despite his years of service all culminated in PTSD and moral injury.

Despite being a chaplain and never carrying or firing a weapon, he experienced trauma much like other service members I interviewed. Like those who were able to adapt their beliefs with new resonant ones, Williams put time into active religious moral work, and he began to read, especially works by Lutheran theologian and philosopher Paul Tillich. "I kind of felt like God disappeared, kind of like Tillich said and then God appears, and the God that appears, is a post-traumatic God, a God that wasn't bound by the morality of my pre-war existence. Sort of that new person has to emerge from that awful experience." This new outlook changed his whole understanding of theology and his relationship with God. It even changed his understanding of the New Testament as a "post-traumatic book written by traumatized people, traumatized by the crucifixion, the betrayal of Jesus and all those things." This new interpretation of God and Scripture allowed him to find peace with his faith, and he pursued a new Episcopalian ministry for a veterans' fellowship. He feels his new way of understanding faith has allowed him to meet veterans where they are. In his words, "trauma has a way of stripping away the crap that we've all believed to make ourselves feel better because the props disappear in those really extreme circumstances." His new framing had major creative potential for healing.

Conclusions

The military experience is one that likely exposes its service members to trauma. Looking at these interviews with post-9/11 veterans who once or currently identified as Christian, trauma is clearly present, and so is religion. As previous studies have shown, the link between the two is complicated. On the one hand, available religious resources can be the cause of distress, particularly when they motivate continued participation in violence. This was true in the stories of veterans who relied on military religious resources for counsel despite having experienced multiple traumas. In addition, some religious resources can exacerbate moral injury when they misalign with the realities of war. In many cases, however, religion provides service members and veterans with resources for mitigating, or even preventing, their trauma.

The experiences of the participants tended to corroborate scholarship that shows religious resources have salutary effects in mitigating symptoms of PTSD and comorbid outcomes like depression, anxiety, and the like (Koenig et al., 2018; Pietrzak & Cook, 2013; Hourani et al., 2012). Only in cases, like divine moral injury, where religious beliefs precipitated the trauma itself were religious coping strategies detrimental, even in the mediation of PTSD. These accounts of PTSD have also shown that an emphasis on a God who existed within the trauma as a co-sufferer in solidarity appeared to be a helpful frame for making meaning of trauma. An emphasis on God providing support for overcoming “obstacles” or preventing worse outcomes also appeared to be a helpful way to frame experience, although such a framing has a potential ethical dimension if it keeps service members in persistently traumatic situations.

Religion’s varied roles come down to a few key factors. For some, religious beliefs provide a meaning-making system for understanding experience. They were able to make sense of what happened to them by viewing their trauma through a specific religious lens. As with the stories of trauma among interviewed veterans above, trauma often triggers active deliberation—the discursive consciousness (Vaisey, 2009)—which may allow service members to find or establish resonance with beliefs and expectations. Perhaps the service member was not sinning; they were doing “good” work. Perhaps God put the trauma in their lives as an “obstacle” for them to overcome, as was the case with SFC Martinez. Religion could be used to justify actions, particularly potentially morally injurious ones, by showing that the warrior role was consistent with a Christian one. This use of adaptation through the discovery of resonant beliefs was common to both moral injury and PTSD experiences; however, there was a distinct difference between the two. In the first case, such resonant beliefs could potentially correct moral dissonance altogether, thus avoiding moral injury. By contrast, resonance could not cure PTSD, but it could reframe experience and lead to a more positive affect and coping.

Alternatively, God may have had nothing to do with the trauma that occurred, but He prevented a worse outcome, as was the case with flight manager Black. In the latter case, an emphasis on a traumatic God was important. This important shift from one of judgment of actions or questions of theodicy to one of God, or Christ, suffering along with the service members’ own suffering appeared to bring service members, like Black and Ch. Williams great comfort. At the heart of this theology is a shift from theodicy to anthropodicy; human action causes suffering, not God (Berger, 1967). Therefore, God suffers alongside humankind. It is what Ch. Williams referred to as a “post-traumatic God” and significant creative potential ripe for discussion in the Conclusion.

These last two chapters have remembered and retold the stories of trauma of post-9/11 veterans and explored how religion helps them navigate those experiences or, conversely, how it upends their cultural toolkits and relationships altogether. There was no monolithic story of trauma; however, we can begin to see these larger pieces snap into place. The military and religion are both significant producers of culture, implicit and explicit. Among the cultural objects they produce are beliefs, narratives, expectations, and justifications that have significant variance, often stemming from the origin of the resources (religion brought to or found in the military) and their goals. Those supplied by military culture and military chaplains are designed to and succeed at keeping service members in the military, performing their jobs. Indeed, this can look like a positive outcome—the service member preempted or mitigated trauma—but the result may be destructive.

Indeed, stories of trauma were of different kinds. Many did *not* report any trauma at all and worked through any PMIEs they faced without problem. Others did, however, experience moral injuries, MST, physical wounds, and they saw, heard, or perpetrated traumatic events, and those traumas led to the development of lasting moral injury, PTSD, depression, and suicidal ideation. At the end of their careers, new veterans then had to face the realities of returning to the civilian sector. In the experiences of returning home, religion again plays a part, and we can begin to see patterns of religious military narratives take shape.

Bibliography

Bagalman, E. (2011, July 18). *Suicide, PTSD, and Substance Use Among OEF/OIF Veterans Using VA Health Care: Facts and Figures* (Rep. No. R41921). Retrieved https://deploymentpsych.org/system/files/member_resource/2011_CRS_Suicide%20PTSD%20and%20Substance%20Use%20Among%20OEFOIF%20Veterans%20Using%20VA%20Health%20Care%20Facts%20and%20Figures.pdf

Bartkowski, J. P., & Read, J. G. (2003). Veiled Submission: Gender, Power, and Identity among Evangelical and Muslim Women in the United States. *Qualitative Sociology, 26*(1), 71–92.

Berger, P. L. (1967). *The Sacred Canopy: Elements of Sociological Theory of Religion.* Doubleday.

Besterman-Dahan, K., Barnett, S., Hickling, E., Elnitsky, C., Lind, J., Skvoretz, J., & Antinori, N. (2012). Bearing the Burden: Deployment Stress among Army National Guard Chaplains. *Journal of Health Care Chaplaincy, 18*(3–4), 151–168.

Chang, B. H., Skinner, K. M., & Boehmer, U. (2001). Religion and mental health among women veterans with sexual assault experience. *International Journal of Psychiatry in Medicine, 31*(1), 77–95.

Conard, P. L., Young, C., Hogan, L., & Armstrong, M. L. (2014). Encountering Women Veterans with Military Sexual Trauma. *Perspectives in Psychiatric Care, 50*(4), 280–286.

Cornish, M. A., Lannin, D. G., Wade, N. G., & Martinez, M. (2017). Can Use of Positive Religious Coping Predict Greater Distress? An Examination of Army Soldiers on Deployment. *Journal of Counseling Psychology, 64*(3), 302–309.

Dewey, J. (1922). *Human Nature and Conduct: An Introduction to Social Psychology*. Henry Holt & Company.

Finley, E. P. (2012). *Fields of Combat: Understanding PTSD among Veterans of Iraq and Afghanistan*. Cornell University Press.

Fontana, A., & Rosenheck, R. (1999). A Model of War Zone Stressors and Posttraumatic Stress Disorder. *Journal of Traumatic Stress, 12*(1), 111–126.

Hourani, L. L., Williams, J., Forman-Hoffman, V., Lane, M. E., Weimer, B., & Bray, R. M. (2012). Influence of Spirituality on Depression, Posttraumatic Stress Disorder, and Suicidality in Active Duty Military Personnel. *Depression Research and Treatment.*

Kelly, U. A., Skelton, K., Patel, M., & Bradley, B. (2011). More Than Military Sexual Trauma: Interpersonal Violence, PTSD, and Mental Health in Women Veterans. *Research in Nursing & Health, 34*(6), 457–467.

Koenig, H. G., Youssef, N. A., Oliver, R. J. P., Ames, D., Haynes, K., Volk, F., & Teng, E. J. (2018). Religious Involvement, Anxiety/Depression, and PTSD Symptoms in US Veterans and Active Duty Military. *Journal of Religion and Health, 57*(6), 2325–2342.

Koenig, H. G., Youssef, N. A., & Pearce, M. (2019). Assessment of Moral Injury in Veterans and Active Duty Military Personnel with PTSD: A Review. *Frontiers in Psychiatry, 10*(443), 1–15.

Levy, H. C., Conoscenti, L. M., Tillery, J. F., Dickstein, B. D., & Litz, B. T. (2011). Deployment Stressors and Outcomes among Air Force Chaplains. *Journal of Traumatic Stress, 24*(3), 342–346.

Litz, B. T., Stein, N., Delaney, E., Lebowitz, L., Nash, W. P., Silva, C., & Maguen, S. (2009). Moral Injury and Moral Repair in War Veterans: A Preliminary Model and Intervention Strategy. *Clinical Psychology Review, 29*(8), 695–706.

Maguen, S., Turcotte, D. M., Peterson, A. L., Dremsa, T. L., Garb, H. N., Mcnally, R. J., & Litz, B. T. (2008). Description of Risk and Resilience Factors among Military Medical Personnel before Deployment to Iraq. *Military Medicine, 173*(1), 1–9.

Mittal, D., Drummond, K. L., Blevins, D., Curran, G., Corrigan, P., & Sullivan, G. (2013). Stigma Associated with PTSD: Perceptions of Treatment Seeking Combat Veterans. *Psychiatric Rehabilitation Journal, 36*(2), 86–92.

Murdoch, M., Polusny, M. A., Hodges, J., & O'brien, N. (2004). Prevalence of In-Service and Post-Service Sexual Assault among Combat and Noncombat Veterans Applying for Department of Veterans Affairs Posttraumatic Stress Disorder Disability Benefits. *Military Medicine, 169*(5), 392–395.

Park, C. L., Smith, P. H., Lee, S. Y., Mazure, C. M., McKee, S. A., & Hoff, R. (2017). Positive and Negative Religious/Spiritual Coping and Combat Exposure as Predictors of Posttraumatic Stress and Perceived Growth in Iraq and Afghanistan Veterans. *Psychology of Religion and Spirituality, 9*(1), 13–20.

Pawelczyk, J. (2014). Constructing American Female War Veterans' Military Identity in the Context of Interviews. *Women & Language, 37*(1), 87–112.

Pietrzak, R. H., & Cook, J. M. (2013). Psychological Resilience in Older U.S. Veterans: Results from the National Health and Resilience in Veterans Study. *Depression and Anxiety, 30*(5), 432–443.

Shaw, A., Joseph, S., & Linley, P. A. (2005). Religion, Spirituality, and Posttraumatic Growth: A Systematic Review. *Mental Health, Religion & Culture, 8*(1), 1–11. https://doi.org/10.1080/1367467032000157981

Surìs, A., Lind, L., Kashner, T. M., & Borman, P. D. (2007). Mental Health, Quality of Life, and Health Functioning in Women Veterans. *Journal of Interpersonal Violence, 22*(2), 179–197.

Vaisey, S. (2009). Motivation and Justification: a Dual-Process Model of Culture in Action. *American Journal of Sociology, 114*(6), 1675–1715.

Wood, D. B. (2016). *What Have We Done: The Moral Injury of Our Longest Wars.* Little, Brown and Company.

CHAPTER 7

Coming Home and the Evolution of Religious Identities

In 2005, Staff Sergeant Trey Underwood found himself in Iraq after years in telecommunications. He had a new job as a convoy operations leader, which provided "personal security" for his battalion between bases but exposed him to "death and destructions" beyond his imagining. He "had a hard time seeing God where [they] were," and it shook his faith. Medically discharged a few years later, the military forced him from the job he assumed would last his professional life. His transition back to civilian life was challenging. He felt he was "expected to come right back to civilian life and act like everyone else," but civilians did not understand the military experience. Outside the military's relentless pace, he had newfound time for reflection. Combat trauma affected his marriage, and vicious behaviors consumed him. "I did not know who I was anymore," he said. "We have a tendency to get caught up in things like we are what we do, we are what other people say we are. And, especially for folks who wear the uniform, when that uniform is taken away, a lot of times, we don't know who we are after that." His identity had been wrapped up so tightly into the role of a National Guardsman, perhaps especially after his trauma, that without it, he did not know what was left.

The military provides tangible resources for active components of the military, but veterans often feel abandoned after they leave. Of course, Veterans Affairs (VA) programming exists and has close to a quarter

T. H. Suitt, III, *Narratives of Trauma and Moral Agency among Christian Post-9/11 Veterans*,
https://doi.org/10.1007/978-3-031-31082-9_7

trillion dollars in funding (US Department of Veterans Affairs, 2020). But program reach and availability vary, and some veterans report bad experiences and attitudes about the VA overall (Britch, 2020).[1] Underwood was one such veteran. He reported being unable to find programs that made meaning of his combat-related trauma—his self-described "soul wounds"—and his feelings of abandonment.

He eventually found a 12-week program outside of VA health care that claimed to attend to those very soul wounds he described. The program helped. It adjusted his thinking about God's role in war, reframing his experiences and adapting his theological understandings from ones he described as "binary" to ones that emphasized a post-traumatic God in a sinful world. Underwood "reclaimed" his faith. This reclamation allowed him to form a new identity as a Christian. "It took me a while to really believe that being a child of God was really what my identity was, and it was sufficient—that there didn't need to be anything else added on to that." The new identity did not compete with other ones. "There's not a distinction or a compartmentalization. My faith now permeates through my whole life, through what I do in my career, and the relationships I have, and everything else. It's all one thing." His identity became one infused with faith, allowing him to reframe his military experiences and find a new community and meaning. He now works for the group that changed his life.

My interview with SSG Underwood revealed a complex narrative of identity. Competing roles and solidarities took different hierarchical positions in his life amid the disruptive military experience, notably when he returned to civilian life. The existential threat of combat experience destroyed the religious toolkit he previously relied upon, and leaving the military upended his sense of self entirely. An adaption of his religious frames to understand his experience and ameliorate his dissonance helped him reshape his sense of self post-service into a new robust one with a religious identity working in tandem with other role identities as a husband and a professional and others. However, his is just one narrative trajectory among many.

This chapter will explore the final piece of the narrative: the role of religion in the lives of veterans returning to the civilian sector. A trauma of

[1] Of the Iraq and Afghanistan Veterans of America (IAVA) members who are enrolled in VA health care and programming, only 54% rated their experience as good or excellent. The remaining 46% rated their experience average to poor.

its own, returning to civilian life brought a loss of meaning and identity for many service members. The loss of applicability of a consistently reinforced and practiced warrior identity and military *habitus* left them unsure of their place in society, leading to a hellacious transition. Religion often played a part in helping them manage, although many abandoned their faith for good, especially as moral injury began to manifest. With the overarching military religious narratives delineated, we can explore the typical patterns of narrative trajectories. This narrative approach will explore how post-9/11 veterans manage different cultural toolkits while navigating among different identities, particularly as a warrior, Christian, and civilian. The trajectories reveal an evolution of religious identity formed and reformed during the arc of a veteran's life, shining a light on how religious belief and moral commitments transform over time.

The Difficulty of Returning to Civilian Life

Reintegrating into civilian life was difficult for most of the service members with whom I spoke. Thirty-seven of them reported having a difficult time making the transition back to civilian life. Only ten said that their transition back into the civilian sector went smoothly. By proportion, the participants in my study had a more difficult time returning to civilian life than those reported in Pew Research that found only about 44% of 700 surveyed post-9/11 veterans felt this way (Morin, 2011: 9). In that study, the contributing factors to a difficult transition were numerous. The leading characteristics were whether the veterans experienced a traumatic event, were seriously injured, were married while serving,[2] served in combat, or knew someone killed or injured. IAVA's (Britch, 2020) recent study similarly found that 40% of post-9/11 veterans reported facing challenges upon transitioning, pointing to a loss of identity and purpose, an inability to relate to non-veteran civilians, difficulty in readjusting to social life, mental and physical health concerns, and difficulty in navigating VA benefits. These trends point to how military experience can make returning to civilian life difficult for veterans.

Many of my interlocutors called returning to civilian life "the hardest thing [they've] ever had to do." As service members transition, they face an incredible challenge of reintegration amid the psychosocial stress of

[2] The study suggests this surprising factor is likely a result of marital strain during deployments.

losing their role identity as members of the US Armed Forces. Anthropologist Zoë Wool explains that the difficulty of this transition stems from American society holding veterans simultaneously as symbols of American moral exceptionalism, violent actors, and non-citizens. The transition, then, is one "marked by instabilities wrought by the incommensurability of being publicly bound to war while moving toward an anonymous American good life to come" (Wool, 2015: 189). Resolving that tension takes time. As Green Beret Marcus Russo explained, "You don't come home and just reintegrate. It's not like you come back and be, like, 'Oh, I'm out of the Army. Okay, good, tomorrow I'm going to wake up and be a civilian.' This is a year or years-long process."

The most significant difficulties by far, however, were the loss of identity, attendant culture shock, and the loneliness this created. The ways of being that marked their behavior and attitudes for years, their *habitus*, had no place in civilian society. Their habits and expectations were not just interrupted by the transition to civilian life; they had no apparent use in it. Often, religious resources that were readily available to most service members while in the service were unavailable upon coming home. SSgt Underwood explained, "The tough questions came after I got home from Iraq and of course there were no chaplains to be found." Finding and joining a new community presented new challenges when faced with the onset of trauma and mental health disorders. Twenty-nine of my participants reported an identity crisis upon reintegrating into the civilian world. There were feelings of rage, withdrawal from the high of being in combat, and disappointment at losing a feeling of worth or power. Life was different.

New veterans must wrestle with the after effects of military experience while managing the severe culture shock of reintegrating to civilian life's slower pace and their new role in it. Foremost among these changes to identity is the loss of status and power. Journalist David Wood (2016: 222) explains, "[F]or some, leadership in wartime, responsibility for a few soldiers or hundreds, is the high point of a lifetime. Yet that skill, and the authority it conferred, seem to belong back there in the war; here at home the sergeant is just another guy nursing a late-night beer." This loss of purpose and importance can precipitate a feeling of a loss of identity. Losing that sense of meaning can make veterans "feel duped or disillusioned and [they may] reject the meaning systems that made them feel part of something bigger than themselves" (Brock & Lettini, 2013: 49). An Army CSM Sam Griffin, for instance, explained to me, "it was very hard for me to transition from being the person who told people what to do and expected exceedingly high standards of execution and mission accomplishment to be involved with failure on a daily basis." Once in charge of hundreds of soldiers in the Army, now working alongside young people who had never been in the military and did not understand his high-ranking position, left him frustrated and distraught. It is difficult for veterans to return to civilian life with none of the clout their position previously conferred or the sense of purpose their role provided.

The loss of identity can also be enhanced by feeling like an outsider to the civilian community. Particularly among combat veterans, there is a feeling that a "tightly closed circle of insiders and outsiders [exists], insiders for whom one is willing to die and outsiders who will never understand the horrific conditions under which that willingness was tested" (Brock & Lettini, 2013: 70–1). Most veterans who had a difficult time reintegrating back to the civilian sector revealed feeling like an outsider and that civilians could not understand what they went through. This was true of those in both combat and support roles among my participants. Army combat veteran Franklin Rivers explained, "Coming back home, again—and this is corny, but this is just my way to say it—there's no lollipops and rainbows out there. Everything's just a blank slate, and no one understands you except those who have been there. Lot of anger, lot of drinking, just trying to cover up and mask things at the time." He isolated himself from the world around him and had difficulty connecting with non-veterans, who could not understand him.

Whether or not a service member experienced a traumatic event, the military experience engrains a new identity in the individual, regardless of their role. Through intense training carefully designed to separate recruits from the civilian world, service members inhabit the warrior identity and enter the military structure by way of a rite of passage (Turner, 2008: 94–5). After that military identity has had centrality, reintegrating into the civilian world can make a veteran feel like an outsider, and they can come to question their identity. Either they remain an outsider, maintaining a warrior identity without the role or responsibilities that helped define that identity, or they must learn to adopt a new identity. This search for a new sense of meaning, while dealing with trauma, isolation, and feeling like an outsider, can create an identity crisis. Theologian Jan Grimell (2018: 193) posits, "[A]s military personnel leave military service the story of who I am calls for a reformulation of self-identity, and this transition initiates some type of narrative identity reconstruction that impacts the self." Grimell emphasizes the transitions veterans must make between different

"I-positions," what we can understand as navigating between different identities, warrior and civilian.

This transition is challenging because the warrior identity can have such centrality. Often the warrior identity, which is engrained in service members from the start of their service, becomes all-encompassing. Military culture produces, inculcates, and reinforces that identity at every turn—even in the religious resources it supplies. Those other identities brought to the service take a backseat to the central identity that finds "success" in the military context. Upon returning to the civilian sector, that identity has less applicability.

Moreover, extensive military training and culture remove individuality and promote unit cohesion and obedience. Upon leaving the military, those norms of behavior make reintegration difficult. The same skepticism of mental health care involved in stories of service members and veterans avoiding a PTSD diagnosis can mean that new veterans avoid help-seeking when transitioning to civilian life. Bryan and Morrow (2011: 17) show how the warrior identity prevents new veterans from seeking mental health care. A military culture that "values strength, resilience, courage, and personal sacrifice, [and] ... inculcates an identity of elitism and superiority" motivates warriors to shrug off injury and illness. If warriors are told continuously, like Special Forces SFC Martinez told his subordinate, "to suck it up and get back in the fight," it is "not difficult to see how a warrior who admits to mental health problems and seeks out mental health care might view these actions as signs of weakness" (Bryan & Morrow, 2011: 17). By holding onto the warrior identity, veterans avoid receiving the help they need, whether due to trauma or an inability to reintegrate smoothly.

The loss of identity and the culture shock of returning to civilian life left service members reeling. As these psychosocial stressors built, many sought other avenues to self-medicate far from VA or civilian mental health and counseling services. At least 12 of the participants reported *years* of drug abuse, alcohol abuse, or dangerous behaviors. Alcohol use disorder affects roughly 7% of veterans overall (Williams et al., 2016), while substance abuse disorders affect roughly 11% of all veterans who use VA health care (Teeters et al., 2017). Rates of alcohol and substance abuse have continued to rise in the past 20 years. This behavior likely extends from habits learned in the military itself. A survey of over 16,000 active-duty military personnel found that about 43% of them engaged in binge-drinking, or drinking five or more drinks for men or four or more drinks for women in one sitting (Stahre et al., 2009). Facing the realities of their trauma post-service, veterans rely on superficial salves for PTSD, moral injury, survivor's guilt, or anger over forced retirement.

Within this new reflective time, PTSD and moral injury begin to manifest, affecting their civilian lives in numerous ways. As all my results show, the military experience is undoubtedly disruptive, particularly for relationships with spouses left at home. Fifteen of the thirty-six veterans I interviewed who were married before or during their military service ended up getting divorced. While combat experience did not appear to be a factor in whether veterans were divorced, trauma did. Every veteran I spoke with who went through a divorce had experienced trauma, whether mental, physical, or both. This squares with Wang et al.'s (2015) study that found divorce and mental health issues associated with trauma (like PTSD) were causally linked among military personnel along with risky behaviors and vice indulgence.

Still other veterans felt unable to participate in faith communities due to a loss of belief in God or feeling like outsiders to moral communities. Lasting moral injuries and trauma upended their meaning-making systems right in the period when such tools could have creative value. The transition home affected their religious engagement, even while it provided new opportunities for it.

Many service members bring anti-individualistic tendencies, destructive masculine cultural frames, and untreated trauma back home to the civilian sector. With the warrior identity still deeply habituated, military cultural tools remain embedded in the new veteran, but they have little use in the civilian world. The loss of status and purpose couple with a realization that the military identity that defined their lives for years is a mismatch for daily life. It is in this transition that reflection on experience takes place, precipitating moral injury if it had not already occurred.

Manifestations of Moral Injury and Post-Service Religious Resources

Moral injury only sets in after a veteran can reflect upon their experiences, and military culture and the high operational tempo of military life often make deliberation and self-reflection difficult, if not impossible. When it is time to reintegrate into civilian life, suddenly, there is a tremendous amount of time, and this is the space when moral injury—and PTSD for that matter—finally arise if they had not already. The potential for moral injury and disrupted moral and religious relationships, then, extend well beyond the actual time of service.

When disruptions in a personal moral narrative do not meet with a cultural account providing strategies for justification or self-forgiveness, the individual can feel unworthy of participation in religious communities. If the situation of moral injury is itself a moment of "anomy," the absence of a guiding sense of moral order (Durkheim, 1933; Berger, 1967), then the absence of a moral community suggests a disruption in the plausibility structure that had made the service member's life narrative coherent. Service members feel that their lack of morality bars them from participating in a moral community, which Litz et al. (2009) have shown to be a common effect of moral injury. This inability to participate with a "pure" community because of one's "impurity" exacerbates a sense of moral chaos, along with feelings of guilt and unworthiness. This echoes Putnam et al.'s (2012) finding that for most Americans, it is a break from traditional religious morals that leads to disaffiliation, rather than disillusionment based on science or even political affiliation. For these veterans, the gap between the religious beliefs and practices service members had available to them and the moral world they experienced was simply too great.

As service members' careers came to an end, some retained a lingering moral problem that needed working through, often years after suffering the moral wound. Seven were unable to reconcile their dissonance. For instance, Paul Callaghan, a former Small Kill Team (SKT) Sergeant, accessed new religious resources after experiencing physical and moral trauma. He had a difficult time participating in moral communities after leaving the service. In his words, "I guess when you're responsible for taking another human's life, and you're trying to figure out, 'Where do I fit in? As a sinner, or a killer?' Whether it's self-defense or just one-offing somebody, it's really hard to understand how you can be accepted for being a terrible human being." He had serious doubts about his moral character as a combat veteran and felt he had lost a piece of his humanity by betraying his sense of right and wrong. This personal betrayal precipitated a break from moral communities and accompanied years of dangerous and self-destructive behaviors.

However, between men's groups and worship services (establishing new relationships), he says, "I understand now that I don't understand, I don't have to understand everything to know that God had a hand in it, right? I'm not angry with anybody or anything anymore. I accept myself, and all my shortcomings, and it's contributed to who I am today."

Callaghan certainly had access to the religious frameworks the military provided and would even have his SKT pray before missions, but he admitted Christianity was not for him at the time. It was not until he realized he had a problem that needed solving that he sought new beliefs, practices, and relationships. By receiving new explicit cultural moral frames, Callaghan was able to find resonance. He solved the haunting salient issue of his moral injury—am I a "terrible human being"?—by finding a new resonant belief in Christian faith that he deployed and redeployed (McDonnell, 2014), thus ameliorating his dissonance.

Civilian religious communities were instrumental. Veterans who had been betrayed by superiors found paths to forgiveness, even for those who had wronged them. In Iraq, Taylor Vaught, an Army recovery specialist, experienced both MST and organizational moral injury during her seven years of service. She was hit in the head with a tank wrench by a superior officer after moving some recovered vehicles that her superiors had decided to leave out on display. "They decided that the vehicles covered in our friends' blood basically and body parts need to sit where everybody can see as they walk by," she said. "And I wasn't having it." After being evacuated from Iraq due to her injuries, she said she felt the military removed her to keep things quiet. In her words, "they decided I have a mouth, I'm going against chain of command, I'm causing problems. If they just get rid of me even though other people had done wrong, then it's more hush, hush." This was organizational moral injury, or a feeling of betrayal instigated by a superior officer or the military organization.

While not religious at the time of the trauma, she found Christianity years later after wrestling with destructive behavior and reflecting angrily on her time in the military. Like Callaghan, she found herself in a church with a persistent minister. She felt like "God kind of really relentlessly pursued" her. Despite her efforts to "shock" the minister, he continued to welcome her, and she is now a missionary. In reflecting on her organizational moral injury, she says, "I've had to spend time with Jesus just going over it and letting God heal the wounds and fix my identity crisis, especially around the military and around the hurt, and feeling betrayed." She says she now feels "peace" and has even found forgiveness. "'God, this happened because they didn't know who you were, and I didn't. And it was a really bad situation.' And everybody was just trying to get out alive." Finding faith and finding access to a resonant religious moral narrative completely reframed her reflections on her military experience.

As novel problems arise in trauma, issues surrounding personal or organizational moral quandaries (i.e., the act of killing or the moral responsibility of leaders) gain salience, engaging a visceral need for narrative coherence (Guhin, 2016; Dewey, 1922). Those who bring a repertoire of religious moral understandings to their service are challenged to find coherence, integrating military religious discourse to account for the disruptions of moral dilemmas. As a result of the military's insistence on high operational tempo and a culture that devalues critical forethought or reflection, dissonance is likely. For those who sought moral discourse while in the military, social interactions with religious guides and communities reinforced military operational goals and resonated with military life. However, those who postpone this moral work until after military service can find resonant cultural packages that do not aim them at military strategic goals. Rather, they can provide new creative tools for the individual that can reframe experience and supply new beliefs and moral expectations that make sense of the past but support a civilian identity.

As we have seen, resonant beliefs found in or after the military provide a post-hoc justification (Vaisey, 2009) for action that guides future accounting of the morally injurious event (Winchester & Green, 2019). The post-hoc justification corrects the perceived breakdown in a significant relationship (with self, superior officer, military organization, or God). This motivates future action, but it is not military action. Instead, it is the act of maintaining coherence in a narrative of moral order. Among the veterans I interviewed, religious resources found after military service, like those found in the military, were likely to incorporate elements of the military religious world. Unlike resources found in the military, however, the new post-service beliefs do not aim for military strategic goals (Waggoner, 2014). The apparent goal of civilian resources found after service is forgiveness and solidarity instead, motivating change and adopting a new religious cultural toolkit.

Post-Service Religious Practice

Having established the trauma of returning to the civilian sector and the ways religion can sometimes reestablish coherence in a narrative post-service, we can now investigate the varied ways post-9/11 veterans interacted with religion in the years following their military careers. It is notable, for example, that there was an overall decline in organizational practice after military service, with only 28 continuing to attend church services after returning to civilian life. As was evident in stories of trauma, many veterans lost their faith even while others discovered it for the first time. This section will explore the kinds of religious communities and practices service members found or continued to practice after leaving the service, revealing a mixed picture of the lasting influences of military religious culture in their lives.

The specific denominational affiliations service members brought with them to the military were often not the ones they found after the service (See Fig. 7.1). The number of those who claimed no religious affiliation doubled from six to twelve, marking the effects of traumatic experiences and shifts in ideology for service members during their careers. By contrast, the number of evangelicals grew significantly, increasing by eight,

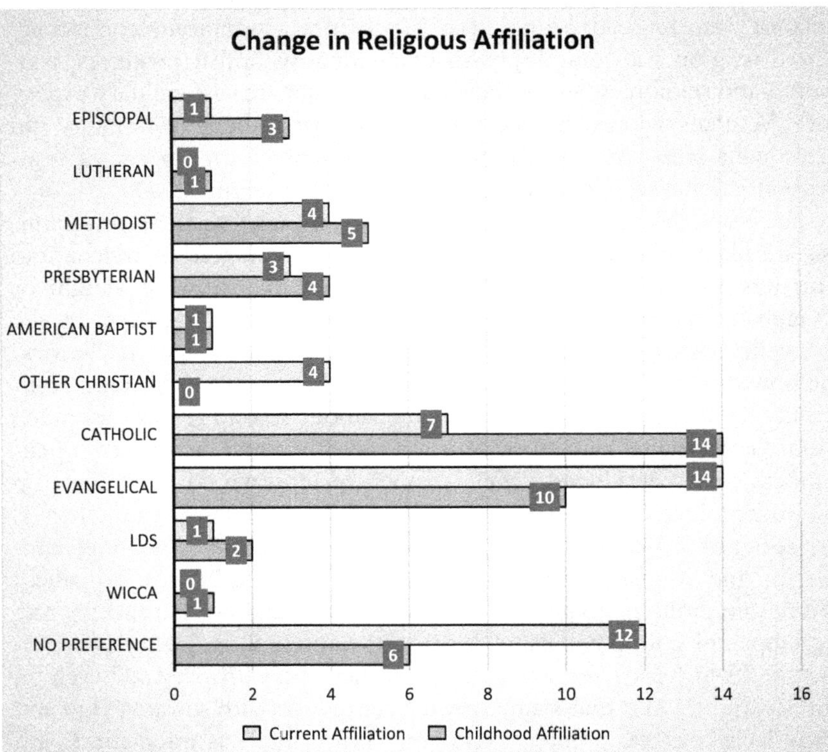

Fig. 7.1 Change in religious affiliation

while only two previous evangelical practitioners lost their faith. These shifts were also noticeable in the changes in their reported religiosity; their organizational and non-organizational practices increased along with a sense of intrinsic religiosity.

Among Catholics and Mainline Protestants, there was some switching tied to significant relationships like spouses, but the majority of those who found religion or converted ended up in evangelical communities. It raises the question of what about evangelical traditions is attractive for service members. Why do service members and veterans find themselves in evangelical settings, even, in one case, like mechanic Taylor Vaught, becoming a missionary and traveling all over the world to proselytize? The answer is the same as the reasons why evangelicalism (and ideologically conservative congregations) were more readily able to motivate military service in the first place. It is also the same for why evangelicalism has such a foothold in military chaplain leadership today. It provides a significant community where religion has centrality with one's identity, and it produces, promotes, and reinforces beliefs and values that resonate with military experience. Veterans who experience trauma find a sympathetic community and a resonant faith. As Ch. Sandberg had described the appeal of non-denominational services in the military, "it honors them."

The evangelical practice of proselytization means that these communities are likely to seek out veterans and to be experienced as welcoming. This was an essential aspect of trauma stories, like those of Vaught or Callaghan, that mentioned persistent ministers welcoming them to the evangelical community. It was a story also echoed by George McClintock, the now former-Wiccan service member. He met a man in his local community named Alex, who was "very much about Jesus. He was very much about God and just being forgiving and accepting, and he was very open-minded." They developed a friendship where Jesus would often come up in conversation. One morning, McClintock bumped into Alex. "Just as I'm about to reach for the door, here comes [Alex] at the same time, coming in, and it just stopped me dead in my tracks." Alex explained, "Something told me to get up, and I needed to get down here to the coffee shop, so I got up and came down to the coffee shop." They sat down to talk. "And I said, 'So, you're going to take me with you to church on Sunday, right?' And that's kind of what started my faith towards God and Jesus." Calling the moment "very, very powerful," his interaction with Alex motivated him to attend church and commit himself to an evangelical community, of which he is still a part today.

Many service members found evangelicalism during their careers because evangelicals had good outreach programs for military members and were so welcoming; and it was no different after the service. Interestingly, evangelical veterans also tended to join or even start veteran small groups to solidify a community further—for instance, Sgt. Paul Callaghan started a men's group that advertised fixing up old cars and creating a Christian community. He wanted to recreate his own experience where God was "leaving breadcrumbs to find Him." Callaghan glowed while discussing his group; "I meet guys every Thursday who aren't believers, who just want to come and try to build a hot rod, and then they hang out for dinner, and then all of a sudden they're telling me, 'Look, man. I haven't talked to anybody in ten years. I've got walls up, I've got this up, but I feel safe with you." This readily available path to community appeals to veterans.

Of course, one did not have to be evangelical to discuss the importance of and benefit of finding a community post-service. Marine engineer Andy Hannon, who became Catholic after leaving the military, highlighted the importance of community. "When I was in the Marine Corps, it was just me," he explained; "Church and I were not the best of friends." After leaving the service, however, he felt a loss of identity and a need for community. His wife insisted he convert to Catholicism, and he went through a confirmation course and became more involved in the community. Upon reflection, he said, "When you're deployed overseas, you're away from your family with whatever the people around you were doing and you lose a lot of yourself. You just concentrate on the job and what's going on; you don't get much free time." He did not feel he even had time for religion while deployed, but not having a community weighed on him when he returned to civilian life. "When all of that stuff is over, once you get back to normal life, you start looking for those things that were making you whole again and … those things that were making you happy and making you whole was just going to church and visiting with people with similar faith and experience. Yes, just that community, I guess." Although he had PTSD and questioned his Lutheran faith from his childhood, the Catholic community he found with his wife helped him feel part of something again. It allowed him to reclaim his sense of self, his identity.

Unlike those who found themselves part of a religious community after service, others experienced an inability to find a religious community, which presented problems. Some felt that they were unwelcome. Still others felt that they could not find the "right" congregation because the community did not have a good veteran outreach program or because the new community's values and teachings did not align with theirs. Veterans reported seeking out community but failed to find one that resonated with their experience or their warrior identity, leading to isolation. Franklin Rivers, an Army cavalry soldier, explained that it has been hard to remain engaged with religious groups since leaving the military, even ones aimed at veterans. He described a PTSD program at his local VA that was run by a Christian chaplain that was too "sensitive" for his macho demeanor. "When you go to these meetings for PTSD, these group sessions, they're very much about, 'Well, let's talk about your feelings,' or, 'Now it's your time, Jim or John, to talk about how you feel.'" Rivers scoffed and said, "Well how about …." He laughed. "They start going into questions you've asked about religion and stuff, and part of you wants to go into that religion and get back with God and whatever—your religion or your beliefs—but let's do it on a soldier's level, like my level." Rivers' dissatisfaction with religious communities was representative of veterans who still claimed affiliation but had not found new religious communities that could capture their warrior identity.

We have seen how resonant beliefs and frames play an essential part in navigating the military experience, but community plays a significant role in veterans' lives as well. Religious communities in and out of the military provide a sense of belonging and purpose. They provide social, moral, and spiritual capital (Ammerman, 1997) as well as shared beliefs, myths, and rituals (Wuthnow, 2013), attendant with a feeling of being saved. However, the difference lies in whether civilian communities can support their identities in ways that overlap with their military experience. For some veterans whose religious identities, or even their warrior identities, do not have centrality, this is not a barrier to entry unless life events or new traumas activate the need to be deliberative about those parts of their *habitus*. For those who have a difficult time, like Rivers, who still claims a Christian affiliation but no longer attends services, it is clear the issue is finding a community that resonates with the military identity he still maintains as a veteran. Unlike the religion readily supplied by the military or found in Christian communities with veteran outreach programs or veteran-led programs like Sgt. Callaghan's car restoration Christian group, communities can be unsupportive of the military cultural package, creating competition between cultural spheres.

Veteran Religious Narrative Trajectories

Having investigated the religious toolkits of veterans, their practices and beliefs, the story of religion in the lives of post-9/11 veterans should now be clear. As a producer of culture—of meaning-making frameworks and moral norms and expectations—religion is often *challenged* by trauma, but it is also often *sparked* by trauma. For many, no trauma occurs, yet the military experience inescapably affects their beliefs and practices. There is not a monolithic narrative that accounts for the role of religion in their lives. This section will propose seven common patterns of narrative trajectory that describe typical life cycles of post-9/11 veterans who once or currently identified as Christian. The religious military narrative trajectories I propose are not static images of a singular identity. They are co-constructed expressions of common themes and mechanisms at work with the various narratives the veterans shared with me. Therefore, while some of the stories share pieces in common, they are ultimately representative of different patterns of religious identity influenced by military experience. These stories represent the ongoing narrative the veterans carry with them today.

The benefit of these narratives is being able to see who these individuals were before, during, and after their military service. Importantly, storytelling accounts for identities taking place in non-institutional locations. As we have seen, religion happens beyond church, and military culture and frames certainly go well beyond a FOB's boundaries. A person's narrative, however subjective, can capture a more robust understanding of identity because it allows us to follow the individual's use of frames through different times and spaces publicly and privately.

The different narratives presented in this chapter come from only a handful of individuals, but they represent "a broader social experience or positionality [that] illuminates a symbolic framework or historical event or process" and reveal "how agency can operate at that locus" (Maynes et al., 2008: 128–9). This approach is interpretative rather than predictive, but it gives us a window on understanding post-9/11 Christian veterans' common life patterns.

In the following pages, I will hone in on these key religious military narrative trajectories by exploring seven case studies that are emblematic of the larger identity patterns. I chose these stories from the 47 veteran interviews for several reasons. First, they were often the most representative of the other veterans that shared similar narrative trajectories. Second, they had distinct voices and were open to sharing their experiences with me in great detail. Finally, they include variation in experiences. The following narratives come from individuals with different jobs (combat and support), ranks (officers and enlisted), years of service, branch of service, and denominational affiliation.

The following narratives will also follow a clear pattern in terms of narrative structure, and this is to capture a "typical" life cycle for a military service member. These different yet consistent episodes in the emplotment of their life stories provide "the logic and syntax of narrative" that will allow us both to make sense of the relationship between episodes and to evaluate and prioritize events and "render meaning to them" (Somers, 1994: 617). With the previous chapters as a base and the new information about the role of religion post-service above, this chapter can make sense of the ways trauma and religious resources impact the life of a veteran. As these are co-constructed narratives, I will insert myself throughout their stories to point out significant patterns in their religious military narrative trajectories, emphasizing how different trajectories compare.

In brief, the seven religious military narrative trajectories I observed in my sample were as follows: *Religion Maintained amid Trauma*, *Religion Adapted amid Trauma*, *Religion Maintained Absent of Trauma*, *Religion Found Post-Trauma*, *Religion Found in Community*, *Religion Lost in Trauma*, and *Religion Lost to Irrelevance*.

Religion Maintained amid Trauma: Thomas Meyer

In the late 1880s, the Swiss Army realized soldiers carrying their ubiquitous service rifle, the Schmidt-Rubin, required a screwdriver to disassemble and clean, but they also needed a way for opening canned rations. Instead of carrying around multiple tools, the Swiss Army contracted a design for one tool for all the necessary tasks common to their soldiers' daily needs. This was the Swiss Army Knife, a universal resource for handling day-to-day problems in one compact package. Like that iconic knife, veterans who maintained high religiosity amid trauma used their religious resources as a universal tool for navigating the disruptive experience of military service. During unsettled times, they could use their faith as a tool, a religious cultural package, for navigating the military experience. It provided the necessary justifications and beliefs to overcome what was, for others, a significant source of dissonance.

These veterans tended to have high religiosity, particularly intrinsic religiosity, stemming from their religious communities before joining. During their service, they maintained high religiosity privately and publicly. At a minimum, attending organizational religious activities was common, though depending on location and job, this was not always possible. They tended to find chaplains invaluable in times of trauma, although if a chaplain did not pass muster for their level of theological understanding, they leveled harsh criticism. They experienced traumatic events, yet the trauma did not shape their religious identity. Instead, their faith allowed them to navigate it effectively, mitigating symptoms. The civilian reintegration process remained challenging, but their religious resources, again, helped them through that experience, allowing them to enter the civilian sector more easily than those without the same resources.

One illustrative example of this trajectory is the story of Thomas Meyer, a Military Police (MP) officer in the Army Military Police Corps who served for nine years. Meyer was raised Southern Baptist and recalled going to church "all the time" growing up, which impacted his sense of morality and community. "The way we was raised and brought up, you always helped your neighbor … just like the Bible says. Help one another and be there for one another instead of turning your back and walking away, like a lot of times they do nowadays," he said. From an early age, he felt a commitment to serving others and being a good community member. Other service members who shared a similar narrative agreed that religion shaped them as people. Usually rooted in Mainline and evangelical congregations, religious culture played defining roles for how they understood the world and how to behave.

"I come from a long line, a family," Meyer said of why he wanted to join the military. "My grandpa and all of them, been in the military. They was drafted of course. My dad was drafted. … [And] I wanted to go to Iraq. I wanted to see what it was like. I just wanted to see how good I was and see if I was good enough." With a history of family members serving and a desire to see what he was made of, Meyer "went straight and joined." Like Meyer, others joined because of a family history of serving in the military, while others felt they needed to course-correct their lives and sought opportunity, or felt a patriotic duty to serve, particularly after 9/11. Overall, these reasons for joining are not unlike those found in national research (Pew Research, 2011; M. Thompson, 2016). A history of family service, patriotic duty, education benefits, seeing the world, and finding direction were the most common reasons for joining.

Training was very intense. "It was mentally and physically hard," he said. He received additional specialized training to become MP. "They break you down mentally and physically … to make sure you adapt to be one of the best." To uphold the law in the military and "go over there, where they spit in your face or whatever they may do to you. To be able to look at them and keep your post and be respectful to them and do your job and then come home alive … it was very rough." He felt it was all necessary because he had to be the example as MP; he had to be the best. That difficulty, however, was too much for some of his fellow cadets. "I've seen guys in my basic training, within the first few weeks, trying to kill their self or trying to find a way out because they couldn't handle it. … They pulled their shoelaces out, tried to hang their self or do whatever they could." Breaking down the cadets was necessary to forge them into the best of the best, but a breakdown of their civilian identity came at a cost. Believing suicide was the only way out, some of Meyer's fellow cadets felt trapped.

Meyer relied on his faith to get through training. Chapel was a real comfort for him and his peers. "If we could go, I would go," he said. "When you walk into church, you felt a peace and camaraderie, and a knowing love and caring and concern was there." It was the only avenue for peace during the intensity of training, and it brought him and his fellow cadets closer. "When you're training five, six, seven days a week … rushing around, trying to figure it out, there's not very much peace, obviously, you're trying to make sure you do everything right because you don't want to fail." There was little downtime or room for reflection or "tranquility," so the chapel services were the oasis amid the gauntlet. Those with a similar narrative universally spoke about chapel as an essential time for worship and finding comfort. Where other trajectories emphasize chapel to get a break, these cadets were there for worship, not merely escaping, highlighting the centrality of their religious identity even as a new military identity developed.

In addition to chapel, faith was his foundation. "Excuse my language, but what it all comes down to is when shit hits the fan, you know you've always got one thing reliable, and that's … always been God." He would read the Bible and pray when he had a few moments of downtime. "Jesus told Peter in the Bible, you know, 'Build your church up on the rocks. The gates of Hell can't prevail against it.' And I remember that verse. That's all I referred back to. I knew I'd go back to church, or I knew God was going to be there. He's my rock," Meyer said.

After training, Meyer maintained his faith during his career; however, a three-month training mission to Egypt tested it. He was working security for COs visiting national landmarks, and the Egyptian military was supposed to protect him and fellow MPs. Meyer and his team wore civilian clothes and were not supposed to have any weapons on them. "Well, we had one concealed weapon we wasn't supposed to have, and if they'd have found out, we'd have probably been in a big bunch of trouble. We was in a close encounter more than once … and never knew while we were there if we'd make it out alive." The fear shook Meyer; he felt his faith was strong but wanted to make sure if the worst happened that he would know exactly where he was going. With an Iraq deployment ahead, he decided to ramp up his church attendance. "I didn't think I was coming home alive [from Iraq]. I straightened myself up, got in the Word, and I did what God would ask of me." Despite growing up Southern Baptist, he had not been baptized. After returning stateside, he was. All the participants with this trajectory increased their religious practice following trauma. Religious toolkits helped them navigate dissonance and maintain their faith. PTSD was still possible, but their religious toolkit helped them navigate it. Their religious identity remained central, and trauma reinforced belief.

While deployed to Iraq, Meyer drove Humvees between FOBs. The threat of fire or IEDs was constant, and he had to once again rely on religious resources to navigate persistent fear. "I was the last vehicle on a convoy," he remembered. "That was usually the last place you wanted to be because actually that's the first vehicle they're going to try to take out because that's the last vehicle you notice is gone. … If they do it right, then it's too late." In these incredibly tense drives, he constantly prayed for strength. "That may sound crazy to you, but when you're … a last Humvee in a convoy, and you get scared, you hesitate, you forget to hit that gas, or you forget to hit the brake when you need to because you're scared of dying. That could be your life or somebody else's life. Where my faith with God was, I was not afraid to die. I knew that he had me, so to speak." Confidence in his salvation helped him perform his job well, preventing more dangerous situations. Other trajectories will show the impact of dissonance between competing identities; Meyer's religious and military identities had consonance, however, allowing him to perform his job. Others with similar stories reported similar justifications; they felt their religious resources supported their job, particularly regarding the protection of fellow service members.

Meyer did not question the morality of the war itself or his actions, which included the use of force. "There was a reason for it. … If we ain't over there keeping them busy, they would come over here and keep us busy. I'd rather be over there, where I'm trained to take care of them." Keeping civilians safe at home was the central justification for military participation. After all, he was trained to make choices that civilians did not. Better to perform his job than to risk endangering loved ones at home, it was a belief that resonated with his religious commitment to serve others. This logic extended to the use of force and emphasized the need to protect loved ones over any hesitation about his actions. "It's easier for me to just say, 'I did what I had to do at the time to take that life,' than have to come home and say, 'Hey, I was trained to bring you home. I didn't bring you home because I thought for .5 seconds and didn't squeeze the trigger like I was trained to do." The thought of wasting time to think critically was unconscionable to Meyer. He would rather do anything to bring his fellow MPs home. "I'm taking my guys home," he said. "I'm sorry, but that's just the way it's got to be."

In late 2006, Meyer left the military after inhaling an unknown substance during his time in Iraq. "I got messed up over there. I don't know what happened to me. They never told me." He was heartbroken at the prospect of going home. He intended to make a career of the military but now found himself "learning how to breathe again." He spent the next 11 months in the hospital with nothing but his thoughts and feelings of survivor's guilt. "I was planning on being tough and strong and sticking with them." He began to tear up. "I didn't. I had to come home. … It's evident there's stuff wrong with me, [but] … that's not an excuse where I come from. It's hard for you to quite understand." He developed severe PTSD. "Being in war, you don't know who's going to take your life. … You've got to be aware of your surroundings at all times." The constant fear response made living in civilian society difficult. "You're jumpy. You watch your back. You're trying to make sure nothing happens, and a lot of people don't understand that." He said relatives were supportive since many were prior service members, but he had a hard time interacting with civilians and even the woman he had married.

Meyer had married a young woman toward the end of his time in the service and had two children. As his PTSD became worse and remained untreated, he turned to "stuff [he] shouldn't have been doing." His wife did not understand, and she filed for divorce. This devastated Meyer, and the situation escalated. "I got accused of trying to kill her," Meyer said. He was found guilty and sentenced to seven years in prison.

Meyer's military identity was so important to him that he was unsure of who he was without it. His injured vocal cords and his PTSD stemming from the trauma he faced abroad made his transition home extremely difficult. A mismatch between the belief that he would be career military and the reality that he was no longer an MP led to cognitive dissonance. This heightened his PTSD, precipitating alcohol abuse and violent behavior. However, that dissonance did not come from his religious beliefs; it came from incoherence in his expected life narrative. He did not question his religious identity, and he credited his faith for keeping him alive through the tragic wake-up call that the incident initiated. "I was still close to God. I found I got closer to him, too, at the time. I have thought about that and reflected back on that a lot because of being sick and stuff. I see people turn up blaming God for that, and these episodes of stuff, but I've never blamed him. I've never cussed him for it." Even in the face of prison time and losing his marriage, Meyer felt his faith allowed him to navigate rock bottom. "My faith always come back to God. I never turned my back on Him. He's always been there for me. That seven years of prison that I did was still a blessing because God was there to help me get through that." Those seven years provided him time to grow in his faith.

After getting parole a couple of years ago, Meyer has had difficulty starting over in life. Being on disability provides some money, but he struggles to pay bills and cannot leave the state, making joining a new church community difficult. "I go to church, but I am not really … I've got a newer church I've been going to," he trailed off. "A lot of people know who I am," he said. Feeling unwelcome at church has created tension in his life. He received support from chaplains and social workers in prison that he now cannot access. However, he insists his faith remains strong. "I learned through prison life that we need to go step forward and not be the tough one anymore." Meyer had the most difficult time after leaving the military of all the participants with a similar narrative, but they all maintain high intrinsic religiosity. Even in the face of trauma, their religious identity was not, at least in the telling of their story, shaken, and it remains strong to this day. Perhaps even more importantly, none of them blamed God for their trauma. Their religious meaning system was never the source of dissonance, and they maintained a consistent sense of their moral selves even amid disruption. They wielded their religious resources like a Swiss Army knife, finding the right tool for every occasion to navigate their lives.

Religion Adapted amid Trauma: Owen Gray

Other veterans found homegrown religious resources incongruent with military experience, marking an impasse when participation in violence sparked dissonance. In these cases, service members needed to adapt, and they did so by either reestablishing moral coherence or learning to compartmentalize, as we saw in the stories of moral injury. They could replace a dissonant belief with a new resonant one, or they could learn to separate religion from moral questions. These adaptations to the disruptive military experience were usually spurred and fortified by military religious resources, where military religious authorities tacitly absolved service members of perceived sin. Where veterans with the *Religion Maintained Amid Trauma* trajectory generally did not doubt their souls when faced with PMIEs, those who adapted their faith maintained it by learning to separate or adjust, as though they needed to change out the tools of their Swiss Army knife to make it better suit their needs.

Marine Colonel Owen Gray is an example of this trajectory. Raised "in a very poor home on a mill hill in a mill house," church was an escape from the doldrums of a Southern "speed-trap town." He went to a traditional church where "to be saved, you had to be saved as Christ was saved, which was to be immersed under the water." Gray frequently attended before joining the military but said it did not "dictate" his life; his parents were religious and instilled that in him and his sister. "It helped me develop some morals that I tried to carry through with me in life. I didn't always follow them, but they were always there." Most who told this story came from Mainline and evangelical denominations before joining, although there was some variation with one LDS member and one Catholic. Moreover, they agreed that religion played a large role in how they were raised and their sense of morality. For them, religion was a source of comfort and a guide for how to treat others.

With few prospects for Gray other than factory work, he looked to the military as an escape. "I wasn't like the kid who, his whole life, said I was going to join the military, and that was my goal in life, but I wanted to go to college, and quite honestly, that was the only way ... because we didn't have the money." Although Gray made high marks in school, the military was a means to get an education. He had no reluctance to joining and obtained a Marine Corps scholarship to go to college, "which is the hardest to get and very competitive." He attended a military academy on track to become a Marine officer. "I didn't plan on spending a career in there, but I ended up doing so," he said. Gray served for 24 years. Those who shared this life trajectory had varied reasons for joining the service, which will be true of all the trajectories moving forward.

As an officer, Gray had significant training. He went to boot camp, trained during his four years at the academy, and attended OCS before commissioning as a Second Lieutenant. Each level of training was more challenging than the last. Boot camp was the easiest; "it was watered down, slowest as the slowest man type mentality." The academy was "more difficult than boot camp ever thought about being." OCS was "an attrition type environment where they want to weed people out." He transformed over the course of his training from a small-town boy to a Marine. "You're ingrained," he said; "it's Marine Corps, Marine Corps, Marine Corps, Marine Corps all day long. Everything is mission-oriented." He left his civilian identity behind but maintained his religious resources from home. Taking on the military identity was common to all the participants with this trajectory. They often mentioned being directionless before joining and ruminated on how the military experience gave them a sense of importance and professionalism, guiding future behavior.

Initially, Gray was a logistics officer, which suited him. "In the Marine Corps, everybody wants to be an infantry officer. Well, I didn't care to be. I didn't really care to go shoot at people or be shot at. Not that I was afraid of it, but it just wasn't what I really wanted to do." The thought of making decisions about the use of force was untenable for Gray. As a Logistics Officer, he oversaw support roles and provided essential resources to keep infantry running smoothly. "I would have an army under me with all the armors and all the weapons, and I would have motor transport and … supply fell under me. Even the chow hall fell under me to be responsible for making sure all the assets were not only prepared, ready, fixed, and operational but that they got delegated out effectively and efficiently." He enjoyed his work. Importantly, it kept him out of combat, which was the point.

He first resigned in 2000, but then 9/11 happened. "I quit my job and went back into the Marine Corps, so I was one of *those* guys. I thought it was the right thing to do." Again, he began as a logistics officer, but he was eventually forced to become an infantry officer. "In the Marine Corps, every officer is what we call unrestricted, so they can make you go do any job they want to make you go do." He was not afraid of the change, but it presented new challenges: life or death decisions for combatants and civilians. Gray's first combat deployment to Iraq presented moral dilemmas immediately. On convoys, he began taking fire, which forced him to return it. "In a lot of cases, our enemy would put women and children out as barricades. They would literally hide behind women and children and shoot at us, and what do you do? You return fire and suppress their fire, and you protect your Marines. But at the same time, you take a chance and likely will kill civilians." He had moments of providence. "At times, I would choose to hold off fire and just hold my breath to get through the ambush zone, and when I wouldn't have any casualties, I knew that God had helped me with that. God had given me the guidance to hold out fire." Other times were harder. "When I would suffer casualties, or … return[ed] fire into areas where I knew that civilians were likely to be harmed, that was something which was hard to live with." Those experiences shook Gray. He was not sure how to move forward. "I saw a lot of things that I never wanted to see, never expected to see and did things that I didn't really want to do." He was only ever supposed to be a logistics officer.

He sought out a military chaplain and attended services to pray with them for "guidance to do the right thing" in unsettled times. The hierarchical structure of the military demanded he "maintain this stoic appearance and not let [his] men know that [he] had the same issues and the same internal conflicts they did," but chaplains shared similar rank. Gray could lower his guard with them. One chaplain became a close friend, and that chaplain's counsel boiled down to this: "You're doing the right thing, and sometimes you have to make decisions and just, again, look internally and do the right thing. And if you do the right thing, then whatever happens, God will understand, and God will forgive you as long as you're doing the right thing and asking … God for help." This reframing of his work as good work resonated with Gray, and he adapted to his combat role, finding forgiveness for perceived sins when collateral damage occurred. Veterans with this narrative shared similar stories of reestablishing moral coherence while others adapted by compartmentalizing religious moral beliefs about killing, focusing instead on military frames like protecting others, or committing to the mission.

The chaplain's counsel helped Gray, and his faith grew. "I did become a little bit more religious at that point in time. I kind of sought out God for some advice and … felt closer to Him during that time." New resonant beliefs helped, but they did not necessarily remove all doubt when new challenges arose. "We would be in locations and would have to paint targets for aircraft to come in and drop ammunitions. Every time, you're praying that … there's not going to be a lot of civilian casualties associated with your having ammunitions dropped on that target." A difficult balance between doing his job and considering the lives of civilians remained. "It's difficult. It's difficult to balance the self-preservation and caring for your Marines and, again, those ethics and the protection of civilians." Moral dissonance and identity conflict required consistent moral deliberation through the triggered discursive consciousness. He simultaneously had to embody the Marine identity while also struggling with dissonant Christian moral frames.

Nevertheless, the words of his chaplain had an impact. "I felt like we were doing the right thing for those people, and sometimes, yes, there were inadvertent consequences. But I believed that we … not believed. I know that what we were doing was the right thing." Besides, he was a good man otherwise. "I didn't go steal. I didn't cheat. I tried to be a good person and abide by the rules of the Bible." If his actions in the military created dissonance, at least an emphasis on social imperatives that did not compete with his warrior identity brought him comfort.

In 2018, Gray resigned. Coming back to the civilian sector was not easy, although he believes he had an easier time than others. He had to "adjust to having a family and doing all those things" after being in the Marines' mission-oriented culture. "I felt like I did okay. Some guys have a hard time," he said. Actually, the months following and between combat deployments were much more challenging than his long-awaited retirement. "I had some baggage," he said of the first time he returned from a combat deployment. "I had some scarring, and I had a tough time. … I won't say a tough time, but there was some tough times but not anything like … People paint this picture about how you come home and all you want to do is sit in the shower and think about killing yourself. I didn't find that to be the case." He had persistent nightmares and unwanted memories, but "where [Gray] had some difficulty … it wasn't' difficulty that [he] couldn't easily overcome." Since retiring, he has had an easier time reflecting on his career and reintegrating into civilian life. He began going to a non-denominational church as well and still actively prays to God for guidance. Admittedly, those prayers are for less morally harrowing situations. He prays to "be successful in something that [he] didn't have experience in" or "to help [him] with [his] family and so on and so forth." Religion still plays a "big role" for him, but he emphasized feeling self-reliant.

Among the veterans with a similar story to Gray, there was variation in how easy it was to return to civilian life. Some participants did not resolve the dissonance until coming home, having chosen to compartmentalize religion while they served. They had not sought a religious authority during their time in the military and left it for reflection later. In those cases, reintegration into the civilian sector was exceedingly difficult, especially with the unmaking of the military identity. It was not until they were able to seek out a religious authority at home that they could resolve their cognitive moral dissonance. Those like Gray, who found resonant beliefs in the military, had markedly easier times transitioning to the civilian sector because they maintained narrative coherence.

In hindsight, Gray has continued to reflect on his time in the military and his views on faith. "I believe that what I did was what God would want me to do. I believe I helped a lot of people. Above and beyond combat, I can't tell you how many kids I've fed and how many generators I've had my Marines fix for local towns and fixing water supplies, just all these things that you lose sight of." He has come to focus on all the good work he did. That has helped him reflect positively on his experiences and overcome the trauma he experienced during his combat deployments. By focusing on his job's positive impact, he has reframed his military experience as wholly beneficent. He felt that religion helped him navigate the different spaces between being a Marine and being a civilian. "Adapting from being a Marine leader and having to make decisions and decisions that sometimes you don't want to make and then adapting back to being a father and a husband and all of those things, I definitely think it helped me to kind of keep things in perspective," he concluded. He maintained his Christian faith throughout his life, but his religious resources looked different. He had to learn to adapt to military experience, replacing beliefs with resonant ones. Religion was a tool for navigating trauma and the transition from civilian to Marine and back.

Religion Maintained Absent Trauma: Lou Granger

Much like the first narrative trajectory, participants that shared this story maintained their pre-service religious resources through the military experience. The critical difference was that trauma never tested their beliefs; instead, they reasoned through hypothetical situations if such moral deliberation occurred at all. In the absence of trauma, they maintained a consistent level of religiosity throughout their lives. While there was variation in religiosity, the majority had moderate to high levels and had much to say about how religion impacted their military lives. The veterans had little in common regarding rank, length of service, affiliation, and other factors. What tied them together was the absence of trauma. They were in roles that did not require frequent combat and did not significantly shift religiosity due to a collapse of its plausibility structure.

Army medic Captain Lou Granger shared this trajectory. Her father was a Protestant Army chaplain, so she had consistent exposure to both military culture and military religious resources. Raised in the Evangelical Free Church of America, she was also exposed to religious beliefs and practices at her Presbyterian school and while visiting her "favorite" grandmother, a devout Catholic. The different forms of Christianity melded together, developing habits of self-reflection and critical thought about her faith. She credits her grandmother with having the most significant impact. "She had a lot of influence on me and my faith and how I saw faith." This exposure to Catholicism motivated her to attend St. Mary's College at Notre Dame and convert to Catholicism for a time. "I found a lot of peace and comfort in the liturgy," she said. She felt committed to "contemplative prayer and meditation," which helped her reevaluate and maintain her religious toolkit. While she is now and has been an Episcopalian for years, she pointed out, "I'm also a Christian who does yoga." She continues to find novel ways to grow in her faith. All the participants with this narrative type talked about religion shaping them regarding morality or a commitment of service.

Granger did not want to join the military at first—"number one because I don't like to run," she joked. More seriously, she reflected on her experience growing up with a father in the Chaplain Corps. "It just did not seem like it was for me. I mean I'm fairly quiet, fairly reserved." Having a real pulse on military culture and expectations, she did not imagine herself fitting into the military world, but attending a private college like St. Mary's required money that her father did not have. "If you want to go to a private school," he had said, "you have to get a full-ride scholarship somewhere, and ROTC might be the only option for you." The ROTC program at Notre Dame did not require a student to pay back a scholarship during the first year if she determined being in the military was not for her, so she could participate in ROTC for one year without penalty. The attack on the World Trade Center changed everything.

Her father deployed almost immediately, ministering to Special Forces operatives in Operation Anaconda, during which the US sustained a high number of casualties. When her father returned home ahead of her high school graduation, he officiated a memorial service for the service members who lost their lives. Granger attended. "I met a soldier who had lost his leg, and he just wanted to get back to his guys. And just meeting him and talking to him, he was just so dedicated … to his friends and to the people that he served alongside." The interaction inspired her. She needed to take her ROTC scholarship seriously and remembered thinking, "You know, they need good leaders, they need people who do have a moral core and can share that with them, … maybe if they can give so much and still have more to give, I should be able to give four years and suck it up and learn how to run."

The religious resources on Notre Dame's campus were immense and always available. They had chapels in every dorm and mass at every hour of the day. She "liked the liturgy" and the "radical feminist nuns." When she arrived, her father was thrilled by her decision to pursue military service, but her own beliefs and the religious resources provided by St. Mary's conjured up doubt. "A lot of my professors had a hard time with it," Granger said. One professor, a Quaker, asked Granger to come by her office. She had worn her ROTC uniform to class for the first time. As a pacifist, her professor was concerned about what Granger could be ordered to do in the service. "She asked me to … really think about what I was doing. And I told her I was, and I always would. And she was like, 'You just don't know what could happen to your soul while you're there.'" The interaction shook Granger, but her active deliberative approach to faith helped her settle the dilemma. She chose to join the Army Medical Service Corps to stay out of combat. "I ended up being Medical Service Corps partly because the Medical Service Corps mission is taking care of anyone who comes into my clinic. I felt like I could get behind that."

Moreover, she came to terms with what she would do if she had to fire her weapon. "My dad always told me that if you're going to carry a weapon, you have to be ready to use it." The thought of killing someone, however, was unconscionable to Granger. "I don't really have a killer instinct at all, and I don't believe that killing is a good thing ever, so I did have some moral struggle." Granger remembered thinking, "hopefully I won't have to fire my weapon, and if I do, it'll be to defend my patients and to defend my soldiers." Her role in the violence would not be one as the aggressor but as the defender. "I had to just always break it down to a smaller level of a mission of service. I had the mission of taking care of people who came to my clinic." Questions about the use of force were secondary to her mission of service. "At the end of the day, we've got to take care of each other, and we have to do what's right on our level." Luckily, she never had to fire her weapon. Both the enlisted and the commissioned service members who fit this narrative tended to be in positions that required little to no combat: medic, social worker, honor guard, civil engineer, and others.

Granger graduated ROTC and was commissioned as a second lieutenant as an ambulance platoon leader for a striker team. She soon switched positions, deploying with the 62nd Medical Brigade in a medical support company where she was a treatment platoon leader at Golby Troop Medical Clinic at Camp Victory in Baghdad. It was a Level 2 treatment facility, a reasonably large clinic with ancillary services, labs, and a pharmacy. She then moved to a clinic she helped set up in the International Zone at the Ibn Sina Hospital. She spent her last year in the military as a battalion staffer, rising to the rank of Captain.

During her career, she noticed she was no longer the introverted young woman she once was. She remembered a soldier seeing her in civilian clothes saying, "Ma'am, I could tell you're an officer anywhere." "What do you mean?" she replied. "Because of how you walk," he said. She laughed, recalling the interaction. "I mean you do, you change. You have to be confident and you have to speak clearly, and I probably didn't have that confidence … in high school or in college." Being an officer gave her newfound confidence, and how she walked and talked changed to match this new military identity, informing a new *habitus*. The military identity gained centrality. Without traumatic experiences to create any identity conflict or dissonance, Granger and those with similar stories were able to maintain their religious identities without a problem. The threat of traumatic exposure remained hypothetical, and she could embody the military identity alongside her religious one without a problem.

She maintained a high religiosity, but her religious expression changed due to her authoritative position. "I probably didn't talk about [my beliefs] super openly, but I know that I did talk about them … where it felt like it was okay." She did not want to proselytize and so kept her beliefs private. However, one soldier's neck surgery occasioned more openness. Previously vocal about his atheism, she felt "he wanted to tell [her] that … to see what the reaction was," but she remained respectful of his beliefs. However, she felt that being more vocal before his surgery was appropriate. "He came to me one day and he said, 'Ma'am, I don't have anyone to be my emergency contact. … Can you be my emergency contact in case something goes wrong?'" His family life was a mess, and she felt that showing support would be meaningful. She acquiesced but with one caveat. "I'm going to be praying for you whether you like it or not." To her surprise, his response was "Ma'am, I really appreciate that." Calling herself a "servant leader," she explained, "I believe that Jesus was a great example of servant leadership, so I try to model my style as a leader after that and focus more on serving my soldiers and … my patients." Her emphasis on servant leadership allowed her religious and military identities to work in tandem.

Access and quality of military religious resources abroad varied. Camp Victory had a chapel within walking distance; the Iraqi hospital in the International Zone did not. Chaplains were available, but she—and others with this narrative—did not seek them out. Her high religiosity, constant self-reflection, and lack of trauma made chaplains less important. Besides, she did not have confidence in some of their abilities. She knew higher ranking chaplains through her father, but she disliked the approach of newer chaplains at her clinic. One event stuck out. After a vehicle rolled over near Camp Victory, two Gurkha soldiers were rushed to her clinic. "It was pretty gory. One of them had brain matter you could see, and he didn't make it." Afterward, a chaplain came to speak with her soldiers. "He seemed scared and like he didn't know what he was going to say. … But we had also never seen him before. I don't think anyone ever took him up on [offers of counsel] because they hadn't seen him before, and they never saw him after. You know what I mean?" She was angry and blamed the lack of open discourse about these and similar events on inconsistency in chaplain quality, experience, and availability.

Overall, Granger's deployments bolstered her faith, especially her call to prayer. "The clinic is hard because you're so busy, you're just going, going, going, and I would try to find those moments where it was quiet. … In a way, you're kind of constantly praying, you know, when something happens. It's in the back of your mind, 'Take care of my guys. Watch over my soldiers'" This constant call to prayer helped her maintain her faith through her four-year commitment, and this was true of all the participants with a similar trajectory. They participated in faith communities when possible, but prayer was the most consistent religious practice.

Her service complete, Granger returned to the civilian world. Like so many, she found the transition difficult, even absent trauma. It was the culture shock and the loss of authority. She attended graduate school, and her classmates "were straight out of undergrad [and] had never even worked. And I had come back from Iraq with a lot of responsibility … more responsibility than a normal twenty-five-year-old would have." Her "very naïve" peers did not understand her or her experiences. Without someone to empathize with her, she experienced a loss of identity. "There is a lot of your identity that's wrapped up in 'I'm a captain and this is what I do,' and all of a sudden, I don't have my rank on me anymore. I'm just a woman in our society." As in other trajectories, transitioning to civilian life proved difficult for most, yet this group included the most stories of people having an easier time. She found an Episcopal Church to help ease the change. "I would just go and sit in there and try to pray [and] find direction because I really didn't know what I wanted to do, where I wanted to go." She was attracted to the congregation's candlelit compline services that "had chanting." New practices were powerful and helped her find a new path forward. She remains an Episcopalian today. While most with this narrative returned to religious communities, some did not. They felt that, without the stress of military life, everything was going well. The need for comfort and prayer diminished; habituated private practice made church attendance feel unnecessary.

Absent trauma or consistent dissonance between identities, these service members maintained faith through the military experience even if practice and belief evolved as part of that maintenance. In fact, this trajectory feels the most akin to a civilian one. Generally, American adults maintain their childhood faith if raised by one or more religious parents in mixed and single religion households (Pew Research Center, 2016: 19–25). Over half of all people maintain their childhood faith, and only about 15% become unaffiliated if raised Christian (Pew Research Center, 2009). This is also true of emerging young adults who maintain their childhood faith 50% of the time (C. Smith, 2003: 282), even if ebbs, flows, and disruptions were common. When the military experience is less disruptive, service members tend to follow general population trends.

Religion Found Post-Trauma: Hunter Doherty

In 2019, scientists noticed a peculiar kauri tree stump west of Auckland. Astonishingly, the old fallen tree was still alive despite not having green foliage to survive. Testing the stump for waterflow, they discovered that neighboring trees were feeding it at night when water's typical evaporation movement is lowest. Those surrounding trees kept the stump alive, helping it maintain waterflow when it could not do so alone (Scully,

2019). Much like the kauri, veterans who experience trauma must rely on community and meaning-making resources to survive. Trauma can precipitate vicious behaviors, used as superficial salves for unseen wounds, and post-service reintegration can be near impossible, straining relationships and exacerbating suicidal ideation. For those with this narrative trajectory, the lifesaving resources of faith found for the first time in communities and beliefs post-service provided necessary waterflow. A new salve for their trauma, Christian faith allowed them to recontextualize their experiences, provided paths to forgiveness, and established participation in new communities.

Hunter Doherty was one of those. Raised by a single mother, Doherty's lack of a prominent father figure shaped much of his youth. Equating anything his mother valued as feminine—including her faith—he sought alternate sources for meaning. "I chalked her faith up to a feminine characteristic, not a masculine one, because I was looking … for what it took to be a man." He did not practice Christianity; it could not provide the masculine identity he sought. Instead, he relished "male affirmation" in football where his coach once pulled him in front of the team and said, "Attaboy! Why can't the rest of you hit as hard or run as hard as this guy?" The affirmation experience from a man he respected changed his life. From that point on, he did three sports every year. It became his "crack, his addiction." By contrast to sports, religion played little part for him growing up, and others with a similar trajectory agreed. Religion was insignificant in their upbringing. They had little exposure to religion or, if they did, felt it was forced upon them. Despite not connecting with childhood religious influences, they claimed Christian values played a role in shaping morals, citing the Ten Commandments and the value of community.

Doherty joined the military two weeks after high school. It was the only way out. "I had no prospects for college, no scholarships. I had this thing inside me that told me I was meant for greater things." The service members he knew in his life had "honor" and "cultivated … inner masculine traits." That emphasis on the soldier as professional stems from a military identity James Griffith classifies as the "soldier warrior." Emerging identities in the post-conscription era motivated the military to make "concerted efforts to alter the image of the soldier … as being a 'professional.'" Raising the bar for new volunteers, this professionalization presented military life as one of "exceptionality" rather than "commonness."

Warriors were now a separate and "desirous class of people" (Griffith, 2009: 264, 272). Doherty wanted those characteristics.

Once at basic, he recalled looking around and determining who had fathers growing up. "They had no desire to fight," he said. "They had this quiet assurance, this self-confidence in themselves, that they'd received from their fathers." By contrast, Doherty found himself constantly wrestling and peacocking alongside inner-city kids who, like him, did not have positive father figures. "We were fighting each other to prove to one another who was tougher and who was more masculine, and we were allowing ourselves to define what masculinity was to us." He worked tirelessly to receive another "Attaboy!" from drill sergeants and judged those around him who appeared weak or took training less seriously. Deeming chapel on Sundays "not very manly," he would "sneer at the guys who went because [he] thought they were only going to get away from extra work duty." He focused on coming in first instead, and the warrior identity was easy to accept and embody. Religion remained undesirable and unmasculine.

Over his two-decade career, Doherty had multiple roles. Beginning in Air Defense Artillery, he became a Special Forces medical advisor after five years. Following 9/11, he transitioned to a combat role, deploying to Iraq during Operation Ugly Baby, where he risked life and limb alongside Green Berets and Kurdish soldiers. He eventually switched to counterterrorism and hostage rescue under Joint Special Ops Command (JSOC) but eventually finished his career training other Green Berets in urban warfare.

His roles demanded tireless dedication. If he was not eating, training, or on a mission, he was sleeping. He functioned on a reverse schedule, waking up at 4 PM to eat "breakfast" before working out. By 6 PM, he and his men were in operations planning that night's mission. "Our last mission was always contingent on sunrise, and our aircraft always had to be back over friendly skies by sunrise." He would plan backward from there, stopping at sunset as the official start time of a mission. When they were not running missions, they trained and competed to keep up their skills. "In Special Forces, you're considered a professional. It's big-boy rules." Physical conditioning was paramount for effective missions along with extensive work in "urban combat, tactics, room clearing, building clearing, urban movement," and more. They needed to be the best; their survival depended upon it. He maintained an "offensive mindset" on rotations that typically lasted 90 days, during which he would do 90 missions.

"I would hit the ground running, and I would do at least one mission every night, sometimes two or three a night."

The high operational tempo prevented reflection. Even if his men were wounded, he kept their minds focused on the mission. "Now, bud, you took a round to the arm. Let me throw a tourniquet on there and a pressure dressing really quick." He would get them to a FOB, "have him sit for a week, get his Purple Heart … and we'd get him back out there on a mission because we didn't want him alone in the hospital and have too much time to think." This process continued year after year, mission after mission. Between deployments, his wife would tell him, "you're already deployed." He replied in terse phrases. His head remained elsewhere. "You always had the next thing to think about, and you had no time to reflect on the morality, the spiritual scarring, that was taking place and building up in your subconscious, in your heart." Rather than reflect on the "brothers that [he had] lost," he thought of "the brothers that [he] could potentially lose." He pushed on harder and harder for years.

The participants who shared this trajectory experienced trauma but buried their soul wounds, leaving moral work for later. By then, "dealing" with trauma came in the form of vice behaviors and avoidance. Sandra Whitworth (2008: 122) proposes that this avoidance is a byproduct of the fatalistic masculinity of military culture that views admission of trauma as "contagious." "Once hypermasculine men begin to experience and share feelings of fear and horror, the myth of the heroic soldier warrior is seen as groundless. This may be a more terrifying idea than PTSD." Admitting to trauma threatens the warrior identity, leading to dissonance. However, not addressing the trauma precipitates risky behaviors and exacerbates mental health issues.

Coming home did not include the banner parade Doherty imagined. "When the curtains closed and the play was over, I found myself sitting at home, … and I'm realizing I had ten fingers and I had ten toes. And I had always believed, firmly, that I would die in one of these places like Iraq or Afghanistan." He imagined, too, that the military would call him and say how much they missed him, how they had "made a life-size memorial statue" of him. That never happened. What did happen was "guilt and shame" over his surviving. "Maybe I didn't try hard enough. If I tried harder, I would at least be missing one limb."

Without a mission, his soul wounds floated up to his consciousness, and he did not have the means to manage them. He self-medicated with "a half-gallon of tequila a day." Persistent nightmares prevented sleep, and he spent days blacked out in front of 24-hour news with "no idea what they were saying." His life was fog and came in flashes. His wife readied the children for school; she made a meal. He attended his sons' sporting events. He was standing; he was sitting. "Life was going on around me, and I didn't want to be a burden, but in fact, that's exactly what I had become." He was not the male role model he wished to be for his sons. Despite himself, he decided to attend his sons' wrestling matches to be there for them even if he was blackout drunk. He would stand on the other team's side in the gymnasium. "I don't want to embarrass my son," he remembered thinking; "I don't want the other parents to smell all the alcohol in me." Overwhelmed by shame, he would vocalize to himself, "I'm in despair."

A chance meeting at his son's match changed his life. A stranger walked up to him while he was shouting, seated on the opposing team's side. "He looked over at me, probably because I was drunk." The stranger asked him, "How's it going?" In response, Doherty "just kind of laid it all out for the guy." Speaking about his despair, he hoped to shock the stranger that he assumed "never experienced any of the pain and crisis." After unloading, the stranger replied, "I have this men's group. ... It's on Tuesday morning at 6:30." To his surprise, Doherty agreed to attend.

He asked his wife to drive him because he would still be drunk at 4:30 AM and assumed he would find a ride home afterward. Arriving at what he soon realized was a Christian men's group, he chose to sit in the back. "I identified all the exits, and I took measure for every man in there." He expected to be "a fly on the wall," but the man who invited him asked him to share his story. "He dimed me out, and he asked me to come forward in front of everybody and, you know, introduce myself and give them my spiel." It all came pouring out, and he feared a critical response. "I had told these guys in this men's group, 'This is who I am, and if you don't like me, then F you. I know the way out of here.' ... What these guys did was they ended up loving on me instead and giving me affirmation that I didn't deserve."

After the meeting ended, the stranger approached Doherty, asking him to reflect. "Think back to your military career on one absolutely no-fail situation you were in where you absolutely could not fail. What was that?" One story came to mind. His team was doing reconnaissance work in Afghanistan and had to crawl on their bellies through herds of livestock, sneaking past shepherds under threat of attack by Al-Qaeda. After crawling into position and smelling "like ammonia because [their] muscles were burnt up," he offered to take the first watch while his men slept. He struggled to remain awake but knew that failure was not an option. His men's' lives depended on it. "I took one of the bullets from my magazine, and I put it underneath my chin. I'm lying down on my belly, looking over the ridgeline over-watching this area full of bad guys, and every time I start to doze off, my chin would dig into this bullet, and I'd wake back up again." He would have rather pierced his chin with the tip of a bullet than fall asleep while his men rested. "Well," said the stranger, "that's the way you need to treat your alcoholism."

He stuck with the men's group. "They were gentle with me," he said. He liked that instead of "you" statements or judgments, they spoke with "I" or "We." They met his perceived shortcomings with love. "They had nothing to gain by investing time and energy into me, nothing," and it was this unbridled love that connected him with his faith. He felt "Jesus' presence" come over him. Jesus "was putting my spirit and my soul back into alignment with my mind and my body." Faith remolded, healed, and shaped him anew. He had once felt emotion a weakness, but new religious resources reframed his masculinity to move away from the military's fatalistic one, which had suppressed his admission of trauma. He now saw emotion, community, and help-seeking attitudes as masculine. "I realize the absolute most masculine thing I've ever done in my life was to step into relationship with God the Father and then give that to other men that are still serving."

The healing he found in the men's group ignited his engagement with religion. "I was really actively practicing giving God my 'yes.'" He prayed for guidance to become the man he needed to be. Doherty began leading other men's ministries and became a mentor for a PTSD foundation. As a mentor, he recalled seeing veterans show up to retreats with nothing but "a big bag full of medicine from the VA." Many of the veterans were "still detoxing, and you could see all the pain and the misery in their eyes." However, during the retreat, they became close. They shared something in common: "they had combat spiritual scarring, and life in the world had taken a dump on them, and they had given more than any other American shy of their brothers who had given their lives." Common ground and understanding provided for effective healing.

For Doherty and those with similar trajectories, finding a religious identity and becoming part of a faith community greatly alleviated trauma and helped them form new identities as Christians replete with new frames and scripts to guide action. They shared a belief that having faith during their careers would have helped them avoid the soul wounds they carried, although their stories show that religious toolkits have a mixed impact on Christian service members' lives. They engaged mainly with evangelical (non-denominational) communities, albeit with some variation. Nevertheless, faith was the salve for their soul wounds, providing lifesaving waterflow through community and new resonant toolkits.

Religion Found in Community: Karen Black

One group of service members found expanded social and meaning-making resources in community during their careers, but not directly because of trauma, even if it remained possible. Unlike those who found religion after trauma, these veterans entered religious communities via interpersonal connections. Coming to the military with low or no religiosity, they found religious communities during their careers, taking on religious ideas, practices, and moral scripts consistent with military culture and strategic aims. They referred to an experience of being "saved" and recalled new religious frames positively impacting military life after that experience. Interestingly, they tended to report having high intrinsic religiosity today, even if finding a new post-service religious community remained challenging.

Illustrative of this trajectory is Karen Black, a former Air Force flight manager of 25 years. She grew up in a traditional Roman Catholic household and attended a strict Catholic girls' school. In her early teens, she became skeptical of the religion around her, showing up late to school to avoid mass. The apparent hypocrisy of it disillusioned her. "I saw nuns getting high and priests getting drunk and nuns getting pregnant. … One of the main principals got pregnant by a janitor, so I just quit. I didn't agree with it. And my parents were very upset about it and always on to me." Despite her parents' attempts to impress upon her the importance of being a good Catholic, Black renounced her faith, a decision which lasted into her military service.

Others who brought few religious resources to the military either had scant religious background or, like Black, felt it was forced upon them. In every case, they did have some exposure to religion, even if it played only a minor role. Regardless, they generally understood faith as a meaning-making system and source of "good" values, perhaps planting the seeds for their shift to a higher religiosity later. Moreover, they reported that

Christianity shaped their sense of morality, even if they did not participate in religious community pre-service.

Black enlisted at the age of 19 looking to escape her small Midwest town. Basic was a challenge. "I look back; it was the Lord that got me through. It was just a miracle I got through because I wasn't prepared at all for it." The physical rigors of training exhausted her, and drill sergeants pushed her even harder when she fell behind. "They made me run twice a day to get used to it." She was also unprepared for the "mind games" and constantly wanted to quit, but when she went to complain, her commander said, "You don't tell me [you want] to get out. I tell you. Who do you think you are?" Giving up authority over herself and being pushed past her mental and physical limits made the first weeks of basic training difficult, but she eventually found renewed determination. Eventually, she "just enjoyed it," she said.

Basic training did its job. She was more confident and internalized Air Force culture, but new challenges arose as she entered a male-dominated organization. In addition to taking on a military identity, she needed to make careful choices about how to present herself to survive:

> In the military, they label women immediately. There's three types of women in the military. Either you're "the slut" or "the whore"—the one that sleeps around—and they use you, pass you around. I worked with pilots, so that's all that I know. And they sleep with you and pass you around and then you go to the next squadron. Or you're what they call "butch," which is either you're gay, or you're not gay, but you dress and act like a man, so they feel safe with you because you act like a man. Or they make you "the bitch." So, I became the bitch, which is the mean woman. I worked hard and made my way up by working hard, and they knew not to mess with me because I was mean. And I stopped being quiet and shy and just became a very mean bitch to take up for myself.

In a male-dominated culture, Black developed an identity that could ensure safety and respect, helping her maintain some authority over others' perception and treatment of her. This framing of a professional woman identity within the military mirrors the challenges outlined by Pawelczyk (2014: 90), that is, the persistent difficulty of maintaining professional and gendered identities simultaneously while not "deviating" from either.[3]

[3] Black's breakdown of woman role identities in the military is much like Rosabeth Moss Kanter's (1977: 3) schema of "managers, secretaries, and wives" with gendered and professional identities influencing one another, particularly among women working in a male-dominated organization.

Like Doherty in the previous section, she pursued a "soldier warrior identity" (Griffith, 2009) that emphasized professionalism and exceptionalism. Unlike him, she had to manage the warrior identity so as to include a female identity as well. To do this, she emphasized her toughness and agency by presenting herself as "mean" but also hardworking and capable of keeping "officers on their toes."

As Black navigated between identities, she still avoided religion, particularly during training. She feared going to Sunday chapel would make her look weak or odd. "There was a girl that did, and she got made fun of. And I felt really bad for her. And she invited me to go to church with her, and I wouldn't do it because I said, 'No, I'm going to fit in. I'm not going to be made fun of. I'm trying to get through this.'" Most veterans reported the benefits of chapel, but Black believed it brought negative attention, which she did not want amid the pressures of male-dominated military culture. Instead, Black pretended to smoke. "Back then, smoking was the thing to do, so I fake smoked to get breaks." She hid a pack of cigarettes by her ankle and even brought one up to her mouth to maintain the illusion, though she never inhaled. "Can you believe that? I will never forget that. I tell everybody that story. I fake smoked," she laughed.

Black maintained her position as a flight manager throughout her entire career. "The name changed, [but] it's basically flight management or scheduler, dispatcher, aviation resource management. I worked with pilots. … I sat on the dispatch desk." She talked over the radio with pilots all day, arriving before them and leaving after them. "You confirm what aircraft they're going to and confirm the fuel and everything." Her job was to confirm flight schedules, fill out paperwork, and keep track of pilot qualifications. Over the years, she worked with different kinds of aircraft, from "trainers in Florida" to B-52 bombers that supported Army Special Forces after 9/11 (the inspiration for the 2018 Hollywood blockbuster *12 Strong*). She eventually commanded other flight managers, controlled flight payroll, and provided paperwork in court cases involving court-martialed pilots.

Religion remained elusive for much of her career until she was stationed at an Air Force base in Louisiana. One weeknight, she accidentally wandered into a Bible study in her dorm. "That's when I got saved and born again and decided to join," she said enthusiastically. "That's when I started going to church." Once, being involved in a church community would have made her an outsider, but she now found a new sense of community and acceptance, becoming a member at a church in Shreveport near the base. "It played the biggest role ever. My life totally changed, totally changed," she said. She started going to church twice on Sundays and once on Wednesdays and took up reading the Bible. "It really saved my life, you know?"

Others who shared a similar trajectory reported finding religion during their careers and reflected on stories of being "saved." Military religious resources and local "military-friendly" communities provided organizational practice for them as their intrinsic religiosity grew. There was variation in the instigating moment that brought them to find religious resources, although the most common reason was a reported desire to overcome the rebellious nature that had lasted through the early parts of their careers. Religion provided resources that would help them find forgiveness for perceived social moral failings. Moreover, many married during their careers, and either their partners expressed interest in them joining a church or the participant felt joining a church would help them remain faithful. In every case, joining the religious community "saved" them, and they found a community supportive of their military service.

Tragically, Black confronted new challenges and trauma in the years that followed. A superior officer assaulted and raped her while she was stationed in England, hundreds of miles from her religious community in Louisiana. Afterward, superiors attempted to remove her from her position lest she try to smear her attacker's name. They falsely claimed she had leaked a classified document, a punishable offense. Black was unsurprised. She had seen this sort of corrupt blaming of MST survivors before. "See, I knew this was going to happen. … About a month earlier, a girl had turned in the commander for grabbing her butt, and she was outside in the dead of winter, [in] snow, painting white rocks brown. So, I knew from then on I had to be on my toes." She provided evidence about to whom the classified document went and where it was at the leak's alleged time, preventing the issue from escalating. She relied on her new religious resources to reflect. "That was the Lord. That wasn't me. That was the Lord making me smart. I really had to be. They did some evil things, evil things to women, evil."

The harassment continued through her career, and she felt trapped. Returning to Louisiana, her mother, religious community, and friends all asked her why she did not leave the military. "How can I leave?" she asked. "I'm enlisted. I can't go. I'll go to Fort Leavenworth. I can't quit." Her community could not understand that trapped feeling, but she still credits her faith community with her survival all the same. These interpersonal relationships provided new resources that created a much-needed social support network amid her trauma, particularly because military chaplains never counseled her. "No chaplain ever came by," she said, "They talked to pilots. They don't talk to a female about nothing. Maybe he said hi." She felt the chaplains cared more for the pilots, mainly ignoring those in support roles, women especially.

Black never blamed God for what happened; instead, she felt that God provided her with comfort and prudence. "The Lord just protected me in certain situations because it could have been a lot worse, a lot, lot worse. At least I wasn't the one that was killed. You know?" She recalled other MST victims, like Army PFC LaVena Johnson whose official ruling of death by suicide has remained controversial amid rape and murder allegations. Black believes God had nothing to do with her trauma. "The Lord can't control these men," she said. "I just see them as evil people, that Satan just has evil people out there, and that's the life that they choose." Out of His control, her post-traumatic God provided determination and skills to survive; her salvation was providential even if her trauma was not. "I realized the Lord put me there in this military, and it put me there into Louisiana to get *saved*. I really do. I really do."

Others who shared this narrative could, like Black, experience trauma during their careers, and religion played a role in mitigating that trauma, mainly because it provided tools for reframing experience alongside community support. Unsurprisingly, like Black, most of the participants who found religion in community, especially those who found religious communities on base, reported an evangelical affiliation.

Although faith helped her survive most of her career, persistent anger and the effects of PTSD began to take a toll. "Most reservists retire at sixty. I retired at forty-five." After years of being worn down, she recounted the final straw: she was forced to continue to wear a uniform to work despite reserve status while the men did not. One morning, Black found herself in a local gun shop holding different weapons in her hand. "I wanted to go to work and just shoot everybody in the office and kill them all. And I said, 'Lord, as a Christian, this isn't right. It's time for me to retire.'" She walked out of the store and went to the base empty-handed.

Walking up to her commander, she worked out a retirement date. Not one to pass up an opportunity to mess with authority, Black said, "I was supposed to retire in civil service. I stayed an extra three months to piss off my commander, so he couldn't hire somebody in my place."

Returning to the civilian sector was not easy for Black. She moved back to the Midwest to be close to family, leaving behind the religious community that meant so much to her. "I just couldn't [reintegrate]. I've never been able to do it. … I couldn't adapt to civilian life. … It's like they had no structure like the military does. I just couldn't adapt to the way people acted and talked. It was driving me insane." Unemployment has remained a struggle due to PTSD. "I was just starting to explode in public and wanting to beat up men that reminded me of pilots or that acted like a pilot. I was physically threatening them, and I just never could cope." Persistent outbursts and a lack of medical support while she fights for VA benefits have led to depressive episodes. "It's just been a nightmare for me. It's been a nightmare."

Unfortunately, she has not found a new religious community. "No, I've never been able to find one since I got out. Everywhere I go, I've tried. … In Louisiana, they would do anything to help you, go out of their way down there in the Bible Belt. They're not like that here." Without similar outreach programs and battles with PTSD, she keeps religious practice private. Despite her hardships, she still maintains her faith. "It saved me. I think it saved me in the long run, and I'm glad I did join the military because it's what changed my life and led me to the Lord." She deeply misses her community where she found support and access to resources, but she continues looking for the right community, grateful to have been saved.

The difficulty of reintegrating varied among these veterans depending on whether they found communities like those they had found during their career. In Black's case, the loss of the community that supported this bridge exacerbated her PTSD. Still, they unanimously felt religion played a positive role in their lives. Faith and community allowed them to frame their experiences positively. While many emphasized a commitment to their jobs and not asking questions of morality while in the service, they all agreed that religion helped them. They'd been saved. Their new religious identities allowed them to manage the dissonance between competing professional, gendered, and civilian identities. If they experienced trauma, they did not blame God.

Religion Lost in Trauma: Damien McDaniel

Many of the stories above included accounts of trauma that forced an adaption of frames or searching for new resonant toolkits and community resources. In this "religion lost" trajectory, veterans shared narratives wherein religious frames exacerbated trauma or were themselves the source of betrayal. Frequently, they felt betrayed by God directly, leading to near-total abandonment of faith, leaving them searching for new toolkits to fill the void. These veterans had moderate to high religiosity pre-service but left with low to no religiosity due to trauma, preventing participation in religious communities and practice. They often reflected on how their religious resources used to help them, but religion was no longer part of their lives. In the following narrative trajectory, I will focus on one veteran's story of faith lost amid trauma, that of Army Sergeant Damien McDaniel, a former forward observer in the Infantry Division.

McDaniel grew up on the West Coast in a Catholic household. Although his family rarely practiced, religion played a "pretty big role." His mother struggled with drug use, and he sought moral foundations elsewhere. A friend from school asked him to attend an LDS church where he was introduced to the missionaries there, and he soon became heavily involved in the community. "I chose, when I was in my freshman year … to be baptized, and then that was pretty much my life after that." He relished the community's inclusive nature. "Not only were they great at teaching lessons and storytelling and that sort of thing, I think they showed compassion and understanding and those things you really expect when you go to church and how they were accepting of new members." Those experiences taught him values of working "together as a team and really look[ing] after each other as a family." Moreover, it helped him "combat the bad influence" of his mother. His surrogate family in the faith community provided the values and support he had longed for earlier in life.

McDaniel enlisted in the Army on September 11, 2001, the afternoon after viewing the attack on the World Trade Center towers on television. It was a "pretty impulsive" decision, he admitted, but deeply engrained church values had inspired his decision. Those values "absolutely played a role because they did make me feel like it was my job to protect my community and my country, and there is definitely some warriors in the Bible. And it made me feel like I was one of them." The attacks themselves were "religiously motivated," and he felt that it was his duty as a Christian to fight Islamic terrorists and protect the community he loved, the LDS community that had allowed him to flourish and helped him escape a difficult home situation. Others with a similar trajectory tended to cite a desire to protect communities as a significant motivator also, although these could just as often be close family and friends in addition to religious communities.

Those with this story of lost faith tended to be Catholic, Mormon, or Mainline Protestant, in congregations that emphasized ritual and sacraments. They varied in their degree of organizational practice but agreed that their religious upbringing shaped their moral development. They came to the military for varied reasons but shared a desire to protect their communities and serve their country. Like McDaniel, they felt they could make a difference in the world and had an idealized image of the military career. Most enlisted, and they were frequently in combat roles.

McDaniel arrived at basic training "highly motivated," doing all he could to be "mentally and physically prepared" to fight. He wanted to excel. "There was nothing that was going to stop me from preparing myself and trying to be the best-trained soldier and most motivated soldier I could be." That can-do spirit paid off. He was the distinguished graduate of his training class, "which is like the valedictorian," he said proudly. A natural leader, even in the LDS youth group in high school, he brought those qualities to basic, bonding with fellow cadets, citing chapel as a key moment for that camaraderie. "Every Sunday, we got to go to services, and I did that, and it was a great experience. I think it helped the guys bond in particular over that."

Faith kept McDaniel motivated and comforted during boot camp's challenges, and he never lost sight of the strength that his faith gave him. He had a tattoo of Jesus over his heart at the time, which was a constant "reminder that he is going to give me strength." His high religiosity and reliance on moral frameworks supplied by his religious toolkit enabled him to reflect on his role in the military positively. "I think I was pretty steadfast in my faith, and I was … a loyal servant of God at that time." This strong commitment continued into his career. Like those who brought in a strong faith and maintained it, those who lost faith had initially found comfort in religious practice. The difference occurred later when the realities of war and military experience threatened their beliefs in a God who would not save them.

McDaniel was a joint fire support specialist, or forward observer. As a "sister" or "FiSTer," his job was to "remain as calm as possible and drop accurate bombs on enemy target locations," using his expertise in land navigation and logistics to ensure his fellow infantrymen's safety. While technically a support role, he found himself deep in the combat zone, looking for enemy combatants alongside light infantry. Over his seven-year career, he promoted to sergeant, in charge of ten fellow "sisters and their training, preparing them for combat and taking them to war." He took his leadership role very seriously and "tried to use the values and morals that [he] had learned both in church and the military to help guide" him. In addition to his LDS values, he took Army values of LDRSHIP to heart. "It's loyalty, duty, respect, selfless service, honor, integrity, and personal courage," and he emphasized personal courage in particular. "We need to have personal courage to do things that we may be scared or frightened to do, that may cost us our lives, and that's a normal thing. The *courage* is where you become extraordinary."

During the initial push to Iraq in 2003, his first deployment was mostly uneventful, apart from sporadic mortar fire. At the same time, he found himself slipping in his organizational religious practice. No less committed himself, the religious community during his first deployment did not have the same closeness that he found at his home church or during basic. "It was good to go there and see the guys and those who shared the faith ..., but I feel because of operational tempo, we didn't exactly get to interact that much. ... There just wasn't necessarily the same camaraderie." Others who shared this narrative began attending services infrequently during their careers, even if they privately maintained their faith. Especially with those in combat roles where missions were frequent, there was no time to attend services.

McDaniel's second combat deployment to Iraq changed everything. This time, he was in Sadr City at the height of sectarian violence in the area. He had been promoted to squad leader in the year before deploying and now had responsibilities that weighed heavily upon him. He was in charge, so if his soldiers got hurt, he felt it was on him. His job was to keep them safe, and to be the leader he had trained to be. Despite lower chapel attendance, however, he brought prayer to his squad-mates. Not wanting to alienate anyone, he admitted, "they were absolutely aware, acutely aware of the fact that, not only was I religious, but that my faith was important to me." This was made evident by his tattoo, of course, but also his commitment to praying before every mission. "Every time we left that gate, I would say a prayer. I had my little Bible, and it went inside my chest pocket. They knew how important it was to me." He recited Psalm 144, "one that talks about God guiding your hand in war," the most. However, what followed, tragically, was entirely out of his hands.

"It was an extremely bloody time" in Sadr City. "We were in constant fights, whether it be small arms, IEDs, EFPs[4] were really big at the time, and our guys were getting tore up." Always in danger, one day was especially horrific. "A couple guys got hurt, and essentially I prayed, and I asked God for help. And at the end of that, I felt that no one was coming, and it was up to us. And that was a very alone, isolating feeling for sure, and I don't know if that went away after that." For all of McDaniel's devoutness, constant prayer, and service, God never showed up. He was alone. "I had put so much faith into this and so much trust, and that trust I felt was betrayed because … no one's coming except us." God betrayed him, and he did not know how to proceed. What hurt him the most was that one of his soldiers, the youngest in the battalion, was injured. "He got hurt, and I felt responsible for not protecting him. I blamed God for not protecting him whenever that was the single most thing I prayed for." He described his loss of faith as "gradual," but that day initiated the loss.

Veterans like McDaniel could not understand how God would allow such evil to transpire. Traumatic experience led to significant moral dissonance, interrupting their habits of faith and initiating discursive consciousness and internal debate. This was a moment of identity conflict between two central identities, the warrior and the Christian. The warrior identity required strict adherence to military values and aims, which conflicted with their religious toolkit's values and moral expectations. As the military identity eclipsed the religious one due to role responsibilities, a series of traumatic events destroyed what remained of the religious identity. All the veterans with this narrative trajectory had their religious identities challenged and lost amid morally traumatic events.

McDaniel attempted to rectify his dissonance by speaking with military chaplains and confidantes. However, the chaplain was unhelpful. "He told me to just stay strong and that my faith will return. I just need to remember that God's grace is there even in wartime and that I was going to get past it." He attempted to frame the evil that he had witnessed as a byproduct of "free will" but could still not understand why God allowed his squad members to die. After all, they were there fighting the good fight. The chaplain asked him to give it time, and he would move on from the

[4] EFPs are explosively formed penetrators, which are specially designed charges or warheads that have the effect of transforming a metal plate into an armor penetrating slug or rod.

pain. "Unfortunately, I feel like I never did." At the time, he did try to take the chaplain's advice and continued to attend chapel services, but he found he "didn't get the same message anymore." He confided in a close friend, his driver, who "was and still is pretty religious," to make sense of it, but it was more of the same. "I talked to him when we were out on mission, actually, and it was just us out there. And, well, … he kind of had the same approach that he thought that my feelings would pass." Unfortunately, his feelings never changed.

At the end of his deployment, his Bradley fighting vehicle had been hit with so many IEDs and RPG missiles that he eventually suffered a TBI. "When I was going to get ready to go back on my third trip, they flagged me, and they said that I was not prepared to go back to a combat zone, which was my life." They also flagged him for potential PTSD, and the career he had built since 2001 was over.

Forced out, returning to civilian life was "absolutely terrible." He developed complications from his TBI and was diagnosed with PTSD. He felt an overwhelming sense of guilt for sitting on the sidelines while his squad continued to fight and guilt for those men who had died under his charge. "I was stuck back home. I drank. I isolated. I got divorced." He despaired and did not know how to escape. As his squad-mates came home, "they started committing suicide." This only enhanced his guilt; he had failed them. "More people from my unit have committed suicide than died in combat." "I lost nine people in Iraq," he said. "We've had fourteen, excuse me, fifteen now suicides since I've been home."

He tried returning to church. "To be honest, I picked a church that I don't think was necessarily a good one; it was like a Starbucks in there and wasn't focused on faith. The community aspect was there for sure, but I didn't feel part of that community. I felt detached." The community could not understand the military experience. "I think if they would've put me in a room full of other veterans at that point, it might've saved me from a lot of turmoil that I went through because I would've found the support." McDaniel did not return to that church or any church after that, and PTSD, divine moral injury, and despair grew worse. McDaniel's loss of a meaning-making toolkit enhanced his trauma, and his inability to participate in new religious communities only isolated him further. He thought fondly about his pre-military faith community but could not find a new one to replicate it.

He had to turn his life around and determined he could be of use to fellow soldiers who came home with soul wounds like him. He wanted to be a leader again. "I needed to … think about how I could best help these guys find inner peace and, most importantly, build their self-esteem and remind them that they're warriors, that they've been through these extraordinary events, and they are absolutely worth something. And they're my heroes." He became a motivational speaker for a veteran non-profit, devoting his life to promoting peer-to-peer mentoring. He spends his time "talking to guys who are in crisis or who don't think there's any hope." He likes to joke that his role as a FiSTer makes him good at his job. "It's because of my expertise in land navigation," he laughed; "I can help these guys navigate. Whether it be the VA or just life in general, I try to help them and give them guidance, some of the stuff I didn't hear when I came home." In the absence of a religious community, he has found a new one that can similarly resolve the dissonance.

Overall, those with this narrative tended to believe religion had played a positive role in their past lives but found it hindered them post-trauma. Upon returning home, the loss of the military identity and moral injury's onset prompted isolation and reliance on vices to cover open soul wounds. Brock and Lettini (2013: 52) contend, "[T]his shattering of the soul challenges what holds life together, and the anguish of moral injury begins." In the absence of viable religious beliefs, religious practices and religious communities were unavailable to bridge their civilian and military identities. Instead, they found new resonant identities housed in professional (e.g., public speaker) and social (e.g., father) roles.

Religion Lost to Irrelevance: Edward Roberts

This final narrative, *Religion Lost to Irrelevance*, follows individuals who slowly left their religious toolkits aside—not because of trauma, but simply because religion became incompatible, even untenable, amid competing cultural spheres. They did not experience moral or spiritual traumas, although PTSD was still possible. Some found another cultural toolkit supported them better, and others found that current resources were no longer useful and were still looking for new resonant frameworks.

Sgt. Edward Roberts shared this narrative trajectory. A counterpropaganda specialist in Army Psychological Operations (PSYOP), Roberts grew up in the Midwest attending "one of the first megachurches" in the area, a conservative non-denominational church over which his father presided as pastor. "We were obviously deeply involved in the church on an extraordinarily regular basis. … The actual organization of the church was so large, there was never really a lack of things to do." However, his father insisted on keeping his family insulated. "I know it's sort of a chimeric answer, but our goal as family was that, to the best of our ability, it wasn't the family that was pastoring the church. It was just my dad. So, when we were home, it was definitely a matter of keeping us kids in our own lives." The pastor's kids were not going to be "props" in his ministry; they were to have their own lives. In that regard, he felt family shaped him as a person more than his church community, which extended to his moral development on "how you treat other people, not simply being right." This moral foundation gave him moral "clarity" throughout his life that he feels others not raised with a religious upbringing missed.

Roberts enlisted his first year of college, postponing higher education for five years. He joined because he felt he "owed something to America to one degree or another." His father had fled Northern Ireland with his family due to sectarian violence there in the early 1960s. "I come from an immigrant family. It had more to do with valuing the country." He felt that serving in the military would be a way to show gratitude for the nation that allowed his family to flourish. Despite an evangelical upbringing shaping much of his early worldview, he said faith had little to do with his decision to enlist, nor did he have any sort of reluctance to join. "No, no, no, no," he laughed. "It's an all-volunteer force. Nobody's making you do it."

Contrary to many of the veterans I spoke with, Roberts did not believe training was among "the single most formative experiences of [his] life." He only recalled the "shin splints"; it was only nine weeks of his life after all. However, he did recall that training's high operational tempo marked the beginning of his shift away from faith. "I went to chapel every Sunday because it got me out of the barracks [but] I would say that would be the start of when I really stopped going to church or wasn't in regular attendance." He was too "busy" in training to make time for it. He also felt military chaplains, during and after training, were "unhelpful" and "consistently found … that most chaplains really don't have enough life experience to speak to someone's condition." Growing up with a mega-church pastor for a father, he had a high standard for what to expect. "I generally found that I knew the Bible, and I knew theology as well, if not better, than most chaplains I ever talked to." As a result, Roberts never sought out chaplains during his career except to have an "hour inside of an air-conditioned room."

Others who shared this trajectory reported a similar deterioration of their religious identity during training, and it represented a failure of religion to make meaning of the realities of military experience. Through the training process, chapel service attendance began out of a desire to go worship but soon was just a way to escape chores and yelling, a subtle but essential difference. Where most other veterans' stories characterized chapel as an escape, these men and women were explicit about their non-religious motivations for going, if they did at all. They "came to realize" they were *just* escaping, suggesting the beginning of the slow decline of their religious identity, perhaps as a byproduct of a new military identity. Those whose shift began later still found that religion provided them with comfort during training.

Roberts' 16-year career included many jobs in the Army and Army National Guard. He reflects most fondly on his time as a counterpropagandist but held support and combat roles at various times. He was a National Guard truck driver, providing convoy security. He did a tour of heavy recoverage in Mosul where he "drove absolutely the largest trucks in the entire military" to retrieve land vehicles weighing more than five tons that got blown up. After that, he stepped away with "every intention of never going back." However, an Army Reserves recruiter convinced him to sign up as a counterpropagandist. It was "genuinely a fabulous job. It was constantly intellectually challenging, occasionally physically demanding but … endlessly fascinating." Unfortunately, as one of the military's smallest career fields, he had to promote out to a different field or leave. As a result, he moved to a different unit in the Transportation Corps. This time, however, he had the pleasure of working from a desk. "It's a great thing. You spend enough time doing the job, you end up not having to do anything at all," he laughed.

After diminishing religious practice during training, the early years of his career accelerated his shift. His religious toolkit no longer supported his outlook; combat experience had changed how he viewed the world. "The more time I spent in combat, the less important I felt [religion] was. It ended up feeling more of a distraction." He recalled having to fire his weapon. "I feel like, my first time, I had to do it. There was certainly a moral struggle, and I had an argument with myself going back and forth. And then after that, it didn't matter. One way or the other, it didn't matter." His faith initially came into play, but became irrelevant. Instead of maintaining his religious resources, adapting his religious beliefs to his new context, burying the moral question to deal with later, or outright abandoning belief because of moral injury, he instead set religion aside. It no longer provided resonant frameworks. There was no great betrayal; the toolkit lost its use. "In the end, when it comes to war, violence is a foregone conclusion. When the thing goes down, it's too late to be a conscientious objector. And I feel by the time you get to that point, your job is more important than an idea. Because the bullets kill you, the ideas won't." He became disenchanted with the world. "Why is there evil in the world?" he asked. "Does it really fucking matter."

Roberts also had negative experiences with military chaplains. "There was a barrier of life experience" that made him believe chaplains could not connect with service members. This included their sermons as well. He attended a Protestant service early in his career, still hopeful he would continue to practice his faith. "The sermon was terrible," he recalled. "It was like the guy had lifted everything he was saying out of a Joel Osteen book. And he, Joel Osteen's the guy, I have always hated his theology because it's not theology. And his whole doctrine of wealth I find egregious and insults the Lord. And being a good Baptist kid at heart, I have no problem calling out people for being heathens," he laughed. With combat veterans in attendance, the Osteen-inspired prosperity gospel made it sound as though if they had just enough faith, good things would come their way. But they had lost brothers and sisters in arms, people often closer than family. How could a chaplain stand there and say if the service members had enough faith, they would have good fortune? "Five minutes after that, we're getting murdered," Roberts said. "I can't imagine anything more damaging to soldiers … than to even give them the chance to think or believe that they didn't have enough faith." He never attended another service.

His shifts were a response to the realities of war and feeling that the world was not morally binary. Like others with a similar story, religious frames were mismatched with the experience of war. Some felt that being overtly religious in the military cast them as outsiders. Others believed religious officials were hypocrites concerning moral behavior or that their conservative ideology, particularly concerning LGBTQ issues, made religious beliefs untenable. In every case, the veterans stopped participating in religious communities and became dismissive of religious frames even if they maintained their theological literacy. Although similar to other stories of lost faith, the absence of reported soul wounds or divine betrayal marked the difference. These individuals still felt a dissonance between reality and moral expectation, but they did not feel betrayed. Roberts did not later reflect on his participation in violence as morally injurious; he dropped those moral frames because they did not match experience.

Roberts did not view his shift away from faith as unfavorable; rather, it showed growth. Parts of his evangelical upbringing still shaped his worldview, but it was not one with a belief in God. "You know, as we get older, our views change, but I feel like faith as a personal thing is a fluid, dynamic thing. And so, yeah, it should change. It should shift. It should morph." Instead of relying on his childhood religious package, Roberts relied on philosophical writings or even Biblical texts that resonated with his outlook. "The longer I've been in, the less faith has played a part. I found Albert Camus to be more helpful than any Biblical writer." Absurdism resonated better; it was an understanding resting in the contradiction of a search for meaning in a purposeless world. In addition to Camus and other existentialist readings, he did continue to reflect on resonant Biblical texts. "My favorite text in the Bible has to be Ecclesiastes, which starts out with a guy screaming into the void that everything is meaningless. And I've always found that to be the most helpful Biblical text under any circumstance," he paused. "I don't recommend reading it at weddings and funerals." Resonant Biblical texts made sense of his military experience, Kohelet's screaming was his screaming too. It was not something Osteen would preach. "I would pay handsomely to watch him try to teach on Ecclesiastes."

Others that shared this trajectory sought out philosophy or nature as well, describing themselves as spiritual or, as one participant joked, "giving up organized religion for Lent." Some held onto religious frames in a piecemeal fashion or tried different kinds of faith communities like Humanist Unitarian Universalism, but the religious identities they brought to military experience were gone, outgrown in a sense. They relied on new frames of understanding the world and making meaning of their experiences, not out of despair or trauma, but out of new outlooks. A new "spiritual" or "humanist" identity takes the place of a religious one. Notably, the shift was chosen. As Roberts explained, "I feel like it's important for me to claim my own agency that I have chosen to change rather than X, Y, Z has changed me. … I have chosen to change." He explicitly felt that the shifts in his views on faith *came from him deciding to shift away* from them.

Roberts is still an Army reservist but mostly works as a civilian now. He, too, found the transition difficult. "You spend so much time doing a really specific thing. And it just, you know, a soldier without a fight just withers away. … There's a piece of that that your body and your heart just long for." The hardest part was the culture shock of interacting with civilians who were indecisive and lacked determination. "It may be the job. It may be the people. It may be the camaraderie. But there is an easy clarity to what we do. There's a straightforward mission, and you do that. And it's over." Interacting with slow-moving civilians remains "incredibly aggravating." He also finds it challenging to be both a soldier and a civilian simultaneously. "There's an old Irish saying that you play the flute or you play the harp depending on where you are. The military has a different dynamic than you'll ever see in the civilian world. It is much more direct. … It essentially requires a different personality." He feels he can act correctly in each setting, but frustration remains.

Unsurprisingly, Roberts said religion played no role in his life in recent years, nor did it play one in his career. On reflection, he felt questions of theodicy were meaningless. "The reality is that war is a self-caused thing. People choose to do it. People make it happen. And even if God was still in the business of miracles, I doubt he'd ever show up to war." Rather than coming home from service with questions about the nature of evil, he accepted the world and his military experience for what he deemed them to be: purposeless. "It was war. It's not a good thing. It's not a Godly thing. It's not a righteous thing. It's a horrible, horrible thing. And understanding God was never going to be there to begin with was what made it easier." His shift in beliefs about God and his faith, while not lost because of trauma, allowed him to manage the disruptive military experience. He summed up his shift by restating his main takeaways, "War is chaos. Religion is structure. And they don't mix. Read French philosophy."

Not everyone who abandoned religious frameworks did so on the same schedule or in the same way. For example, those who shifted away from their faith early in their careers, as Roberts did, dismissed religion's role entirely. Compared with the new toolkits, religion's impact was small. If the transition happened later, veterans were likely to resent religion's role for hurting their careers or their relationships, even while they maintained a positive memory toward the religion they used to have. Theological frameworks or religious literature could still provide insight, but the religious belief and practice of their youth or found in the military no longer resonated with salient issues.

Conclusion

These stories reveal great variety in what we can consider the "typical" life cycles of post-9/11 veterans who once or currently identified as Christian. Most commonly, veterans maintained their faith. About half shared narratives of faith maintenance. Among those who maintained their faith in some capacity, three distinct religious military narrative trajectories emerged. Some maintained their faith because their civilian religion, the religious life present in the military, and faith communities provided them with tacit and explicit measures for managing unsettled times. Faith-based justifications supplied built-in mechanisms for handling feelings of doubt, shame, or the use of force. They maintained their faith using Scripture and theological grounding to mediate and navigate moral issues, often in ways that aligned with military culture. Others maintained their faith by adapting dissonant beliefs. Some wrestled with dissonance immediately by relying on moral guidance from religious military authorities. Others compartmentalized their dissonance, leaving moral work for later. Regardless of timing, they eventually found resonant beliefs and cultural packages that allowed them to resolve their moral dissonance, reframing experience using post-hoc justifications that absolved them of perceived sin. Still others never experienced trauma and maintained their religious resources throughout their military career, thus experiencing no dramatic religiosity shift. Mostly untested, they could continue to participate in the moral order with uninterrupted warrior and Christian identities. Most veterans with this trajectory were in non-combat roles, although service roles do not preclude someone from experiencing trauma, as we have seen.

The second-largest group in the study was veterans who found religion at some point during or after their careers. Despite little exposure to religion growing up, they reported not being Christian at the time of joining. Typically, their civilian identities would be characterized as directionless or rebellious, even dismissive of religion, particularly in their teen years. Among these stories were two major religious military narrative trajectories. Some found faith following trauma. Typically, these traumatic events meant leaving the military altogether. They found faith often years after having time for reflection following years of alcohol and drug abuse. They tended to have high religiosity today and found that religion provided a remedy for dissonance. There were also veterans who found welcoming religious communities during their careers. Faith communities supported their military participation and supplied them with cultural toolkits that resonated with their experience.

Finally, there were those participants who lost their faith. These narratives often began as veterans who maintained religion, but due to traumatic experience or disillusionment with organized religion stemming from incongruence with experience, veterans abandoned their faith. Here, there were also two distinct paths to abandonment. Some tended to be veterans with high religiosity, whose moral injury initiated a loss of faith, especially if the source of the betrayal was God. Other veterans more matter-of-factly chose to leave behind their Christian religious resources. Unlike those who lost faith due to trauma, they were not concerned so much with the existence of evil as they were with social or philosophical considerations that their Christian religious resources could not adequately manage, leading them instead to a different meaning-making toolkit. Many veterans here continued to hold onto theological and ethical frameworks but otherwise became dismissive of God and organized religion. New identities—like humanist, pantheist, nihilist, or simply military ones—eclipsed the religious one, providing the individual with alternative frames to understand the world and interact with others.

Husking off old identities, veterans emerge with a new sense of self. These identities—still composed of different toolkits and perhaps multiple *habitus*—find coherence in post-hoc justifications and new resonant beliefs that then guide future action. Narrative identity is an ongoing representation of the social process of managing and ensuring coherence in one's life story amid the navigation of multiple cultural spheres and roles. Different role identities or cultural packages find centrality among a litany of I-positions, but along the narrative arc of veteran stories, which identity has centrality at any given moment is somewhat beside the point. The social process is one that takes place over years and years.

The military experience tests civilian habits and resources amid trauma and violence. Simply working with the military implies exposure to morally disruptive events, even if they are never reported as trauma. Training and moral discourse purposefully limit reflection and moral deliberation, aiming recruits at the military institution's strategic goals. They develop new habits, held unconsciously as much as not. After leaving the military, they find these warrior habits mostly have no place in the civilian sector, challenging them yet again. While many cannot reconcile the dissonance of the challenges to their habits, whether in the military or after returning to the civilian sector, others adapt their beliefs into new resonant ones or find new meaning-making systems altogether. Finally, these adjustments culminate in a new amalgamation of cultural toolkits that form the basis of a new *habitus*. If their deliberative practices settle their interrupted habits, they successfully establish coherence, allowing them to look back at their life narrative and sense of identity with a connective through-line that makes sense of their experiences.

These stories are the culmination of the life chapters that came before, showing the evolution of religious resources and trauma on veterans' lives and personal narrative identities. Meyer, Gray, Granger, Doherty, Black, McDaniel, and Roberts each had vastly different military experiences. Some were officers, while others enlisted. Some were always Christian, while others found Christianity during their careers or following trauma. Others disaffiliated after confronting atrocities in war. However, what united each of their stories were the looming shadows of trauma and the need to make sense of their lives.

Bibliography

Ammerman, N. T. (1997). *Congregation & Community*. Rutgers University Press.

Berger, P. L. (1967). *The Sacred Canopy: Elements of Sociological Theory of Religion*. Doubleday.

Britch. (2020). *10th Annual IAVA Member Survey: Perceptions and Views of Iraq and Afghanistan Veterans on the Challenges and Successes of the Next Greatest Generation of Veterans* (Member Survey). Retrieved https://iava.org/survey2020/IAVA-2020-Member-Survey.pdf

Brock, R. N., & Lettini, G. (2013). *Soul Repair: Recovering from Moral Injury after War*. Beacon Press.

Bryan, C. J., & Morrow, C. E. (2011). Circumventing Mental Health Stigma by Embracing the Warrior Culture: Lessons Learned from the Defender's Edge Program. *Professional Psychology, Research and Practice, 42*(1), 16–23.

Dewey, J. (1922). *Human Nature and Conduct: An Introduction to Social Psychology*. Henry Holt & Company.

Durkheim, E. (1933). *The Division of Labor in Society; Being a Translation of His De la Division du Travail Social*. Macmillan.

Griffith, J. (2009). Contradictory and Complementary Identities of U.S. Army Reservists: A Historical Perspective. *Armed Forces & Society, 37*(2), 261–283.

Grimell, J. (2018). Advancing an Understanding of Selves in Transition: I-Positions as an Analytical Tool. *Culture & Psychology, 24*(2), 190–211.

Guhin, J. (2016). Why Worry about Evolution? Boundaries, Practices, and Moral Salience in Sunni and Evangelical High Schools. *Sociological Theory, 34*(2), 151–174.

Kanter, R. M. (1977). *Men and Women of the Corporation*. Basic Books.

Litz, B. T., Stein, N., Delaney, E., Lebowitz, L., Nash, W. P., Silva, C., & Maguen, S. (2009). Moral Injury and Moral Repair in War Veterans: A Preliminary Model and Intervention Strategy. *Clinical Psychology Review, 29*(8), 695–706.
Maynes, M. J., Pierce, J. L., & Laslett, B. (2008). *Telling Stories: The Use of Personal Narratives in the Social Sciences and History.* Cornell University Press.
McDonnell, T. E. (2014). Drawing out Culture: Productive Methods to Measure Cognition and Resonance. *Theory and Society, 43*(3/4), 247–274.
Morin, R. (2011, December 8). *The Difficult Transition from Military to Civilian Life.* Retrieved from https://www.pewsocialtrends.org/2011/12/08/the-difficult-transition-from-military-to-civilian-life/
Pawelczyk, J. (2014). Constructing American Female War Veterans' Military Identity in the Context of Interviews. *Women & Language, 37*(1), 87–112.
Pew Research Center. (2009, April 27). *Faith in Flux.* Retrieved from https://www.pewforum.org/2009/04/27/faith-in-flux
Pew Research Center. (2011, October 5). War and Sacrifice in the Post-9/11 Era. *Pew Research Center's Social & Demographic Trends Project.* Retrieved from www.pewsocialtrends.org/2011/10/05/war-and-sacrifice-in-the-post-911-era
Pew Research Center. (2016, October 26). One-in-Five U.S. Adults Were Raised in Interfaith Homes. pp. 19–25.
Scully, R. (2019). Tree Stumps That Should Be Dead Can Be Kept Alive by Nearby Trees. *New Scientist.*
Smith, C. (2003). *The Secular Revolution: Power, Interests, and Conflict in the Secularization of American Public Life.* University of California Press.
Somers, M. R. (1994). The Narrative Constitution of Identity: A Relational and Network Approach. *Theory and Society, 23*(5), 605–649.
Stahre, M. A., Brewer, R. D., Fonseca, V. P., & Naimi, T. S. (2009). Binge Drinking Among U.S. Active-Duty Military Personnel. *American Journal of Preventive Medicine, 36*(3), 208–217.
Teeters, J., Lancaster, C., Brown, D., & Back, S. (2017). Substance Use Disorders in Military Veterans: Prevalence and Treatment Challenges. *Substance Abuse and Rehabilitation, 8*, 69–77.
Thompson, M. (2016). Here's Why the U.S. Military Is a Family Business. *Time.*
Turner, V. (2008). *The Ritual Process.* Cornell University Press.
US Department of Veterans Affairs, Office of Public Affairs Media Relations. (2020, February 10). *VA Strengthens Care and Benefits for Veterans with $243 billion Budget Request for Fiscal Year 2021* [Press release]. Retrieved from https://www.va.gov/opa/pressrel/includes/viewPDF.cfm?id=5393
Vaisey, S. (2009). Motivation and Justification: a Dual-Process Model of Culture in Action. *American Journal of Sociology, 114*(6), 1675–1715.
Waggoner, E. (2014, September). Taking Religion Seriously in the U.S. Military: The Chaplaincy as a National Strategic Asset. *Journal of the American Academy of Religion, 82*(3), 702–735.

Whitworth, S. (2008). "Militarized Masculinity and Post Traumatic Stress Disorder." Rethinking the Wo/Man Question in International Relations. In J. Parpart & M. Zalewski (Eds.), *Zed Books* (pp. 109–126).

Williams, E. C., Gupta, S., Rubinsky, A. D., Jones-Webb, R., Bensley, K. M., Young, J. P., Young, J. P., Hagedorn, H., Gifford, E., & Harris, A. H. (2016). Racial/Ethnic Differences in the Prevalence of Clinically Recognized Alcohol Use Disorders among Patients from the U.S. Veterans Health Administration. *Alcoholism: Clinical and Experimental Research, 40*(2), 359–366.

Winchester, D., & Green, K. D. (2019). Talking Your Self into It: How and When Accounts Shape Motivation for Action. *Sociological Theory, 37*(3), 257–281.

Wood, D. B. (2016). *What Have We Done: The Moral Injury of Our Longest Wars*. Little, Brown and Company.

Wool, Z. H. (2015). *After War: The Weight of Life at Walter Reed*. Duke University Press.

Wuthnow, R. (2013). *Small-Town America: Finding Community, Shaping the Future*. Princeton University Press.

CHAPTER 8

Conclusion

The son of a United Church of Christ pastor, Tim Bester "was absolutely determined not to be" one. As fate would have it, that is precisely what he became. Growing up in New England in the 1950s, he recalled constantly moving while his father served multiple parishes. He loved literature and attended college to pursue English and an advanced degree in Library Sciences. However, "Vietnam intervened," as did his draft board. He joined the Navy to "avoid the Army and a sure ticket to Vietnam," but his plan failed. He served a tour in Vietnam from 1971 to 1972. Upon reflection of what motivated his call to the ministry, he posited two reasons: "a book by Peter Marshall and an encounter—well, more than one—with human brutality."

After returning from the war, he finished his obligation to the military by teaching at the Naval Academy Prep School, a college preparatory school that feeds directly into the Naval Academy. Afterward, he went to seminary in New England, married, and began his career at "a naughty little church that chewed up pastors." He survived three years before they "spit" him out. Luckily, he found new churches to call home and had a rewarding career. Along with ministering to congregations from Maine to Louisiana, he put together veteran retreats and programs to help veterans who, like him, never felt welcomed home or who never healed from their soul wounds. His primary interaction with 9/11-era troops occurred

T. H. Suitt, III, *Narratives of Trauma and Moral Agency among Christian Post-9/11 Veterans*,
https://doi.org/10.1007/978-3-031-31082-9_8

when the Canadian Armed Forces offered him a contract to "brief various 'Royal' units before they deployed for the first 'rotos' [rotations] to Afghanistan." Canadian Armed Forces were largely peacekeepers following the Korean War, so Bester's experience as a combat veteran and a pastor motivated that contract. As he explained, "the need for an outside voice with some authority was obvious."

After a decades-long career, a diagnosis of Parkinson's disease stemming from Agent Orange exposure forced him to retire in 2010. He has spent time writing and gathering resources useful for his veteran healing retreats in the years since. His interactions with veterans and wrestling with his own trauma gave him perspective. He boiled it down: "PTSD, moral wounds, and spiritual isolation … upset the *Imago Dei* I had been issued by my faith by robbing me of my identity of someone who physically did good things … and by putting me in the position of having to keep secret the identity of the person—the errant warrior—I had become. … My self-image as being made in the image of God was taken away." Like many veteran participants, he had buried his trauma for moral work later in life and did not reconcile those wounds until an emergency stay at a VET Center in 1990. His experience transformed his ministry; "it allowed me to undertake a regime of healing and outreach, a process which opened a field of ministry with the wounded souls, the abused, and the addicted, souls that I found I could now touch as I fit in." He has worked out new ways of seeing the world in the years since. "Note that I speak of creation and destruction, not 'right' and 'wrong'—the latter terms have no meaning for me; I lost them in Vietnam. But 'creation' and 'destruction' I understand, especially 'destruction.'"

Bester was not a US military chaplain and did not match the interest form for this study by the look of it. All the same, it seemed worthwhile to speak with him, and I remain glad that I did. His insights as a veteran who experienced trauma, as a civilian minister who led veteran healing retreats, and as a Canadian Armed Forces military chaplain working alongside those deployed in the first years of the Global War on Terror coalesced in challenging insights. Along with providing one last veteran story, his thoughts also shape some of the conclusions of this ongoing project. Questions of right and wrong, creation and destruction, agency and incapacity are ever-present in the oft-traumatic stories we have encountered. They demand an exploration of how the military organization and the military experience upend the life of a service member. We must challenge the religious meaning-making systems service members bring to or find in the military that no longer reflect the realities of war—if they ever did—and often exacerbate trauma themselves.

Summary

This book began with an exploration of the ways religion is (and always has been) present in the military. In addition to the role and history of military chaplains, we explored ethics education and moral training, and finally looked at the formal and informal religious practices of post-9/11 service members. These various pieces of the larger military religious tapestry revealed an image of competing religious resources—brought to or supplied by the military. In the stories that followed, we saw that this array of religious resources often provided formal and informal support amid the disruptive experience of military life. They helped establish a community based in shared resonant beliefs, frames, and expectations. They were a means by which the military could persistently aim service members at the military's strategic ends using shared narratives and myths, the authority of institutional religious guides, and religious rituals and practice. As much as it was a source for comfort and meaning, religion could also fuel the dehumanization of the enemy and encourage the othering of fellow non-Christian service members. Religion plays a pervasive role in the lives of service members—even non-religious ones—because of its continued presence at every level of the US Armed Forces.

Religion has been a part of the US military since its infancy under the Continental Congress, and chaplains have always been there too. They started out with more limited and explicitly religious roles, specifically guiding worship. As the numbers of chaplains have grown and the role has become more formalized, they have absorbed other functions. They are teachers, formal military event leaders, social workers, mental health counselors, aids to command, and more. Chaplains have become integrated into the military ethos. They are the military's symbolic representation of moral exceptionalism. The oft-cited "two-collar problem" chaplains discuss is nominally about feeling torn between commitments to their faith and to the military organization. However, it is really about managing deeply habituated theological and moral commitments (one collar) that have been redefined by the military (the other collar) through a process of cultural bricolage (Waggoner, 2014). When asked, chaplains claim resolute commitment to the well-being of individual service members, but they are also aware of and obliged to promote the strategic goals of the military. In this way, the clear symbol of religion in the military is inseparably representative of the military institution and its goals.

The consequences of their institutional affiliation play out in various ways. Chaplains do both good and ill. Reports among service members noted their courage and persistent presence along with their incredible insights into the well-being of subordinates and the camaraderie they provided among commanding officers. The identity and military *habitus* shared between chaplains and service members provided invaluable relationships that carried service members through trauma. Problematically, the hierarchical structure of the various Chaplain Corps means that inexperienced chaplains interact the most with lower ranking service members, who often need the most help. In addition, facile and often self-serving justifications for traumatic experiences in war have exacerbated moral injury for many.

Of course, service members bring a range of moral norms, beliefs, and expectations to the military, but these are often immediately met with military ethics education and moral training rooted in a long history of Christian religious theory that can challenge or reaffirm their prior moral toolkits. What they encounter and how much time they spend in this training varies across branches, rank, and enlisted versus officers. Officers, for instance, receive a robust value-based ethics education with explicit links to its Christian roots along with more modern secular frameworks. Conversely, enlisted service members receive only rule-based ethics education with little nuance beyond the confines of their role-specific obligations. Treated as compulsory during training, some enlisted service members did not remember receiving ethics education or moral training at all. Worse, rule-based obligations were often treated as laughable and bendable prescriptions. Despite evidence that consistent ethics education among officers makes a difference in attitudes and decision-making (Bell, 2014), its persistent variation—down to differences in number of contact hours, courses, and instructors—leads to inconsistency.

In addition to religious authorities, symbols, programs, and the Christian theological scholarship that underlies ethics training, the religious life of the military is one with a much larger array of formal and informal religious practices, rituals, stories, and symbols. There are significant institutional formal religious offerings like chapel services and religious accommodations for a broad range of religious commitments. Along with these are also music performance opportunities through bands and choirs, as well as small-group Bible studies. Fellowships, books, devotionals, and even religious communities designed specifically for active service members and supplied by local communities and religious organizations supplement these resources. Extending from these more formal resources are also persistent institutional myths and stories related to material objects that take on sacred meaning (Lamothe, 1998; Pargament, 1997). Pocket Bibles and Psalm 91 bandanas are widely circulated throughout the military by outside organizations and chaplains alike. Such formal practices supplied by the military and pro-military religious organizations found the most communal resonance with service members.

Informal religious practice and symbols are also found in the everyday lives of service members. Often rooted in religious commitments brought to the military, service members found different ways to express their religious beliefs even within the high operational tempo of the military. Outside of small communities and lay-led Bible studies, service members tended to keep these religious practices private, shared only with close confidantes or practiced only alone. Prayer was by far the most common practice, particularly among those in combat roles, although many found that even such practices could take a backseat to the commitments of the military workload and tempo. Some also relied upon personal symbols of meaning, like tattoos, to express their faith commitments.

Looking at religious belief and practice in the military, it also became clear that the religious resources brought to and found in the military could be cause for harm when they led to the othering of those outside the service member's religious community. In promoting commitments to their own religious communities, particularly the religious community found in the military, service members could become intolerant of those not perceived to be in their group. Stemming from a long history of dehumanizing the enemy—especially one characterized by a different religion—religious intolerance of non-Christian traditions, particularly Islam, has been a persistent problem of the Global War on Terror. Among participants, this intolerance and othering extended to the military's own as well, with one Wiccan service member reporting persistent threats to his life.

Looking at the religious resources of the military overall from chaplains to training to religious practice, religious military culture is one that simultaneously does good and ill. The same resources that can provide positive coping, counseling, moral frameworks, moral prescriptions, and community can also endanger the moral equilibrium of service members. In addition to othering of the enemy and of fellow service members deemed outside of that religious culture, religious commitments could exacerbate trauma if not cause trauma themselves. They can motivate service members to continue participating in violence despite experiences of moral injury. They can cause service members to blame themselves for actions in war. They can upend their sense of meaning in the world when reality misaligns with deeply held moral expectations.

In view of the military religious backdrop, the remaining chapters of the book explored the role of religion amid traumatic experience, moral injury, PTSD, and while returning to the civilian sector. We found that religious beliefs and practices have a varied impact on service members confronting PMIEs. They can preempt or mitigate moral injury for some while exacerbating it for others. While most veterans experienced PMIEs, the differences between those with moral injury and those without depended on whether they could find resonance with meaning-making toolkits amid trauma. This investigation of religion amid moral injury revealed a social process of culture in action. Dissonance stirred by incoherence in one's moral narrative and the betrayal of significant relationships (self, organization, or God) spurred manifestations of moral injury by interrupting a deeply held *habitus*, one replete with habits of belief, expectation, narrativity, and identity. Unsettled times initiated Type II cognition—the reflexive consciousness—forcing service members to confront moral trauma in varied ways. While many compartmentalized moral work for later, those who achieved resonance relied on religious moral frames brought to or supplied by military culture, or they engaged in explicit moral deliberation. This complex process of belief maintenance resulted in an adaptation of beliefs and moral toolkits to settle interrupted habits. Importantly, religious resources were the salve for some and the cause of injury for others.

Moral injuries—particularly those stemming from a divine betrayal—could result in the abandonment of religious frameworks altogether, signaling the potential harm of religious resources in exacerbating trauma. However, in reports of other forms of trauma—physical injury, MST, or other exposures to traumatic events that can result in PTSD—religion tended to play a more uniformly positive role. Religious resources supplied by the military could still prove problematic—particularly in some negative interactions with military chaplains—but religious practice and community tended to ameliorate the severity of lasting trauma through positive coping and a reframing of experience. For both lasting moral injury and PTSD, post-hoc justifications that absolved individuals of perceived sin or reframed theological understandings of theodicy and God's role were reportedly the most helpful.

Most veterans reported experiencing a difficult time returning to the civilian sector. The return home is usually the period when PTSD and moral injury first manifest; the persistent fast pace of military life makes reflection during one's career difficult, which was the point. However, the return home can present unique challenges beyond moral and physiological responses. A loss of status, community, and purpose can challenge one's identity. The warrior identity that so completely overtook their lives for at least four years, if not four decades, had little purchase in the civilian realm, and abandoning one's *habitus*, even if other toolkits were waiting in the wings, was not easy. Community was certainly important for service members throughout their careers, and it remained so upon returning to civilian life, particularly when communal experiences and beliefs could resonate with their military identity. In fact, even amid severe trauma, those with a sense of belonging in community fared better post-service than those who remained isolated.

There were key differences between those who found Christian faith during their career and those who found it following trauma and returning to the civilian sector. Typically, the military service members who became Christian while in the military had a difficult time finding a new community upon returning to the civilian sector. They gained a moral framework that was resonant with military service and culture, but not necessarily with religious life outside the military. By contrast, those who became Christian after being in the military worked out more varied paths toward healing. They tended to continue to have high participation in faith communities, even forming their own or taking on leadership positions. The timing of religious moral work and explicit moral discourse are shaped by particular religious communities and their proximity to military culture and to the traumas that challenge moral relationships.

Bringing these strands together, we investigated seven distinct narrative trajectories representative of "typical" post-9/11 veteran lives. What emerged through these narratives was a constant pattern of identity maintenance and adaptation occurring throughout their lives. Identities included role (e.g., father, civilian), professional (e.g., soldier, warrior, public speaker), gendered (e.g., woman), and religious identities (e.g., Christian, Southern Baptist). At various points, service members and veterans maintained or navigated these identities as needed. The social process indicated by the stories of moral injury—of interrupted habits necessitating deliberation and adaptation—played out again and again. Even for people with no reported trauma, the instillation, adoption, and eventual loss of the warrior identity, for example, initiated the process of toolkit maintenance amid dissonance. Simply put, the military experience was unquestionably a disruptive and unsettling experience in their lives.

Religion—as a military framework, as a toolkit unto itself, and as a cultural sphere—had a major part to play in the stories recounted by the veterans I interviewed. As a creative force, it could powerfully heal veterans in their trauma. It connected many with communities that helped them manage the disruption of military life. It provided essential frameworks that allowed service members to navigate PTSD or reframe moral trauma, providing them with self-forgiveness or a new sense of meaning in the world. However, it was also a destructive force. Some service members relied so heavily upon faith that confronting evil on the battlefield or perpetrating it themselves left them reeling. Unmet moral expectations upended coherence in their life narratives, and trauma and a loss of identity ensued.

Religious and ethical systems make meaning of war when they supply beliefs, narratives, and expectations that resonate with service members and veterans surrounding salient issues in their lives. It is as Dewey (1922: 76) said, when dissonance occurs, habit "swells as resentment and as an avenging force." People would rather do anything to correct that dissonance, and religious and ethical systems often supply those needed correctives. When they do not, service members seek other salves—like alcohol or risky behaviors. Others seek new meaning-making systems altogether. That is, religion works when it works, and it does not when it does not. However, that is a misleading tautology. Kinds of religious resources matter.

Inseparable from the remembering and retelling of these stories is an image of the military institution that persistently aims service members at strategic goals using whatever resonant beliefs they can supply amid a purposeful inculcation of the warrior identity. Military culture and the warrior identity it supplies are all-encompassing; other identities, by needs, fall to the wayside, especially if they do not similarly support military aims. However, support for that warrior identity often disappears as service members become veterans. The military efficiently and systematically expends resources to engrain and support the warrior identity, but its plausibility structure crumbles when service members leave.

A Path Forward

The question remains of what one ought to do with these stories, for they do not sit in a void and should not be kept locked away as patterns repeat. There is some idealism in the just war tradition and normative ethics broadly, so perhaps what I propose remains a chimera. Despite this, I will propose some path forward, one which places these stories back in the hands of those who told them to me, back to those to whom they belong.

While it would be easier if we could end warfare and stop making new veterans altogether, we must face the reality of today by learning from the past and forging new paths forward. Similarly, we ought to push back on scholars, like Robert Meagher (2014: 132), who would have us throw out the just war tradition for its self-serving modern application and arguable irrelevance because "war has its own rules, and they don't include fair play, moral limits, or an agreement that right trumps might." Such arguments dangerously edge us toward throwing out any authoritative system of limiting warfare.

Instead, we ought to address the issue head-on, even if changes to existing ethical frameworks appear like piecemeal solutions or too difficult. Change will indeed be difficult. This is again Crawford's (2013: 315–317) "problem of 'many hands'" that explains why changing organizational frameworks is difficult since no one individual can alter the cultural products of an organization. It would take an entire cultural shift spurred by an organization-wide moral discursive consciousness to make such a change. However, if we view the military organization itself as an imperfect moral agent capable of thinking and acting as a "collective or corporate moral agent," change ought to be possible. It is with that idea in mind that we can begin to address the ethical issues present in military religious culture.

Perhaps the most significant consequence of military culture and its all-encompassing warrior identity is the removal of service member agency. The new warrior identity supplies a new warrior *habitus* and larger cultural toolkit that service members draw upon. The issue is that, as that warrior identity takes centrality, the tools service members draw upon look like choice—in terms of thinking on their feet under incredible duress—but limit their moral agency overall as they abandon previous moral commitments. To create the warrior identity, the military unmakes others. Their prior narrative construction—a defining feature of agency—is upended by the warrior identity. What comes to define their perception of "future possibilities in relation to more or less coherent causal and temporal sequences"

(Emirbayer & Mische, 1998: 989) is one that places all moral consideration and trust in the decision-making of superiors. As one Navy cryptologist explained:

> There is a point where things just happen, and you're going to shut your morality off because you're going to have to do things that you don't think are right. And you're going to have to do them. I know this for a fact that people do this because they put their morality on their sergeants, or their officers, or whatever. And they say, "If this person says that I'm supposed to be doing this, then it's something I have to do." ... If they don't, they go insane because they literally sit there and think about every trigger pull. And I don't think people can actually justify that. Most people at least.

The warrior identity requires one to supplant their own moral deliberation with a trust in someone else's. The job requires it. High operational tempo, lack of sleep, intensive training, and duress in conflict support it. Masculine culture that mocks sensitivity and emotion support it. Military religious resources support it or even defer that trust to a higher power altogether. It is no wonder, then, that a betrayal of that trust precipitates moral injury and lasting trauma.

On a macro-level, this lack of moral agency among service members ought to shape our understanding of *jus in bello* and the moral responsibility of individual warriors. Although military culture demands and produces trust in superiors' morality, it simultaneously emphasizes individual moral responsibility over organizational moral responsibility. This is rooted in the just war tradition that has shaped military operational policy. Historically, the just war tradition places blame for unjust actions on individual service members, even while the justice of going to war remains a question for military and government leaders (Walzer, 2006: 39). The "standard answer" to questions of moral responsibility consistently lays the blame on individual service members "understood to be autonomous moral agents" and "solely responsible for their behavior in war" (Crawford, 2013: 225). Military culture demands trust in superiors, in obedience, effectively stripping away moral agency. Service members must endure constant yelling, shoot at targets in the shape of human beings without thinking, and obey orders without hesitation or doubt. They must learn to kill, and they must swear an oath upon enlistment that they will "obey the orders of the US President and the order of the officers appointed over [them] according to regulations and the Uniform Code of Military

Justice" (Enlistment Oath). They must swear obedience, yet service members are held responsible for all their actions. Military law even codifies this emphasis on individual moral responsibility. According to the Operational Law Handbook, "the 'I just followed orders' defense usually fails. By training and common sense, Soldiers must recognize unlawful orders and act appropriately" (Kouba, 2017: 39).

Yet military training and culture limits individual agency. Crawford (2013: 226) argues that service members' "individual agency is constrained by military training, the rules of engagement, and the deference to command authority that is required of soldiers" along with the "fear and fatigue that characterize war." The constant influence of military culture, along with the duress of military experience, limits the ability of service members to act differently, so when decisions or actions lead to an immoral consequence, all of that moral blame lands squarely on the shoulders of individual service members. Peers, commanders, and even chaplains laud them for their actions, yet if moral questions arise within the one who acted, it is the individual service member who feels the blame. Military law codifies individual blameworthiness, yet service members do not readily have an outlet for seeking help for the inevitable dissonance they experience because military culture looks poorly on seeking it. We have seen this blameworthiness play out in the stories among veterans who experience lasting moral trauma.

More than that, we have seen the effects of military culture that systematically uses its resources—training, education, religion, symbols, mythic narratives, and more—to frame military strategic ends as good, thus making participation in violence easy. Simultaneously, we have seen how the hegemonic masculine culture of the military makes emotion—particularly reactive moral emotion—unmanly. Service members lose their agency. These resources and advances in technology not only make violence easier but they also socialize and normalize doubling in service members (Lifton, 1986). Amid this splitting of their *habitus*, they create a separate moral reality—one in which killing and violence are justified—or else use "dissociative defenses" that can "block out the horror of the enterprise" and ignore the pesky feeling of empathy (Lifton & Markusen, 1990: 195). As a result, even the mostly deeply held meaning-making frames service members possess are secondary to the military frameworks that define their warrior identity at the cost of individual moral agency.

To correct this, military organizational frameworks must shift away from their emphasis on individual responsibility as a model for blame in favor of one that places moral responsibility on collectives or the military organization itself. The culture that overwhelmingly produces feelings of self-blame, guilt, and weakness amid the moral crises service members face in the military must instead produce and reinforce help-seeking attitudes and supply avenues for framing experience in healthy ways that also take seriously the lasting moral wounds of participation in violence. Simply, if service members are not autonomous moral agents, then just war considerations of blameworthiness in war ought to fall on superior officers and the military organization overall. Such a reframing could have a lasting impact on persistent moral shame and guilt among service members while also affecting attitudes among the public toward the military organization, which ought to be the target of such blame.

Pastor Bester helped illustrate this point. During his combat deployment to Vietnam in the final years of the war, he confronted what he referred to as "human brutality." He explained, "It was my unfortunate—that word seems so inadequate—lot to kill a fifteen—or so—year-old girl who was shooting at me with an AR-15. It was an ambush, and I discovered that I had killed a child as I was searching the bodies for documents. Killing a person I considered a child was hard to take—I should have known better; I should have held fire, I should have—and the 'should' go on." His experience led him to feel lasting and overwhelming blame, shame, and guilt. In response, he abandoned the moral framework of right and wrong that was so "heavily freighted with judgmental overtones" and stirred in him a skepticism of someone "should-ing" on others. For him, "the phrase 'you should' carries with it the implication that the answer is simple, and one is just too stupid to not have done it already." In effect, the frameworks that rely on individual blameworthiness in the context of war force persons who have been involved in wartime violence outside the accepted moral order for acts they were commanded to perform. "It is just like dropping a load of shit on someone, or upon oneself, and then blaming the one dropped upon for being in the way or not moving, or shaming them for smelling like shit, or making them feel guilty for being covered in shit—that's the idea."

The question of justice of and in war remains, of course. Providing and refining limits on warfare remains a necessary project as we continue to participate in global conflicts. Moral prescriptions in war need new codifications, and training must be reimagined. However, such an overhaul of the tradition is not the work of this book. Determining how best to reimagine the tradition for the modern context is a wider ranging project for another time. Still, I hold up Pastor Bester's story to illustrate the need to reconfigure how we assign blame to individual service members, who have been stripped of the moral agency to act otherwise. It is, as theologian Brian Powers (2019: 109–10) explains, a matter of the "universality of sin" and its power to "distort one's life-intentionality ... [that] questions the fixity of demonstrable moral categories of 'victim' and 'perpetrator.'" As we have seen in experiences of moral injury, it is the utter lack of moral agency as victim or perpetrator that spurs moral injury. Guilt and betrayal in the context of war signal the loss of that agency and ought to make us question the moral categories associated with them. When PMIEs and other traumatic events occur, the societal blame—even the way we frame feelings of self-blame—need to change to reflect the culpability of the military organization and superior officers. The "standard" just war framework of individual responsibility needs to change.

There are also theological lessons to be learned from the stories of these post-9/11 veterans. I am not a theologian, but as a sociologist, ethicist, and religious studies scholar, I can observe how theology has been employed by military chaplains and military religious organizations and to what effects. A significant part of the picture here is that not everything about religion is beneficial or "good"—it can be the source of religious intolerance, and it can exacerbate trauma. Religious rhetoric and strategies of military community formation have employed notions of "us" and "them" that draw harmful boundaries. Military culture often mocks, ridicules, and otherwise dehumanizes any person or group not seen as "us," and religious beliefs and practices can support and exacerbate that dehumanization.

The latter is particularly acute when the divine is adopted as part of "us" but fails to protect as promised. Moral injury, particularly divine betrayal, stemmed from the disconnect between inevitable wartime tragedy and the military religious resources that kept service members in the fight by making them feel as though God was present with them in violence. That the warrior God theology alienated many service members and chaplains should give us pause. It was literally the cause of trauma. Sgt. McDaniel's story of losing the youngest member of his unit illustrated the failure of this outlook. The widespread reporting of failed vital objects and service members dying despite wearing Psalm 91 bandanas or carrying pocket Bibles on their person illustrated this failing. The total abandonment of faith by those who repeatedly felt they received only facile justifications for their experiences in war and empty explanations for questions of theodicy all illustrated this failing. I argue that such a framing has failed service members in need of resonant frameworks that match their lived reality.

How do we reframe military theology to aid chaplain support of service members? How do we re-establish the first collar's primacy (the call to serve service members) over the second (commitments to the military organization) among military chaplains? The answer must stem from the insights conjured from our process of remembering and retelling, by seeing the patterns, frames, and narratives that can supply a new imagined future. It is the process that Fluker (2016: 169) calls "imaginative and analytic bricolage" that uses memory to create "new signs, symbols, and visions in new spaces and in new rhythms of time." This pragmatic approach to ethics is one rooted in community and tradition.

Fluker draws on several ethicists—particularly Alasdair MacIntyre and Jeffrey Stout—to conceive of his positive bricolage. Unlike the bricolage of the military that used religious symbols and narratives to aim service members at strategic ends, Fluker's (2009: 54) bricolage emphasizes "reflection on and retrieval of tradition." In the spirit of MacIntyre (2007: 208, 219), Fluker's process of memory, vision, and mission takes seriously that "narrative history … turns out to be the basic and essential genre for the characterization of actions." Indeed, it is our narratives that shape virtue and show us what the "good life is" and what practices aim us to it. Housed in the traditions of a community, these narratives invite what Stout (1988: 74) describes as the "process in which one begins with bits and pieces of traditional linguistic material, arranges some of them into a structured whole, leaves others to the side, and ends with a moral language ready to use, possibly a quite novel one." Fluker (2009: 54–5) describes this process of moral bricolage as a "continuous creative cycle of remembering, reframing, and learning … [where] values that have been the long stay of a said tradition find resonance in new contexts of meaning and are enabled." In a sense, this process is a way to harness the discursive consciousness to find resonant beliefs and values that can settle a community during unsettled times. It is from this perspective of creative moral bricolage that I wish to suggest a path forward for service members.

In my view, this new vision and mission rests in the post-traumatic God identified by Ch. (Maj.) John Williams, the chaplain who experienced trauma for his perceived failure to help service members as much as he felt he should have. Framing God as one who suffers and remains in solidarity with service members has the creative potential to restore moral agency to service members by freeing them of what is organizational blame. This theological turn is one that requires a view of human suffering rooted in "anthropodicy"—the argument that good and evil are matters of human character and action; God suffers as humankind suffers (Berger, 1967). A post-traumatic God is not one aiming them at strategic ends or able to come to their rescue on the battlefield. Instead, such a theological framing captures the reality of suffering in war—both the sadness of one dying and the soul wound of the one pulling the trigger. It removes God's perceived judgment on individuals and the destructive belief that God fights for American political aims.

The need to shift away from a present violent God to a present suffering one ought to be clear. It resonates more with the realities of war. Pastor Bester explained the post-traumatic God:

> We all want to be able to say "God is good. God is all powerful and in control. And I am good." Then something bad happens; a child dies. Why would God allow a child to suffer and die like that? What kind of a God would do that? If God is good and all powerful, he wouldn't allow it to happen, unless God has a bad streak. But God is good, then it must be that I am not good and deserve this. And so the argument goes on. So, my point is that I will advance the goodness of God and affirm that I am a good person. I am willing to sacrifice the position that God is all powerful and in control of everything. God's will doesn't mean a hill of beans. What I will affirm is God's presence. When I am caught in the midst of war making a choice that in order for me to survive someone else must die, and having to do it in the blink of an eye, I affirm that God is present both for me and the one I am killing, receiving the dying and crying for me.

The power of this theological framing is not that it makes war easier. Rather, it effectively captures the reality of war in which combatants are not autonomous moral agents. Their suffering and the suffering of their enemy is a moral tragedy, and the post-traumatic God resonates.

These new theological frames can allow service members and chaplains to articulate the truth of their wounds and the reality of suffering. More than that, by articulating the wounds brought on by military culture, acknowledging the wounds on the battlefield, and suffering together as God suffers with them in demanded violence, service members can develop a story of post-traumatic suffering that captures the reality of war.

Limitations and Recommendations

Interviews with service members have provided a rich picture and series of stories about their religious and military lives. They cannot, however, represent the whole of the military or of those who have served since 9/11, so there are some key limitations to consider. The veterans and chaplains are a self-selecting population, people willing to share their experiences, who have perhaps already come to terms with their trauma or who have previously spoken with strangers (perhaps publicly) about their experiences. They were also people willing to talk about faith and religion, suggesting that others for whom religion was irrelevant would not have volunteered for the study.

What you hear from the veterans who agreed to speak with me is also a story shaped by my position as an outsider to the military. As one social media commenter professed in all-caps, I am a "civilian puke" and am simply an outsider to the military and veteran community. While I found that most of the veterans with whom I spoke were courageously honest and open about their experiences, I do believe being an outsider to the community hindered me as I tried to find people to speak with and in the interviews themselves. Not being an insider likely meant certain experiences and reflections on them were off-limits for the interview. This was, of course, the right of the participant, but it does likely mean my accounts of the realities of religion in the military are a somewhat filtered version.

This is also largely the story of Euro-American service members. Because I did not intentionally account for demographic considerations when recruiting for the project, racial diversity is significantly lacking in my self-selecting sample. I am, therefore, missing an important dynamic—race—and the distinctive experiences of service members from African American religious traditions. I cannot know what religious resources are available to BIPOC veterans or how they affect their military and life experiences, particularly relating to traumatic events.

What this project addresses are the internal mechanisms that link religious beliefs and practices to experiences in military service. The emphasis of this study was on the role of faith in navigating transitions between identities and other disruptive or traumatic moments, that is, on the mechanisms in play and what they reveal about religious identities within the military population. Neither the narrative trajectories nor the range of military experience are generalizable, but the ways in which these lives are shaped and re-shaped can tell us a great deal.

Among these veterans, however, Christian faith consistently had a part to play in navigating the military experience and trauma. The findings of this research demand further research on the dynamic between resonant and dissonant belief amid trauma across different religions, demographics, ranks, and eras. Additional research can extend the arguments here to different sites beyond religion and contexts beyond war. Experience in the military disrupted the moral narratives of these veterans and called for resources often supplied by religion but tested in their lives—mechanisms for justification of actions, obtaining forgiveness, seeking absolution of transgressions by an authority, finding belonging and community, and making meaning in the face of existential moral challenges.

One Last Story for the Work Ahead

Pastor Bester, having been contracted by the Canadian Armed Forces, worked with active-duty service members during a particularly violent time in the War on Terror in 2007. Following failed attempts at adapting his veteran retreat material to the lives of active personnel, he opted for a different approach. This new approach was tested by the unexpected death of a "respected Sergeant Major," who had been killed in action. "Some of the men had been with him; others had handled the evacuation-medical end of it, other transportation, and so on." Bester and his peers took the moment head on and broached the subject with those involved and gathered them to speak in a large group.

Distraught but stuck together, they had to respond. "There was a good deal of anger that we would bring up such a painful topic. … The first group spoke about the reality that the war moved on and they had no opportunity to understand what happened. However, present were representatives who had attempted treatment, then recovered and moved the body, as well as some from the back who were facilitating communications." Despite some open complaints and reflections, the service members were not really hearing one another. They all sat together with their smaller role groups, and Bester could sense distrust over sharing emotions among them.

However, a revelation changed the course of the night. The Sgt Maj's body had been accompanied by various units through the "ceremony of a fallen warrior's return, which is part of the Canadian tradition." The repatriation ceremony involves a large procession with pallbearers carrying the flag-wrapped coffin of the deceased from the aircraft to the transport with the sound of bagpipes in the background. It involves many units and moving pieces to pull off as it simultaneously pays respect for the fallen. One of the chaplains in attendance had actually led the procession in the airfield. "Each unit, hearing the part played by other units, and mutually acknowledging the communal depth of loss and grief, changed the entire aspect of the retreat. … No longer did people sit separated, but they mingled and shared stories, spoke of other losses, and asked for information from other units." The evening was so successful and meaningful that several of the service members in attendance then volunteered to lead similar debriefings for returning personnel. A community of solidarity and the embodied ritual of the fallen warrior's return (Rambo, 2017) allowed service members to find peace in their despair. "To be a part of that process and to witness that healing was an experience of grace," Bester said.

With that thought, I too wish to express the grace I felt working with veterans and chaplains. That they have survived their traumas, found love, maintained communities, consistently had good humor, or were, at the very least, willing to talk to a stranger about their lives is astounding to me. I am deeply grateful for their trust and for their stories that illuminate the endless bravery and resilience they claim not to have.

At the end of our conversation, Bester sighed, "Ah well, time goes on." He had to leave to go to his improv comedy class. "My instructors are all in their twenties. I have shirts older than they are," he laughed.

Bibliography

Bell, A. (2014). Leashing the "Dogs of War": Examining the Effects of LOAC Training at the U.S. Military Academy and in Army ROTC. *Proceedings of the Annual Meeting (American Society of International Law), 108*, 370–373.

Berger, P. L. (1967). *The Sacred Canopy: Elements of Sociological Theory of Religion.* Doubleday.

Crawford, N. C. (2013). *Accountability for Killing: Moral Responsibility for Collateral Damage in America's Post-9/11 Wars.* Oxford University Press.

Dewey, J. (1922). *Human Nature and Conduct: An Introduction to Social Psychology.* Henry Holt & Company.

Emirbayer, M., & Mische, A. (1998). What Is Agency? *American Journal of Sociology, 103*(4), 962–1023.

Fluker, W. E. (2009). *Ethical Leadership: The Quest for Character, Civility, and Community.* Fortress Press.

Fluker, W. E. (2016). *The Ground Has Shifted: The Future of the Black Church in Post-Racial America.* New York University Press.

Kouba, D. (Ed.). (2017). *Operational Law Handbook* (17th ed.). International and Operational Law Department The Judge Advocate General's Legal Center and School.

Lamothe, R. (1998). Sacred Objects as Vital Objects: Transitional Objects Reconsidered. *Journal of Psychology and Theology, 26*(2), 159–167.

Lifton, R. J. (1986). *The Nazi Doctors: Medical Killing and the Psychology of Genocide*. Basic Books.

Lifton, R. J., & Markusen, E. (1990). *Genocidal Mentality: Nazi Holocaust and Nuclear Threat*. Basic Books.

MacIntyre, A. (2007). *After Virtue* (3rd ed.). University of Notre Dame Press.

Meagher, R. E. (2014). *Killing from the Inside Out: Moral Injury and Just War*. Cascade Books.

Pargament, K. I. (1997). *The Psychology of Religion and Coping: Theory, Research, Practice*. Guilford Press.

Powers, B. S. (2019). *Full Darkness: Original Sin, Moral Injury, and Wartime Violence*. William B. Eerdmans Publishing Company.

Rambo, S. (2017). *Resurrecting Wounds: Living in the Afterlife of Trauma*. Baylor University Press.

Stout, J. (1988). *Ethics after Babel: the Languages of Morals and Their Discontents*. Beacon Press.

Waggoner, E. (2014, September). Taking Religion Seriously in the U.S. Military: The Chaplaincy as a National Strategic Asset. *Journal of the American Academy of Religion, 82*(3), 702–735.

Walzer, M. (2006). *Just and Unjust Wars: A Moral Argument with Historical Illustrations* (4th ed.). Basic Books.

Index[1]

[1] Note: Page numbers followed by 'n' refer to notes.

T. H. Suitt, III, *Narratives of Trauma and Moral Agency among Christian Post-9/11 Veterans*,
https://doi.org/10.1007/978-3-031-31082-9

Printed in the USA
CPSIA information can be obtained
at www.ICGtesting.com
LVHW060519070823
754480LV00007B/457

9 783031 310812